RADICAL PHILOSOPHY

2.09

Series 2 / Winter 2020-21

Editorial collective

ISSN 0300-211X
ISBN 978-1-9999793-8-6

Of what is Bolsonaro the name?

Rodrigo Nunes

[O]ne might refer to the fascist movements as the wounds, the scars, of a democracy that, to this day, has not lived up to its own concept.

Theodor Adorno

What's in a name?

First things first: to speak of 'Bolsonarismo' is not the same as speaking of Bolsonaro voters. Evidently, whatever we can call 'Bolsonarismo' must have been a factor in Jair Bolsonaro's November 2018 election; but the former army captain's victory was overdetermined in all sorts of ways, and the electoral coalition that brought him to power is broader than any phenomenon we can accurately describe with that name. In short, not every Bolsonaro voter is a Bolsonarista – a distinction that it is both analytically and politically essential to make.

Smaller than Bolsonaro's actual or potential electorate, Bolsonarismo is at the same time bigger than Bolsonaro himself: neither created by nor solely dependent on the individual from whom it borrows its name. This means that the link between 'leader' and 'movement' is synthetic rather than analytic, and its strength hinges not on some essential bond but on the contingent fact that, having found himself at the crest of a groundswell at a critical time, Bolsonaro now has more power to shape it than anyone else. In short, my contention is that Bolsonarismo is a real convergence of different trends in Brazilian society, with the potential to consolidate itself as a major force for quite some time; but the arrangement of political forces that expresses it is neither coherent nor necessarily stable. In fact, one of its key sources of instability is precisely Bolsonaro and his sons, owing to their divisiveness, shady connections and constant attacks on potential challengers to their control over this political capital.

'Bolsonarista' thus refers to a social segment that has acquired an explicit political orientation in the last eight years or so through an interactive relation with leaders like Bolsonaro, even if the fact that the latter came to dominate it is itself contingent. It can be estimated at around 15% of the population; considering Bolsonaro's approval ratings have never dropped far below 30%, it comprises the solid, unwavering half of that percentage.[1] Though less than one sixth of the adult population, this group has a disproportionate political weight by virtue of the high electoral floor that it offers, its commitment and permanent engagement. Though composed of atomised individuals not organised in any major political structures, it is the vocal, militant core from which the gravitational pull of the far right radiates to the rest of Brazilian society.

Insisting on a contingent, synthetic link between Bolsonaro and Bolsonarismo might beg the question of why call the latter by the former's name. But following Laclau's remarks on naming as retroactively constitutive of its object, we could turn the question on its head and reply that it is exactly that contingency that justifies this choice.[2] Not, of course, that Bolsonarismo emerged fully formed the moment the name was uttered. For polemical and ontological reasons, Laclau tends to exaggerate the passivity of things and the spontaneity of leaders, minimising the horizontal ties that pull people together in favour of a shared vertical bond with the figurehead or the empty signifier. The truth tends to be more prosaic:

instead of naming as the foundational act that inaugurates a linear causal chain, a feedback process through which people begin to gravitate towards one another and represent themselves as doing so until one or more representations 'stick'. While the political operation 'at the top' was essential to giving it shape, Bolsonarismo should be seen as the coming together, under the aegis of the political factions that coalesced around Bolsonaro's campaign, of social trends that had for some time been imbued with a certain mutual tropism. And while they are certainly far from constituting a consistent theory or worldview, they have a lot of common ground to connect them.

Most accounts of Bolsonaro's rise to power tend to stay at the more superficial level of the sequence of events that led to his triumph. While it can enrich our understanding of the political decisions that produced Bolsonarismo, this approach is insufficient when it comes to identifying the deeper social shifts that were both precipitated by these decisions and made them possible. A comprehensive look at Bolsonarismo must work on more than one timescale and take into consideration at least four different levels of analysis:

- the different *discursive matrices* that came together in its formation;

- the *common grammars* that ensured these matrices' communication and mutual compatibility;

- the *affective conditions* or collective moods that gave them something to latch on to;

- the *organisational infrastructure* – encompassing churches, radio and TV shows, YouTube influencers, WhatsApp groups, Twitter bots etc. – that they rely on.

In this article, I will focus primarily on the first two, alluding to the third in the conclusion. My goal throughout will be double. Firstly, to present Bolsonarismo perspectivistically, as a phenomenon that can take on different meanings depending on the position that one occupies within it. Secondly, to highlight what is generalisable in this story. To the extent that similar conditions can be found elsewhere, that of which Bolsonaro is the name is in no way a uniquely Brazilian phenomenon.

Elective affinities

What, then, are the elements that went into the composition of Bolsonarismo? Sociologist Gabriel Feltran offers us a starting point by listing three 'discursive matrices' he calls 'police militarism' (support for law-and-order policies and the extrajudicial use of force), 'Evangelical anti-intellectualism' (rejection of science and formal education in favour of religion and personal experience), and 'entrepreneurial monetarism' (an 'entrepreneur of oneself' ethos for which precarity equals autonomy).[3] This is doubly useful, as it not only pinpoints long-term tendencies that Feltran has identified in his fieldwork in the periphery of São Paulo, but does so by resorting to the concept that Eder Sader advanced in his analysis of the early 1980s' 'social movement boom' out of which the Workers' Party (PT) emerged.[4] The same caveat raised above about Laclau applies here: to speak of 'discursive matrices' is not to claim some fundamental priority for language over embodiment or affectivity, but to propose that we think the two spheres in a circular, reciprocal relation. Language has the power to give names to things that are already vaguely sensed in everyday experience, and resonates to the extent that it does so; in so doing, however, it renders that experience communicable, enhances its publicness and reframes sensibilities accordingly.[5] Discursive matrices should therefore be considered as generative not only of statements, but of affective structures (likes and dislikes, hates and loves, objects of admiration and repulsion; what Spinoza would call *ingenia*), identification and belonging, ways of understanding and narrating oneself – all the latent conditions for what may or may not develop into fully conscious, mobilised political subjectivity.

Yet Feltran's conclusions, valuable as they are for showing the fertile ground Bolsonarismo has found among the poor, are needlessly constrained by the way he generalises (or fails to generalise) his ethnographic findings. As he himself recognises, anti-intellectualism is not exclusive to the Evangelical population and is just as visible among the predominantly Catholic upper class. As for militarism and entrepreneurialism, though they are each a single matrix shared by rich and poor, they take on such different connotations depending on class and racialisation as to result in very distinct subjective posi-

tions: it is not because people are using the same words that they are saying the same thing. In short, Feltran's observational bias puts him at risk of (correctly) countering the idea that Bolsonarismo is merely 'a mobilisation of the elites against the poor' with the (incorrect) suggestion that 'sectors of finance, agribusiness, religious and rural elites' joined this 'totalitarian movement' late in the game, 'possibly without realising what they were doing'.[6]

A formulation like this misses three crucial things about Bolsonarismo. Firstly, its character as a cross-class alliance around a few common identitarian and political reference points that have, until now, far outweighed the contradictions among the divergent interests that it brings together. Secondly, the fact that what makes this balancing act possible is both the pervasiveness of certain discursive matrices and their having enough grammar in common as to be compatible with one another. Thus, although there may be an upper- and a lower-class militarism or anti-intellectualism, the two sides can still understand and identify with one another, especially when set against what they oppose (criminality, drug use, unbridled sexuality, leniency with 'marginals', leftist indoctrination etc.). This means, thirdly, that we should

not speak as if there were a pre-existing movement to which some groups latched on to in 2018, but rather think of what happened as the confluence of different vectors, 'from above' as well as 'from below', that already had much in common. The top 10% of the electorate were in fact the first sector Bolsonaro won over, very early on, and if the 1% did not have him as their first choice, they had no qualms about embracing him when it became clear he could win. To sum up, Bolsonarismo is a cross-class project held together at the top by politics and at the base by strong elective affinities.

This means that we can distinguish among the discursive matrices that compose it three different types: those that are restricted to a particular class or group; those that are widely shared but whose meaning remains constant across groups or classes; and those that are shared but take on different meanings depending on one's position in the social structure. As we have seen, anti-intellectualism, militarism and entrepreneurialism all cut across strata, but the latter two belong to the third type.[7]

As regards militarism, the difference is obvious. For those living in dangerous areas, the hankering for unrestrained state violence supposes a clear demarcation between the 'working people' and the 'criminals' in the neighbourhood, with some collateral casualties in between. For those in well-off areas, policing is about protecting them from the poor, making the grey zone of potentially disposable life much larger. As for entrepreneurialism, whereas for the rich it often acts as a meritocratic narrative disguising inequality of opportunities, among the poor and much of the middle class it is more akin to what Verónica Gago has called 'neoliberalism from below'. This ambivalent dynamic, through which individuals engaged in inventing strategies of survival in an environment reconfigured by neoliberal policies come to understand themselves according to 'the logic of the microentrepreneur',[8] is in fact a major factor in the sea change that Latin American politics has seen in recent years. Largely unchallenged and often elicited by the progressive governments in the region, this 'mass self-entrepreneurship'[9] was effectively reinforced by the growth of informality and indebtedness of the Pink Tide years, making neoliberalism even more 'anchored in territories, strengthened in popular subjectivities, … expanding and proliferating within popular economies'.[10] Phenomena like Mauricio Macri in Argentina and Bolsonaro in Brazil are partially understandable as the encounter between a radicalised version of the 1990s 'neoliberalism from above' and a neoliberalism from below that flourished during the neodevelopmentalist interlude of the 2000s, which continued to pose the market as the primary arena for the pursuit of recognition and material satisfaction. As Rosana Pinheiro-Machado and Lucia Scalco show, the empowerment produced by PT's 'inclusion through consumption' was so imbricated with the capacity to buy things that, once the economic downturn took that capacity away, many of 'the very citizens that had symbolised Brazil's rise'[11] under PT readily shifted allegiance from Lula to Bolsonaro.

Not only does Bolsonarismo openly espouse entrepreneurialism, it is an entrepreneurial phenomenon in its own right. The quintessential Bolsonarista is neither rich nor poor, but a member of a downwardly mobile 'lower upper middle class' (to borrow Orwell's turn of phrase) among which 'failed businessman' is perhaps the most common occupation. Extremely sensitive to negative fluctuations in the economy, they are by that same token especially prone to a politics of resentment that blames others for their frustrated expectations. Since

2014, many have followed a career path that went from becoming a right-wing influencer on social media to going into politics. 85% of the senators and 47% of federal representatives elected in 2018 were first-timers, most of them successfully riding on Bolsonaro's 'outsider' discourse – even though the latter had been a congressman since 1991. Among these were 22 policemen or members of the military, a retired porn actor and an heir of the Brazilian royal family.

Constructing the upstanding citizen

Despite being more socially circumscribed, two other matrices play an important role in establishing narrative connections among the others: economic libertarianism and anti-communism. Whereas anti-intellectualism, militarism and entrepreneurialism developed in parallel across social strata, in these two the direction of diffusion is more evident, going from the upper classes to the poor. Besides, their propagation is more obviously the result of coordinated action.

The seeds of the staggering resurgence of anticommunism in Brazil started being sown during PT's first term in power. At a time when the economy was booming and most people's material standards were improving, red scares manufactured with the aid of the media were among the few weapons in the opposition's armour. The contrast between these and the embracing of Lula by the international establishment produced a cognitive dissonance that conspiracy theories about a global leftist conspiracy would subsequently help solve. It was the social media-fuelled spread of the latter that operated the shift from Cold War discourse as a tool in parliamentary struggle to anticommunism as an overarching geopolitical narrative pitting Trump and Bolsonaro as the Asterix and Obelix of the struggle against 'cultural Marxism-driven economic globalisation'.[12] The very fact that no concrete threat existed only made this discourse more efficient, as its 'abstractness' meant that 'anything that somehow [did] not fit [could be] subsumed under [an] all-purpose term' like 'communism' or 'globalism'.[13]

While market libertarianism is in one sense merely the theoretical counterpart to entrepreneurialism, it merits independent consideration because of its importance as a rallying point for a young, university-educated middle class that played a protagonist role in the events leading to Bolsonaro's election. This too was a process that began shortly after PT came to power, the creation of Instituto Millenium in 2005 being a major landmark. Funded by some of the most powerful financial, industrial and media groups in the country, this think tank worked to popularise ultraliberal ideas and, alongside players like Instituto Mises Brasil (founded in 2007), contributed to a veritable editorial boom in the field. (A boom in conservative literature was happening around the same time.) This created the environment in which young, media-savvy ultraliberal activists started to organise, drawing on grants from international funders like the Cato Institute.[14] The most important of these groups is the Students for Liberty-trained Movimento Brasil Livre (Free Brazil Movement, or MBL), which emerged during the June 2013 protests as the right-wing answer to Movimento Passe Livre (Free Fare Movement, or MPL). Two years later, MBL were key to organising the marches calling for the impeachment of Dilma Rousseff; in 2018, they elected seven congressmen.

At first, this sector's selling point was the cosmopolitan, socially liberal attitude that set them apart from the traditional right: 'liberal in economics and in social mores' was how they described themselves. As power beckoned, however, they increasingly converged with social conservatives, not only finding areas of cooperation but adopting some of their discourses and tactics. Conversely, their newfound clout was one of the factors that pulled Bolsonaro, whose economic views had previously appeared to lean statist, towards an ultraliberal agenda. Despite the former army captain's unequivocal authoritarian tendencies, they continue to support him with varying degrees of enthusiasm, invoking a distinction between the government's 'technical' (economic) and 'ideological' areas as an excuse.

The most universal of these discursive matrices, anticorruption, illustrates the power of libertarianism and anticommunism in tying Bolsonarismo's different strands together. In Brazil, corruption has long worked in the public imaginary as a sort of meta-problem, the magical cause which, once eliminated, would cure all other ills. In this account, the weight of structural constraints and differences of political orientation are entirely disregarded in favour of a voluntaristic, individualised vision of politics: the country would be prosperous and there would be money for everything if only there were honest individuals in charge.

Although Brazilian elites have used anti-corruption rhetoric to destabilise progressive governments in the past, until recently it was widely understood that misappropriation of public funds was endemic to the political profession. Having usually been far from positions of power, left-wing parties were, if anything, deemed more trustworthy. Yet the vast institutional sleaze uncovered in 2014 by the now-famous Operation Car Wash presented libertarians and anticommunists with a unique opportunity to promote a new narrative. It combined a Hayekian mistrust of social justice as '[amounting] simply to the protection of entrenched interests'[15] with the notion that the left's universal modus operandi is to buy off interest groups such as minorities and artists in order to install corrupt totalitarian regimes. The sheer size of the schemes Car Wash revealed thus functioned as evidence not of PT's definitive incorporation into the country's political elite, but of how far they had advanced in their plan to 'turn Brazil into Venezuela' – exactly as the right had been warning they would for a decade.

It helped that one of the largest corruption scandals in the country's history unfolded in parallel with one of its worst economic crises ever, indelibly connecting the two in most people's minds. If there was a recession, the thought went, this was not due to bad economic policy or a global slump, but to an unprecedentedly large attack on the state's kitty. It became easier on this basis to cement the association between left-wing governments, sleaze and economic inefficiency, even though the scandal actually involved all mainstream parties. The political advantages of this account were obvious. In one fell swoop, it turned what was deemed to be a universal, endemic problem into a particularly left-wing vice; it painted even PT's cautious reformism as part of a communist threat, making anything but the most pro-market libertarianism potentially suspicious; it legitimised opposition to progressive policies by reframing it as resistance against a slide towards tyranny; and it nurtured a feeling of imminent danger that created the demand for urgent, radical action.

The final element in the Bolsonarista constellation is another discursive matrix that plays an important role in tying together the rest: social conservatism. Like anticommunism, it came from the fringes of the political spectrum and was progressively mainstreamed by politicians and vehicles interested in denting PT's popularity.

Unlike anticommunism or market libertarianism, it did not spread downwards, but was already well established across all classes. Spurred by the advances made by feminists and the LGBTQ+ community in the last decade on the one hand, and by fabricated moral panics on the other, it too relied on a sense of urgent threat to expand. Growing steadily over the Lula years, the defence of 'family values' proved to be a force to be reckoned with the 'gay kit' episode in 2011.[16] By 2015 it was so strong that many invoked it as a reason to support the impeachment of Dilma Rousseff, one congressman in particular claiming to be acting against 'programmes that aim to make children change sex and learn sex at school'.

As Isabela Kalil has noted, Bolsonarismo's greatest achievement was to make all these different elements – militarism, anti-intellectualism, entrepreneurialism, anticommunism, market libertarianism, anticorruption discourse, social conservatism – converge around a single figure, the 'upstanding citizen' (*cidadão de bem*).[17] If there is an empty signifier that represents the Bolsonarista base to itself, it is that.[18] On the other side of the antagonistic frontier, the concept of *mamata* (from *mamar*, 'to suckle') does the same work when it comes to identifying the enemy. Meaning 'easy life' or 'undue advantage', *mamata* can apply to anything from perceived leniency with criminals to the exorbitant salaries of politicians and the judiciary; from labour rights to the supposedly charmed existence of artists and academics; from the job stability of civil servants to sexual freedom and the questioning of traditional gender roles; and from the misuse of public funds to affirmative action at universities. Its capacity to establish equivalences between basic rights and elite privileges, and to present the former in terms of the latter, is key to building the class alliance on which Bolsonarismo depends. Its constitution of a continuum between private and public morality allows it to be the *point de capiton* that makes changes in societal attitudes resonate with rising crime rates, corruption, progressive social policy and even contemporary art as gathering evidence of a single process of moral decadence that it behoves the upstanding citizenry to stop.

It bears repeating that, although these discursive matrices overlap at various points, not every Bolsonarista (let alone Bolsonaro voter) subscribes to all of them with the same intensity, or at all. Not only are there inconsistencies between them, none of them is fully consistent either. This matters little, as the power of the metanarratives that establish their connection lies in association more than logic, and coherence derives less from any actual content than from the feeling of being on the same side in a struggle.[19] Whether one believes or not in all that is said about the enemy is less important than believing that there is an enemy and it must be defeated. And precisely, what these metanarratives promise is more than just certainty amidst change and sensory overload. The perception of imminent existential threat that they cultivate intensifies subjective commitment, presents their adherents in a heroic light and frames politics as a fight to the death in which all means are justified in advance.

A common grammar

Although *mamata* has a very Brazilian flavour, the operation it makes possible is the far right's quintessential conjuring trick everywhere: promoting the confusion between anxiety around the loss *of rights* and the fear of losing *privileges*. This is what has allowed it in recent years to gather the support of both those sectors that have few material concerns but resent the advances made by some groups, and those that are haunted by falling standards and the prospect of no longer enjoying rights they once had. In that, it was evidently abetted by the fall-out from the 2008 crisis coming on the back of a 'progressive neoliberalism' that combined a 'plutocratic economic program' that left millions of people behind with a 'liberal-meritocratic politics of recognition' and mostly symbolic improvements for some minorities.[20] The concomitance of severe losses for some and modest gains for others is what helps the far right convince the 'losers' of globalisation that if they are being deprived of *rights*, it is because others – women, migrants, ethnic groups, LGBTQ+ people etc. – are gaining *privileges* off their backs.

It is this triadic structure of right populism – not 'the people' versus 'the elite', but the people against an elite that unduly favours some other group[21] – that explains how, in the United States, a billionaire could appear as the candidate of the common man against an 'establishment' consisting of Hollywood actors, newspaper columnists and graduate students on Twitter. It also helps us make sense of the confluence, particularly sharp in Brazil, of

social conservatism and no-holds-barred neoliberalism. When the loss of certain privileges (white, male, heteronormative etc.) is associated with the conquest of rights by others (affirmative action, for example), the desire to see the status quo restored finds a natural ally in the rejection of redistributive policies.

Not that this confluence should surprise us too much. In places like Brazil and the United States, the coming together of social conservatism and neoliberalism has long been prepared, on the one hand, by the 'prosperity gospel' of Neopentecostal churches, which provides divine justification for the accumulation of wealth and 'reinforces the Calvinist tenet of individual responsibility for material success'.[22] And, on the other, by a 'neoliberalism from above' that has never ceased to invest the family as disciplinary institution, counterweight to the market's disaggregating tendencies, safety net that could take on functions previously exercised by the state (education, health, well-being), and part of a *dispositif* for the privatisation of risk.[23] Ultimately, however, what Bolsonarismo helps us see is that, if neoliberalism and neoconservatism can be relatively easily welded together by politics, it is because they share to a large extent the same moral grammar.

Once again, to speak of 'grammar' is not to stay at the level of language only. A grammar, following Wittgenstein, is part of a form of life. Thus, if the way one lives conditions what one can say about the world, what one can say about the world provides the grounds for decisions and institutions that condition the way one lives.[24] Indeed, the moral grammar of the far right at once reflects how its adherents see the world and demands that the world be remade according to that vision. Its key elements are *individualism*, *punitivism* and *the valorisation of order above the law*.

Ideas like self-reliance and becoming an 'entrepreneur of oneself' are of course among the highest values posited by neoliberal discourse. But in a world reconfigured by these ideas, they are also essential to the strategies required to navigate relationships, institutions and work, and integral to how individuals perceive themselves. As safety nets shrink and uncertainty grows, the sheer 'strain of risk-bearing'[25] forces people to internalise the idea that they are solely responsible for their own fate. By rendering invisible both the interdependencies that sustain individual trajectories and the structural constraints that hold them back, this individualistic grammar voids the notion of a social space beyond the immediate private sphere: there are only individuals and (at best) their families, as someone famously put it. This not only deprives people of the language in which to address structural injustice, but induces them to interpret positive changes in their economic environment as their own achievement and structural demands as special pleading: 'if they have to battle through life alone, then everyone else should too'.[26]

Perversely, individualism is an ideal that works as well in success (narrated as heroic self-realisation) as it does in failure (in a 'therapeutic' mode that restores dignity by locating emotional development in adversity).[27] In our societies, individual sovereignty is the site of 'cruel optimism'[28] *par excellence*, the frustration of its expectations only making its grip stronger. Inadequacy is therefore less likely to lead to a reformulation of the ideal than to a doubling down that can be turned inward as self-aggression and outward as resentment and negative solidarity.[29]

This is where the grammars of individualism and punitivism intersect. In a world where everyone feels they are (and ought to be) out on their own, non-conformity is seen as eschewing personal responsibility or seeking special treatment, and therefore worthy of punishment.[30] This tendency is compounded by the increasingly punitive features of post-2008 (in Brazil, post-2014) neoliberal governmentality.[31] If neoliberalism has managed to hold on since, despite a huge loss of legitimacy, it is because the disciplinary mechanisms that sustain it have become starker, even as – or precisely because – the normative claims behind them have become more suspect. What many failed to appreciate a decade ago is that crisis itself can be a highly effective source of discipline, given its power to rescind alternatives, mobilise subjective investment, intensify economic coercion and reactivate neoliberalism's founding myth of being the rational, technocratic cure for the excesses of a previous period. This metanarrative proves that the retributive element in neoliberalism is not entirely new and has in fact been there from the start. Yet what is different now is that calls to tighten the belts come with only the faintest prospect of ever loosening them again, and whereas sacrifice was once a means to a better life, it increasingly appears as end in itself: the naked imperative to adapt

to a diminishing horizon. This has reached a paroxysm with the Covid-19 pandemic, when the official discourse in places like Brazil and the United States has *literally* been that people have to choose between the economy or their lives.

As a product of internalised discipline, punitivism is highly respectful of established authority, social roles and divisions; organised crime and social movements are potentially equally loathsome and despised. Among the rich as well as the poor, the punitive animus is directed against those at the base of the social pyramid more than those at the top, whose transgressions can be shrugged off as part of their reward for having 'made it'.

It is here that individualism and punitivism intersect with a notion of order as something above, and ultimately against, the law. Many have identified this as a founding trait of Brazilian culture of which Bolsonaro is merely the latest, obscene flower.[32] It goes back to the early days of the country's formation, when local landowners were at once representatives of state power and the most powerful men in their areas, fostering the confusion between public and private interests.[33] The agrarian, slave-holding structure of the plantation economy not only divided society into individuals endowed with rights and pieces of common property, but meant that even free men often owed their fortunes to attracting the favours of the property-owning elite. This meant that liberal discourse and a modern state apparatus developed not by supplanting but by appeasing, and often providing cover for, this archaic structure of command.[34] Even after the abolition of slavery – which Brazil was one of the last countries to enact – the permanent and assured exercise of one's rights was a privilege reserved to those of a certain social standing. Punishment, conversely, was certain only for those whose status did not exempt them from observing the same rules as everyone else.

In a society in which the guarantee of equality before the law is a privilege, the demand for order is thus usually not about applying the law, but about revoking the rights of those who do not 'deserve' them and granting special treatment to those who do. This was visible in the way the media and the public cheered Operation Car Wash on through its numerous procedural infringements, which have exposed its legal results to revision and annulment even if its political effects are irreversible.[35] It is also visible in four themes dear to Bolsonarismo: the call for 'human rights for the right humans',[36] not criminals; the flexibilisation of gun laws, which amounts to privatising the sovereign power over death; the dismantling of environmental protections, understood as obstacles to entrepreneurship; and the crusade against speed cameras and traffic fines, seen as impinging on car owners' liberties.[37]

On the one hand, the pre-modern logic that places the right to flaunt common rules as the greatest right of all fits in well with the libertarian absolutisation of individual freedom. This was made explicit by Bolsonaro's rejection of movement restrictions or mask enforcement during the pandemic, which he has since followed on by insisting that 'nobody can force anyone to take the vaccine' once it is available. On the other hand, as this type of order supposes not the formal equality of laws but the arbitrary exercise of authority, it combines perfectly with the defence of a 'private life of power'[38] premised on a traditional distribution of roles between men and women, white and non-white, straight and not straight, etc. As Wendy Brown has noted, nihilistic revanchism against the inroads made by oppressed groups 'releases the will to power not only in subjects, but in traditional values themselves, baldly revealing the privilege and entitlement they encode'.[39] 'Those who can, rule; those who have sense, obey', as the Brazilian saying goes.

This too is a moral grammar, but one indexed less on codes than on the power of a 'strict father' to lay down the law.[40] This confluence of the pre- and the post-modern, traditional authority and the neoliberal voiding of the social, creates the basis on which the ruling elite and the excluded can meet. It is a meeting between those who have given up on waiting for the democratising promises of modernity and those no longer even nominally interested in pursuing them; those who have ceased to expect accountability and equality, and those unwilling to make concessions to such values.

It is in this sense that Bolsonarismo is the scar of a democracy that has failed to live up to its concept, as per the Adornian aphorism I have chosen as the epigraph for this text. Bolsonarismo converges around the paradoxical dream of a state of nature presided over by a paternal figure at once strict (with those who are not 'upstanding citizens') and permissive (with those who are); in which authority is both exercised decisively from above and devolved to local powers that are free to act in their own sphere of influence (the pastor, the landowner, the cop, the *pater familias*, the crime or paramilitary boss); in which conflicts of jurisdiction are nonetheless unlikely, because 'everyone knows their place'. The supreme leader thus really is at once a 'father of the horde' and a 'great little man'.[41] If he is entitled to a surplus of obscenity, it is not because of any intrinsic quality, but simply because he 'made it to the top'. He is therefore free to use his position in his own favour, *as any of us would*. ('If I can give my son steak, I will', as Bolsonaro said of his intention to make his middle son the Brazilian ambassador to the United States.)

The problem, of course, is that such a dream cannot work for everyone. If dog-eat-dog is made the rule, dog *will* eat dog, and the strong will feed on the weak. It is at this point of convergence, then, that Bolsonarismo (and even more so Bolsonaro's election) reveals itself as a huge misunderstanding. Whereas some (mostly poor) supporters tend to see him as the sheriff who will restore respect, others (mostly middle class) perceive him as a self-made chancer who will make life easier for go-getters like himself. The elite, finally, identify him above all with that figure from the plantation whose function was historically superseded by the army and the police. Unable to find a viable candidate in their own ranks, they chose to elect the *overseer*; and as long as he fulfils his duty of containing demands from below while ensuring even more draconian conditions for capital accumulation, he can manage his political capital as he pleases. A dangerous bargain, to be sure, as the overseer is given free rein to combine this political capital with the armed support of overseers like him in the police, paramilitary and armed forces.

Characteristic as it may be of Brazilian society, the confusion between order and law is hardly exclusive to it, and neither are any of the other elements considered here. Bolsonarismo is not reducible to either a national atavism or a simple repetition of historical fascism. It is a very contemporary tragedy, the conditions for which are given far and wide today, and tend to worsen as political and economic inequality grows and the effects of climate change intensify. Some form of overseer capitalism may well be part and parcel of that 'Brazilianisation' with which the developed world is menaced from time to time.

Dark moods: the rationality of the irrational

Among the thorniest problems in analyses of historical fascism is the interplay of deceit and desire, rationality and irrationality at its heart. To what extent were people duped into doing certain things? To what extent did they actually come to desire them – and how conscious were they of doing so? Were irrational justifications such as conspiracy theories mere attempts to rationalise anti-social urges run rampant? Was stirring and performing these urges merely a cover for base interests and calculations, such as appropriating the wealth of persecuted groups? Although it is not hard to notice that there is a certain 'phoniness' about fascists – a category that 'applies to the leaders as well as to the act of identification on the part of the masses'[42] – it is not always easy to tell who is faking what to whom, and when.

Thinking through these questions demands that we consider the discursive matrices and grammars on which the far right relies in relation to the affective conditions that give them something to latch on to: the shared affects or moods that enhance receptivity to far right politics and make it appear as a plausible answer in a concrete situation. Given that the recent resurgence of far right politics is a global phenomenon, we should expect to find the same affective conditions in several different countries, and be able to trace them back to processes taking place globally. And indeed, everywhere we look today we will find feelings of humiliation in the face of joblessness, underemployment, poverty and debt; fear of losing one's place in the world; wounded male pride; resentment against groups perceived as benefiting from transformations occurred in the last decades; abandonment and being taken for granted; and the diffuse, unfocused anti-systemic sentiments that follow from that. It is not hard to see the processes set in motion by neoliberal globalisation and accelerated by the 2008 crisis at the root of all of these. Yet there are other components to our present ambient mood that are less salient because the changes to which they respond unfold on a timescale that is longer and less immediately obvious. Among these, I would like to focus on one in particular that provides an interesting angle on the issue of phoniness; I will call it *denialism*.

Many have already drawn connections between the resurgence of the far right and denialism – about the holocaust, the crimes of the military dictatorship in Brazil, the climate crisis.[43] What I am calling by this name does not, however, refer exclusively to the lies that those who deny the existence of such things consciously spread. It also involves the public that consumes them and what attracts this public to them in the first place. My intuition here is that the state we describe as 'being in denial' – an unconscious attempt to protect oneself from a traumatic experience or thought by refusing to recognise its reality, or what Freud called *disavowal* – creates a demand for the commodity that conscious "denialists" supply. A booming market for the latter should therefore lead us to suspect an increase in the former. This would mean that it is no coincidence that a sizeable fraction of the Brazilian upper class would turn to those who blamed social conflict on 'cultural Marxism' when the modest gains made by historically marginalised groups forced them to confront their place and role in the country's extremely unequal social structure. Disgusted by the sight of his face in a mirror, Caliban chose to believe those who said that the mirror was broken. Likewise, it is no coincidence that the rise of leaders who eschew even the usual insincere platitudes about the environment comes after states and markets have failed to adequately address global warming for decades. It may be easier to imagine the end of the world than the end of capitalism, but it is much less costly psychologically to just wish its reality away.

Of course, the picture that the far right paints of the present is far from rosy. On the contrary, it is a narrative of war, of slow-building civilisational conflict finally coming to a head. But this is exactly where its perverse rationality lies. For while it on the one hand meets the demand for disavowal by fabulating easier problems with easier solutions, it does not fail, on the other, to acknowledge just how bad things are. In so doing, it speaks to the atmospheric dread of a world haunted by climate change, a stagnating economy, precarisation, the lack of democratic oversight and global pandemics much better than most well-meaning liberals would. It may well be that one of the reasons why Bolsonaro's popularity went up among the poor despite his disastrous handling of Covid-19 was that framing the situation as a choice between life and the economy was, for them, *objectively true*. It showed him as more in touch with their reality than anyone telling them to stay at home when they had no option but to go work.

This is not all there is to this rationality. In what I am calling denialism, disavowing the enormity of the challenges facing humankind is made all the more necessary by the conviction that no major structural transformations are possible. Now, if none of the big variables can change – because a real challenge to those at the top is inconceivable – all that is left for those at the bottom is to fight each other for ever-diminishing scraps. And this is exactly what the alternative reality that the far right puts in place of the disavowed traumatic content prepares its adherents for. By locating the source of the problem in the misappropriation of resources by various others (countries, ethnicities, religions, cultures, genders, sexualities) and framing the distributive conflict as a war, it provides justification for going after the weak and inoculates against the psychological burden of any excesses one might perform or support in the future. It is a '*conservative politics of antagonistic reproduction*', as Alberto Toscano aptly summarised it, in a world in which social reproduction tends to become ever more antagonistic.[44]

In denialism, then, we find what is ultimately the greatest, most ironic misunderstanding on which the far right relies: the fact that it seals an alliance between those gearing up for surviving in worsening conditions and an elite increasingly at ease with the idea that 'the earth no longer has room enough for them and for everyone else'.[45]

Rodrigo Nunes is Professor of Modern and Contemporary Philosophy at the Pontifical Catholic University of Rio de Janeiro. He is the author of Organisation of the Organisationless *(Mute, 2014) and* Neither Vertical Nor Horizontal: A Theory of Political Organisation *(Verso, 2021).*

Photography courtesy of Lara Mancinelli.

Notes

1. The estimate was made by statistician Reginaldo Prandi based on polls from the end of June 2020. Reginaldo Prandi, 'Adeptos Fiéis a Bolsonaro São 15% da População Adulta, Indica Datafolha', *Folha de São Paulo*, July 2 2020, www1.folha.uol.com.br/poder/2020/07/adeptos-fieis-a-bolsonaro-sao-15-da-populacao-adulta-indica-datafolha.shtml. Bolsonaro's popularity has remained fairly constant even though rejection of his administration has grown, reaching a peak at the height of the Covid-19 pandemic, when Brazil had over 1,000 deaths a day between early June and August. What changed in the meantime was the social profile of his support, the losses incurred among the upper class being recouped by gains made among the poor. Against most expectations, at the time of writing Bolsonaro enjoys the highest approval ratings since the start of his term (37%). Igor Gielow, 'Aprovação a Bolsonaro Sobe e É a Melhor Desde o Início do Mandato, Diz Datafolha', *Folha de São Paulo*, August 13 2020, www1.folha.uol.com.br/poder/2020/08/aprovacao-a-bolsonaro-sobe-e-e-a-melhor-desde-o-inicio-do-mandato-diz-datafolha.shtml.

2. Ernesto Laclau, *On Populist Reason* (London: Verso, 2005), 101ff.

3. See Gabriel Feltran, '"The Revolution We Are Living"', *HAU: Journal of Ethnographic Theory* 10:1 (2020), 12.

4. See Eder Sader, *Quando Novos Personagens Entraram em Cena. Experiências e Lutas dos Trabalhadores da Grande São Paulo, 1970-1980* (São Paulo: Paz e Terra, 2010).

5. We could thus say, misappropriating Raymond Williams somewhat, that 'discursive matrices' and 'structures of feeling' always presuppose one another. That would not be a problem for Sader, who speaks of 'demands about social reproduction and symbolic recognition' as enjoying a 'virtual existence', that is, actualised in conscience once they are articulated in language and become objects of reflection. See Sader, *Quando Novos Personagens*, 58.

6. Gabriel Feltran, 'Formas Elementares da Vida Politica. Sobre o Movimento Totalitario no Brasil (2013-)', *Novos Estudos* (2020) novosestudos.com.br/formas-elementares-da-vida-politica-sobre-o-movimento-totalitario-no-brasil-2013

7. As for anti-intellectualism, if its meaning does not change, its source and reference points do: among the upper class, religious authority often takes a back seat to contempt for knowledge without immediate economic utility and the conspiracy theories spread by YouTube celebrities like far-right guru (and avowed Bolsonaro influence) Olavo de Carvalho.

8. Verónica Gago, *Neoliberalism from Below: Popular Pragmatics and Baroque Economies*, trans. Liz Mason-Deese (Durham, NC: Duke University Press, 2017), 36.

9. Ibid., 6.

10. Ibid., 11.

11. Rosana Pinheiro-Machado and Lucia Scalco, 'From Hope to Hate: The Rise of Conservative Subjectivity in Brazil', *HAU: Journal of Ethnographic Theory* 10:1 (2020), 21–22, https://www.journals.uchicago.edu/doi/full/10.1086/708627

12. This is how obscure diplomatic kook-turned-Foreign Minister Ernesto Araújo defines 'globalism'. See Ernesto Araújo, 'About', *Metapolítica Brasil* blog, https://www.metapoliticabrasil.com/about. For a well-informed look into the role of YouTube in the rise of Bolsonarismo, see Max Fisher and Amanda Taub, 'How YouTube Radicalized Brazil', *The New York Times*, August 11 (2019), https://www.nytimes.com/2019/08/11/world/americas/youtube-brazil.html.

13. Theodor Adorno, *Aspects of the New Right-Wing Extremism* (Cambridge: Polity, 2020), 19; translation modified.

14. Camila Rocha, 'Think Tanks Ultraliberais e Nova Direita Brasileira', *Le Monde Diplomatique Brasil* 124 (2017), diplomatique.org.br/think-tanks-ultraliberais-e-nova-direita-brasileira.

15. Friedrich von Hayek, *Law, Legislation and Liberty: A New Statement of the Liberal Principles of Justice and Political Economy*, Volume 2 (London: Routledge, 1998), 97.

16. See 'Religion and Politics in Contemporary Brazil' by Carolina Evangelista in this issue of *Radical Philosophy* 2.09.

17. Isabela Kalil, 'Quem São e no que Acreditam os Eleitores de Jair Bolsonaro', Research Report, Fundação Escola de Sociologia e Política de São Paulo (2018).

18. This is corroborated by Débora Salles' analysis of the discourse of the Bolsonaro campaign on Twitter using a methodology developed by Sara Walton and Brownyn Boon to apply Laclau and Mouffe's insights to data analysis. Débora Salles, *The Twitter Effect. The Politics of Tweeting During the 2018 Brazilian Presidential Election*, Doctoral Thesis, Graduate Programme in Information Science, Federal University of Rio de Janeiro (2020).

19. Among the different types of Bolsonaro voter identified by Kalil there were, for instance, the poor people who defended a 'minimal state', which they explained as minimal intervention from the state in religious or moral matters rather than the reduction of public services. See Kalil, 'Quem São e no que Acreditam', 20.

20. Nancy Fraser, 'From Progressive Neoliberalism to Trump – and Beyond', *American Affairs* 1:4 (2017), americanaffairsjournal.org/2017/11/progressive-neoliberalism-trump-beyond.

21. See John B. Judis, *The Populist Explosion: How the Great Recession Transformed American and European Politics* (New York: Columbia Global Reports, 2016), 10.

22. Jason Hackworth, *Faith Based: Religious Neoliberalism and the Politics of Welfare in the United States* (Athens, GA: University of Georgia Press, 2012), 45. This is in fact an important component in the constitution of a 'neoliberalism from below', which Gago curiously overlooks.

23. See Melinda Cooper, *Family Values: Between Neoliberalism and the New Social Conservatism* (Cambridge, MA: MIT Press, 2017).

24. This is what Foucault had in mind when he wrote that 'a society made up of enterprise-units is at once the principle of decipherment linked to liberalism and its programming for the rationalisation of a society and an economy'. Michel Foucault, *The Birth of Biopolitics. Lectures at the Collège de France, 1978-1979*, trans. Graham Burchell (Basingstoke: Palgrave, 2008), 225.

25. Jennifer Silva, *Coming Up Short: Working Class Adulthood in an Age of Uncertainty* (Oxford: Oxford University Press, 2013), 155.

26. Ibid., 150.

27. On the therapeutic narrative, see ibid., 114ff.

28. See Lauren Berlant, *Cruel Optimism* (Durham: Duke University Press, 2011).

29. On the concept of negative solidarity, see Jason Read, 'Negative Solidarity. The Affective Economy of Austerity', *Unemployed Negativity* blog, October 24 2019, http://www.unemployednegativity.com/2019/10/negative-solidarity-affective-economy.html.

30. On the combination of class anxiety, meritocracy and punitivism among Lula voters turned Bolsonaristas, see Pinheiro-Machado and Scalco, 'From Hope to Hate', 27.

31. See Will Davies, 'The New Neoliberalism', *New Left Review* 101 (2016), 121–34.

32. For an overview, see Tales Ab'Saber, 'Ordem e Violência no Brasil', in Bernardo Kucinski et al., *Bala Perdida: a Violência Policial no Brasil e os Desafios para sua Superação* (São Paulo: Boitempo, 2015), 97–102.

33. See, for instance, Sérgio Buarque de Hollanda, *Roots of Brazil*, trans. G. Harvey Summ (Notre Dame: Notre Dame University Press, 2012).

34. See Roberto Schwarz, 'Misplaced Ideas: Literature and Society in Late Nineteenth-Century Brazil', *Misplaced Ideas. Essays on Brazilian Culture*, ed. and trans. John Gledson (London: Verso, 1992), 19–32.

35. It is worth remembering that Bolsonaro only became the frontrunner in 2018 after Lula was ruled out of the race. The Car Wash Operation judge who convicted Lula, Sergio Moro, went on to become the Minister of Justice, but resigned a year later, accusing Bolsonaro of trying to interfere with criminal investigations against his oldest son.

36. This is a slight détournement of the slogan *direitos humanos para humanos direitos* ('human rights for "straight", as in "upstanding", humans').

37. '[T]o "respect" connotes an option, and is therefore the more appropriate word for those who think themselves as superior'; "to obey" is compulsory, and is therefore much more appropriate for those who have learnt to think themselves or as classified and thought as inferior'. Roberto DaMatta, *Fé em Deus e Pé na Tábua. Ou Como e Por que o Trânsito Enlouquece no Brasil* (São Paulo: Rocco, 2010), 69. Roberto Andrés connects the growth of this attitude to the 255% rise in the number of motorised vehicles during PT's administrations, which the party held up as evidence of success in the fight against inequality. Roberto Andrés, 'Jeitinho sobre Rodas', *Piauí* 154 (2019), 32–35.

38. Corey Robin, *The Reactionary Mind: Conservatism from Edmund Burke to Donald Trump* (Oxford: Oxford University Press, 2018), second edition, 10ff.

39. Wendy Brown, *In the Ruins of Neoliberalism: The Rise of Antidemocratic Politics in the West* (New York: Columbia University Press, 2019), 173.

40. On the strict (versus 'nurturant') father as metaphorical model for conservative politics, see George Lakoff, *The Political Mind: A Cognitive Scientist's Guide to Your Brain and Its Politics* (New York: Penguin, 2009), 77–81.

41. See Theodor Adorno, 'Freudian Theory and the Pattern of Fascist Propaganda', in *The Essential Frankfurt School Reader*, eds. Andrew Arato and Eike Gephardt (London: Continuum, 1997), 125–8.

42. Adorno, 'Freudian Theory', 136.

43. See, for example, Déborah Danowski, *Negacionismos* (São Paulo: n-1, 2018).

44. Alberto Toscano, 'Notes on Late Fascism', *Historical Materialism* blog, April 2 2017, http://www.historicalmaterialism.org/blog/notes-late-fascism#_ftn25. (Italics in the original.)

45. Bruno Latour, *Down to Earth: Politics in the New Climatic Regime*, trans. Catherine Porter (Cambridge: Polity, 2018), 1.

Amefricanity

The black feminism of Lélia Gonzalez

Raquel Barreto

Though a quarter of the total population, black women represent just 2% of the legislative body of Brazil's federal government, the National Congress. Yet their visibility in public debate has grown radically in recent years with younger activists beginning to occupy spaces in media, academia and the arts. Lélia Gonzalez (1935-1994) has become a major point of reference for this new generation, and not only because of her pioneering position as a black woman intellectual in the 70s and 80s, or the example set by her political commitments and engagements. It is also because her thought foreshadowed contemporary debates concerning race relations in Brazil and beyond. Bolsonaro's Brazil is in many ways stuck at a crossroads between such processes of social transformation and political forces determined to stop them at all costs.

Gonzalez took the experience of black people in Brazil as the point from which to articulate an original perspective on the country's formation that both contested and resituated official accounts. She drew both from Marxism, in order to understand the implantation and development of capitalism in the colonial Americas, and Lacanian psychoanalysis, to interpret a national unconscious revealed in cultural and linguistic elements imprinted by colonialism and the disavowal of African and indigenous origins. She brought together the disavowed experiences of African descendants and indigenous into a single category – *Amefricanity* – which questioned the 'Latin' identity that suppressed both, thereby offering a contribution *avant la lettre* to the conversation on decoloniality taking place today. In her insistence on always thinking race, class and gender in relation, she not only was an early practitioner of what would become known as 'intersectionality', but she laid the basis for a black feminism in Brazil – a facet of her work so influential now as to risk overshadowing the rest. It is as a tribute to

Gonzalez's ongoing relevance and her rediscovery today that this paper uses her trajectory to comment on the continuities and discontinuities between two disparate moments in the history of Brazil and the struggle for social and racial justice.

Trouble in paradise

Born Lélia Almeida on 1 February 1935 in Belo Horizonte, capital of the state of Minas Gerais, she was the penultimate daughter of a large family with few economic resources. Her father died when she was a child; her mother, of indigenous descent, was a domestic worker. Brazilian society imposes a marked racial and sexual division of domestic labour: not only do women perform it almost exclusively, but poor black women often do it in the homes of wealthier white families.[1] Like many in her position, Gonzalez began her professional life as a nanny, though she managed to break with the path laid out for her by finishing her studies and attending university. As she would later recall: 'The only way I found to overcome these problems was to be the first student in the class. We all know the story: "she's black but she's smart"'.[2] She studied History and Geography and then Philosophy at what is today the State University of Rio de Janeiro, teaching at several colleges and higher education institutions. In the late 1970s, Gonzales became one of the few black lecturers at the Pontifical Catholic University of Rio de Janeiro (PUC-Rio), where she worked until the end of her life.

Gonzalez's trajectory personified several of the changes taking place in the political, academic, artistic and cultural circuits of the 1970s and 80s. The spaces in which she circulated and the encounters she had encapsulate the period. In the late 70s, while the military dictatorship began a slow thaw, the political and cultural fields in Brazil started opening up to a plurality of new ideas. It was during this period that indigenous, feminist, black and gay movements began to emerge, each contesting the centrality of the working class as the subject of social transformation.

Examples of the effervescence of that moment were the creation of the Parque Lage School of Visual Arts in 1975, an epoch-making experimental art school at which Gonzalez taught the country's first institutional course on black culture; and the Freudian School of Rio de Janeiro, one of the first institutions in Brazil to popularise Lacanian psychoanalysis. From Lacan she would take concepts such as 'disavowal' and 'cultural neurosis', and give them her own distinctive elaboration. Gonzalez, also in 1975, participated in the foundation of the Quilombo Samba School, initiated by important artists from the world of samba as a way to contest the growing commercialisation of Carnival and return the popular festival to a more political, popular and black perspective.[3] Her respect for and interest in popular culture would result in a book, *Festas Populares no Brasil* (1987).[4]

Gonzalez played a significant role in the reorganisation of the Left in later years, participating in the formation of the Workers' Party (PT) and joining its National Directorate from 1981 to 1984. She ran for a federal congressional seat in 1982 and received enough votes to place her as an alternate. She would soon leave PT, however, for what she saw as a lack of commitment to the antiracist struggle, accusing the party of 'racism by omission' in an open letter that became well-known.[5] Instead she joined the Democratic Labour Party (PDT), for which she ran for state legislature in 1986, once again becoming an alternate.[6] She explained her commitment to institutional politics by saying: 'It is a space that we have to conquer. ... It is necessary to fight and guarantee our places, which, of course, have never been ceded to us.'[7]

Among all of Gonzalez's engagements, the most significant was undoubtedly with the black movement, just as it was going through its process of reorganisation after the 1964 military coup that dismantled all social movements and opened a gap between political generations.[8] The dictatorship not only restricted freedom of association and persecuted leaders, but also banned the debate on racism through a legal trap in the National Security Act of September 1969 which prescribed the crime of

'incitement to hatred or racial discrimination'. It might seem anti-racist, but this would be used to criminalise anyone who proposed to discuss race at all, since any accusation of racism could be interpreted as a subversion of the 'paradise of racial democracy'.[9]

Although it began to be elaborated as a foundational ideology during the Imperial period (1822-1889), the discourse of 'racial democracy' received its canonical formulation in 1933 with the publication of Gilberto Freyre's *The Masters and the Slaves* [*Casa Grande e Senzala*.][10] In the country that received the largest contingent of enslaved Africans (around 4 million, or 40% of the transatlantic traffic between the sixteenth and the nineteenth centuries) and was the last in the Americas to abolish slavery, this discourse played a major role in minimising the centrality of racial domination and exploitation in the formation of Brazil, constructing the notion of a supposedly more benevolent Portuguese colonisation and a miscegenated country in which racism had no place. One of Gonzalez's contributions to this debate was to point out that the romanticisation of miscegenation was effectively a way of covering up the trauma of colonial rape.

Yet the Brazilian elite were not the only ones to repress the racial question. In the context of the Cold War, the racial question was eschewed both by the Right and the Left. If for the military it was a subversive topic that the Left used to sow division, for the latter it was a US import that threatened the centrality of class struggle. Although this did not prevent the black movement from building alliances with others in the struggle for re-democratisation, it forced them to stress that full democracy would not exist so long as blacks were excluded. To end that exclusion it would be necessary for them to have distinct organisations of their own.

The reorganisation of the black movement began in 1971 with the creation of the Palmares Group in Porto Alegre, one of the whitest and most racist regions in the country – nowadays part of Bolsonaro's heartland. In the following years, other groups would spring up in capitals like Rio de Janeiro, São Paulo, Belo Horizonte and Salvador. Gonzalez took part in the foundation of one of these, the Institute for Research on Black Cultures (IPCN) in 1974. The main reference points for this new black movement were the Civil Rights and Black Power movements in the United States and the anticolonial struggles taking place in Portuguese colonies like Angola, Cape Verde and Mozambique. Extremely popular soul music parties in working-class neighbourhoods at the time spread the cultural influence of North American black culture and ideas of ethnic pride and belonging. These elements – plus a Marxist influence that was embraced by some and rejected by others – led this new movement to break with the emphasis on respectability and integration that had been characteristic of the organisational efforts of previous generations.[11] This process would culminate in 1978 with the creation of the first national organisation to coordinate anti-racist struggle, the Unified Black Movement (MNU); Gonzalez would be a member of its national leadership until 1982. And she she would found the N'Zinga Black Women Collective in which anti-racist, anti-sexist and popular struggles were further combined.

The Amefricanity category

In Brazil as elsewhere, the circulation of intellectual production is organised according to a gendered, racialised logic that renders invisible the work of black women. On the few occasions when their names are inscribed in the canon of intellectual thought, that inscription is in the margins, a 'peripheral place at the centre'[12] which acts as an exception that confirms the rule. To this structural exclusion is added another, deliberate, exclusion derivative of the fact that in many situations their narratives confront hegemonic assumptions in their field. This is a fate that befell Gonzalez, as her dissident account of race in Brazil contested two pillars of national identity: the myths of racial democracy and miscegenation.

Like other black intellectuals of her generation who had a dual affiliation to the black movement and academia, she stood out for her efforts to de-centre Eurocentric hegemony in the production of knowledge, and this also led her to subvert the impersonality of academic language. In an attempt to create a style of writing that incorporated features of speech, she impregnated some of her academic texts with Afro-Brazilian orality, incorporating other rationalities in academic discourse, without abandoning rigour and seriousness. Besides, her analysis of the relation between capital, labour and race in Brazil was deeply rooted in a Latin American reality and took a rather critical position on the work of US-based African-American intellectuals, partly because, like many in her generation, she shared a certain anti-imperialist rejection of the role of the US in the world. This is an important difference to the current generation, in which an often uncritical and decontextualised reception of the North American debate is noticeable. Today's discussion of colourism, for example, more or less directly imported from the United States, runs against the grain of the Brazilian black movement's struggle in the 1970s to educate black people to recognise and take pride in their African ancestry regardless of the tone of their skin.

The originality of Gonzalez's contribution resides in her formulation of an alternative perspective on the social and cultural formation of Brazil that moves black people from the margins to the centre. In doing so, she makes protagonists of black women, something unheard of at the time.

> If we pay close attention to some aspects of so-called Brazilian culture, we'll notice right away that, in its more or less conscious manifestations, it hides, while simultaneously reveals, the marks of the Africanity that constitute it. ... From there, we can also spot the place of black women in this process of cultural formation, as well as the different modes of rejection/integration of their role.[13]

In this process, she mobilises the psychoanalytic concept of *Verneinung* ('disavowal' or 'denial') to address the way in which the recognition of racism is repressed. For Gonzalez, racism is integral to the unconscious structures of Brazilian society, and disavowing that, as well as the African roots of its culture, is precisely the purpose that the myth of racial democracy serves.

> To better understand the tricks that racism plays ... it is worth remembering the Freudian category of denial

(*Verneinung*): 'a process through which the individual, although formulating one of his desires, thoughts or feelings that were until then repressed, continues to defend themselves from it, denying that it belongs to them'. As a disavowal of our *Latinamefricanity* [*ladinoamefricanos*], 'Brazilian' racism turns precisely against those who are its living witnesses (black people) whilst claiming not to do so (Brazilian 'racial democracy').[14]

In this text we find the concept of *Amefricanity* [*amefricanidade*], which Gonzalez proposed as a key with which to think the specificity of the experience of Africans and African descendants as it was historically constituted in American soil.

> Beyond its purely geographic character, [Amefricanity] designates a historical process of intense cultural dynamics (resistance, accommodation, reinterpretation, creation of new forms) referenced in African models but referring to the construction of a whole ethnic identity.[15]

Amefricanity not only proposes to think the black experience in the Americas in a unified way, but also brings to light what is, alongside the contribution of indigenous culture, silenced and disavowed in the notion of a shared 'Latin' identity. It refuses the idealisation of the African continent for a perspective in which diasporic displacement is essential to the formation of a black identity. Finally, it challenges the centrality and hegemony of the United States in the creation of models of analysis and conceptualisations of blackness.

Double trouble

Gonzalez's work from the 1970s is also concerned with the function and structure of Brazilian capitalism from the perspective of race relations. That is the moment when she was in close dialogue with Marxist thought, particularly Louis Althusser, a dialogue that would cease in the following decades when her main points of reference became psychoanalysis and Afrocentrism.[16] An important debate in which Gonzalez became involved in this period, responding in part to dependency theory, was that of the 'unequal and combined development' of Brazilian capitalism. Referring to W.E.B. Du Bois, Gonzalez depicted how blacks, post-slavery, had been driven by 'a long process of marginalisation ... to the condition of the most oppressed and exploited sector of the Brazilian population', coming to constitute an industrial reserve army in a context where remnants of pre-capitalist productive formations coexisted with neocolonial dependency.[17]

Gonzalez kept touch with black intellectuals and activists from around the world, such that in her 1982 campaign she could present herself as the first black woman to represent the Brazilian black movement abroad – a reference to her participation in the fourth meeting of the Latin American Studies Association (LASA) at UCLA in 1979. She held exchanges with Angela Davis, Aimé Césaire, Molefi Asante and Carlos Moore, a staunch critic of the Cuban Revolution's failure to address racism.

Her pioneering role in the formation of Brazilian black feminism is due in large to the way she disturbed a hegemonic feminism based on the universalisation of the experience of middle-class white women – a feminism incapable of contemplating the complexity of gender and class relations in a racist society built on slavery. Years before the African-American scholar Kimberlé Crenshaw's reflections on intersectionality, she had already discussed the impact of raciality on gender relations, the racial and sexual division of labour, as well as the triple discrimination and economic overexploitation to which the interconnection of race, class and gender exposed black women.[18]

> There is a double discrimination against non-white women in the continent, African and Amerindian. The double character of their biological – or racial and sexual – condition makes them more oppressed and exploited in a region dependent on a patriarchal-racist capitalism. Precisely because this system transforms differences into inequalities, the discrimination they suffer takes on a triple character, given their class position: Amerindians and African Americans are part, for the most part, of the immense Afrolatinoamerican proletariat.[19]

Looking at the statistics of the 'Brazilian miracle' of the 1970s, which produced rapid economic growth without affecting the nation's concentration of wealth, Gonzalez observed that the greatest distributive disparity occurred between whites and blacks and not between men and women. This questioned a pillar of white feminism, which conceived of patriarchal domination in a one-dimensional way. Not only were different types of masculinity shaped by variables such as class, race and sexual orientation, but the mediation between race and gender placed black men simultaneously in the peculiar position of dominant subjects (in relation to women in their own community) and subordinate subjects (in relation to white power). On the other hand, and this was certainly one of the thorniest issues she raised within the feminist movement of her time, the economic and social emancipation of white women could also be understood as being based on the exploitation of black women as domestic workers:

> There is an unmistakeable political backwardness in Brazilian feminist movements, as they are led by middle-class white women. Here too one can see the need to disavow racism. … Here too one can see the need to hide from the scene the crucial issue: the liberation of white women has been done at the expense of the exploitation of black women.[20]

'Everyone knew their place'

The black movement that Gonzalez helped constitute in Brazil in the 1970s distinguished itself from that of previous generations by openly confronting the myth of racial democracy, proposing an alternative account of national formation and reclaiming an identity specific to black Brazilians. The movement vigorously denounced racial discrimination and its socio-political consequences, as well as political violence, proposing an alternative project for the country as a whole (at least as far as the Unified Black Movement was concerned), and demanding historical reparations for the black population in Brazil. The latter would bear fruit over the last decade, particularly with the establishment of affirmative action for poor, black and indigenous students at federal universities in 2012.[21] The effects have been remarkable: between 2010 and 2018, the number of black and brown undergraduates at public universities went up by 10.5%, and for the first time in history they are now the majority (51.2%); 41.9% of undergraduates in 2018 had used the quota system to get into university.[22]

Yet it is precisely such long-term victories of the black movement which have sparked responses in the opposite direction. A case in point is the Constitutional Amendment of 2012 which lifted domestic workers out of informal labour agreements and granted them basic rights such as retirement and paid holidays. This was a cause of the black movement since the 1940s, when a group of black women instituted the Association of Domestic Workers in Rio de Janeiro with the support of Abdias do Nascimento's Black Experimental Theatre company. To many upper- and middle-class employers, however, the Amendment amounted to an attack on their right to have cheap household labour and created a rift with Dilma Rousseff's PT government. Partly, it was in this context that the mentality which lead to Bolsonaro's victory began brewing. Rights for the black population were perceived as privileges that should be restricted to a small class; demands for equality were perceived as claims for special treatment. Thus, even though the actual balance sheet of the PT years is ambiguous – the same period saw a sharp rise in mortality rates among black youth, and the 2006 Drug Law has hit the black community disproportionately and increased incarceration[23] – policies like affirmative action lit the fuse for a *politics of resentment* that would explode when a sharp economic downturn began in 2014.

The crossroads at which Brazil finds itself now is the opposite of the one that Lélia Gonzalez experienced. The late 70s and early 80s were filled with the promise of the end of the dictatorship and a new constitution, as if the dam which the military regime erected could no longer hold and demands long ignored were to burst forth irresistibly. Today, it feels as though old Brazil has judged that even the modest victories which the historically-excluded have won were too much and the clock must be set back to a past in which 'everyone knew their place'. Symptomatically, Bolsonaro has closed the Special Secretariat for the Advancement of Racial Equality created in 2003, and he has appointed as head of an institution for the promotion of African-Brazilian culture a black man who denies the existence of racism in Brazil and describes the black movement as 'scum'. (A good reminder, if one was needed, of the limits of tokenism.) Yet the rediscovery of Gonzalez' thought is a consequence of precisely the kind of transformation that these forces are resisting: the democratisation of education and the rise of a new generation of black activists and intellectuals. While the conflict in which Gonzalez fought has come out in the open once again, her thought and trajectory can be a weapon and a compass for those who continue the fight.

Translated by Rafael Mófreita Saldanha

Raquel Barreto is working on a PhD on the Black Panther Party and visuality, politics and power, at the Fluminense Federal University (UFF). She was co-curator of an exhibition on the pioneering Black novelist Carolina Maria de Jesus at the Moreira Salles Institute, for the 2020 São Paulo Biennial.

Notes

1. In Brazil it is common for middle class families to employ domestic workers and for them to sleep at their job – a legacy of slavery.

2. Lélia Gonzalez, 'Entrevista', O *Pasquim*, 871 (20-26 March 1986), 9.

3. Samba Schools are the associations that organise carnival parades. They are organised by neighbourhoods or communities and maintain a strong territorial, social and cultural identity. *Quilombo* (maroon community), with its connotations of organisation, freedom, resistance and equality, is a central idea for the black movement in Brazil.

4. Lélia Gonzalez, *Festas Populares no Brasil* (Rio de Janeiro: Índex, 1987).

5. Lélia Gonzalez, 'Racismo por omissão', *Folha de São Paulo* (13 August 1983).

6. During the process of restructuring the Brazilian party system following the dictatorship, PDT was the heir of a Left populism (*trabalhismo* or 'labourism') whose origins date back to Getúlio Vargas in the 1930s. In the period in which Gonzalez was affiliated to it, PDT boasted a sizeable popular base and important black leaders as members, among whom was Abdias do Nascimento, a pioneering figure in the 1940s. Its social and political composition is starkly different today.

7. The platform of her two campaigns was similar, featuring demands that were radical for the time and remain relevant today. These include the depathologisation of homosexuality (which eventually took place in 1985), giving land titles to slum-dwellers, and the decriminalisation of abortion, still illegal today except in a few circumstances.

8. Michael George Hanchard, *Orpheus and Power: The Movimento Negro of Rio de Janeiro and São Paulo, Brazil, 1945–1988* (Princeton: Princeton University Press, 1994).

9. Gonzalez was surveilled but never arrested or tortured, both common at the time. She was first investigated in 1972 under suspicion of 'recruitment of adherents to the Marxist doctrine'. No evidence was found. Subsequent mentions in reports made by the Department of Political and Social Order (DOPS) are related to her activities in the black movement and, later, in PT. The documentation is available at the Rio de Janeiro State Public Archive. Sector: Comunismo, Folder 112, Sheets 211-217 (Fundo de Polícias Políticas no Rio de Janeiro, DOPS Archives).

10. Gilberto Freyre, *The Masters and the Slaves: A Study in the Development of Brazilian Civilisation*, trans. Samuel Putnam (Berkeley and Los Angeles: University of California Press, 1986).

11. See Paulina Alberto, *Terms of Inclusion: Black Intellectuals in Twentieth-Century Brazil* (Chapel Hill: University of North Carolina Press, 2011).

12. I take this concept from Fernanda Miranda's work on the place of black authors in the Brazilian canon. Fernanda Miranda, *Silêncios Prescritos. Estudos de Romances de Autoras Negras Brasileiras, 1859-2006* (Rio de Janeiro: Malê, 2019).

13. Lélia Gonzalez, 'Racismo e Sexismo na Cultura Brasileira', *Movimentos Sociais Urbanos, Minorias Étnicas e Outros Estudos* (Brasília: ANPOCS, 1983), 226.

14. Lélia Gonzalez, 'Categoria político-cultural da amefricanidade', *Primavera Para as Rosas Negras: Lélia Gonzalez em Primeira Pessoa* (São Paulo: Diáspora Africana, 2018), 321–322.

15. Lélia Gonzalez, 'Nany', *Primavera Para as Rosas Negras*, 336.

16. The reception of the debate on Afrocentricity in Brazil was still incipient at the time. Most references to it in Gonzalez's work are taken from Molefi Kete Asante, *Afrocentricity* (Trenton, NJ: Africa World Press, 1988).

17. Lélia Gonzalez, 'Mulher Negra', *Jornal Mulherio* 3 (October/-September 1981).

18. What Crenshaw gave a name to was of course already present in such forerunners as the black feminism that had developed within the Communist Party of the United States of America (out of which emerged Angela Davis), the Third World Women's Alliance and the Combahee River Collective.

19. Lélia Gonzalez, 'Por um feminismo Afro-latino-americano', *Primavera Para as Rosas Negras*, 314.

20. Lélia Gonzalez. 'Cultura, etnicidade, trabalho: efeitos linguísticos e políticos da exploração da mulher', presented at the 7th Conference of the Latin American Studies Association. Pittsburgh, (5-7 April 1979), 20.

21. Although the Brazilian system is similar to the North American, public universities in Brazil are entirely free. Curiously, the first university in Brazil to autonomously implement a quota system was Gonzalez' *alma mater*, the State University of Rio de Janeiro, in 2003.

22. Associação Nacional dos Diretores de Institutos Federais de Educação Superior, 'V Pesquisa Nacional de Perfil Sociêconomico e Cultural dos/as Graduandos/as das IFES' (2018), 210–12, http://www.andifes.org.br/wp-content/uploads/2019/05/V-Pesquisa-Nacional-de-Perfil-Socioecon%C3%B4mico-e-Cultural-dos-as-Graduandos-as-das-IFES-2018.pdf.

23. The problematic law leaves it to judges to decide the circumstances that distinguish users from dealers, leaving room for racist interpretation.

'Brazil above everything, God above all'

Ana Carolina Evangelista

Religious influence in the Brazilian state is hardly new, but it has become more evident with the 2018 campaign and subsequent election of Jair Bolsonaro, whose slogan was 'Brazil above everything, God above all'. It was not the first time a presidential candidate had run a campaign with straightforward religious overtones, but it was the first time such a candidate was elected. Bolsonaro was the first to receive overt support from evangelicals, among whom he won 70% of the vote.[1] But the influence of other Christian groups over his administration has also been enormous, such that a simple opposition between fundamentalist evangelicals and progressive Catholics is misguided. Nuances, dissidences and disputes exist on both sides. However, despite the bases of both having become more conservative in recent years, the main protagonist and beneficiary of this conservative shift has been the evangelical leadership.

The 2018 Brazilian election represented a sea change for the party system that had been in place since the country's re-democratisation after the military regime in the 1980s. Congress has never been so fragmented – thirty different parties are now represented in it – and the present legislature has the largest number of first-time congresspeople in history. The elections also marked the end of a two-decade pattern in which the main political disputes would take place between party blocs led by the Workers' Party (PT) and the Social Democrats (PSDB). More surprisingly, the Social Liberal Party (PSL), which in twenty years of existence had elected only one congressperson, suddenly found itself with 52 members of Congress as well as the president himself – who had only been in the party for twenty months when he decided to split and start his own extreme right political grouping, the Alliance for Brazil.[2] The latter, according to their official statement, intend 'to fight in the trenches to defend Judeo-Christian values, national sovereignty, democracy, and entrepreneurship as the driving force behind our economy.'

What do these elements mean regarding the relationship between religion and politics in Brazil? Is there a greater coordination between conservative movements in Brazilian politics and, at the same time, a deepening of interaction between Christian political forces? Current Brazilian public debate mostly addresses the influence of evangelicals in politics, but we ought to remember they were neither the first to go into politics, nor are they the only religious group present in the legislative, executive, or judiciary branches. A proper discussion of this issue demands that we understand the characteristics of the different religious groups in Brazilian society and politics today – their profile, composition, demands, presence and territorial expansion – and consider the religion-politics relationship, in Brazil as elsewhere, in greater historical depth.

Evangelicals and religious transition

Brazil officially became a secular state with the creation of the Republic in 1891. However, politicians have always had the Catholic Church as a major ally and have favoured it in several political, administrative acts and decisions.[3] Crucifixes have always been prominent in public schools, courthouses and in legislative houses at the municipal, state and federal levels. These are not just symbols, and many legislative houses continue to open their sessions with the sentence: 'We start our works under God's protection.' This phenomenon, which we could name a 'Catholic occupation' of the public arena, has most often appeared natural and gone unremarked, in part also due to the absence of any other major religious groups. For as long as this was the case, secularity hardly ever seemed to be an issue. The naturalisation of this link between Catholicism and state power only started coming into question with the growth of evangelicalism.

The latest national survey by the Brazilian Institute of Geography and Statistics (the 2010 Census) pointed to increasing religious diversification in Brazil, as well as a steady evangelical growth. Over 40 years, the percentage of evangelicals has gone from 5% to 22%, representing more than 16 million people.[4] Simultaneously, Catholics, long the overwhelming majority, have significantly declined. The number of those who claim 'no religion' has risen from 1 million people in 1970 to 15 million in 2010.[5] And the amount of participants in Afro-Brazilian faiths like Candomblé and Umbanda, as well as spiritist movements and global religions such as Buddhism and Islam is also on the rise.

An evangelical belt has emerged in the urban outskirts of Brazil. Although it is growing across social strata, it does so predominately at the base of the social pyramid, in urban and peripheral areas where the population experience a lack of government support and welfare. In this ongoing religious transition, evangelicals do not stand out only for their numbers but also for the intensity of their religious commitment. This is, in short, a growing population that is also more active in its faith in a country with a lapsed Catholic majority.

The evangelical universe is more heterogeneous and broad than usually imagined. The so-called 'Brazilian Evangelical Church', spoken of as a unity, does not exist; what the term supposedly refers to is neither a homogeneous nor a uniform group. It is an assortment of churches and groups whose classifications can be made based on distinct historical and theological heritages, governance models, practices and rituals. It has been estimated there are more than 179,000 evangelical denominations in Brazil – an expression of the autonomous spirit and fissiparous tendencies of the Protestant DNA.

These denominations vary in organisational structure, from the rigidly hierarchical to the horizontal. As for politics, some groups steer clear from it, others pursue covert agendas, a few have open political projects. This is the case of *Igreja Universal do Reino de Deus* [Universal Church of the Kingdom of God], a Pentecostal church founded in Brazil in the late 1970s and present today in almost a hundred countries. Though far from the most popular, since it began to move into institutional politics Universal has become one of the most visible, and has always had the second or third largest number of representatives in Congress.

Universal is part of a subgroup of pentecostal churches characterised by the use of media outlets to broadcast services, the emphasis on exorcism and divine healing and looser moral and behavioural codes that associate upward social mobility with devotion and grace.[6] Such pentecostal churches tend to be intolerant of other religious beliefs, considering them either obsolete or a channel through which demons intervene in the world.[7] Universal, organised as a business conglomerate, adopts aggressive marketing and communication techniques in order to attract more followers. Its founder and principle leader, Bishop Edir Macedo, controls the church in an entirely vertical manner, controlling over 10,000 temples with 14,000 pastors and millions of believers.

Igreja Universal's political project is overt enough for it to be the subject of Edir Macedo's 2008 bestseller *Plano de Poder* (literally 'A Plan for Power'), in which he talks about awakening 'the numerical potential of Evangelicals' to 'decide any election'.[8] It is oriented towards increasing the church's sphere of influence through territorial presence, media control and political participation. As a political force, Universal has learned to navigate the Brazilian electoral system rules and has consolidated its legislative presence and influence over administrations at all levels since 1990. Pragmatic, it has worked with progressive and conservative governments alike. Its greatest triumph to date was the 2016 election of former bishop and Macedo's nephew Marcelo Crivella as the mayor of the second largest city in the country, Rio de Janeiro. Deploying a characteristic communication tactic of overestimating the segment's size, Crivella's inaugural speech 'thanked God and the 90% of Evangelicals in Rio de Janeiro'.[9] As Ari Pedro Oro has argued, its capacity to infuse with new meaning the act of voting and politics in general by means of its institutional charisma has been key to Universal's electoral success – which has, moreover, produced 'a mimetic effect on other evangelic churches'. Combined with the fact that its presence in politics 'has not gone unnoticed' by political parties, this makes it a relevant actor in the current Brazilian political conjuncture.[10]

The evangelical segment is not sealed off from the rest of society, nor driven exclusively by faith. Those who are a part of it have demands towards the state and public institutions beyond just religious matters. Public safety, the economic crisis and the fight against corruption, for example, have all been prominent themes among evangelical candidates in the last federal and state elections, reflecting strong demands and preoccupations coming

from their constituencies. It is unlikely that evangelical political leaders could establish themselves if they were not responding to these constituency concerns, and they are certainly attentive to the movements of their base – which they are well positioned to ascertain, given the constant contact at the churches – in order to decide which way they will go. To outsiders, this often only confirms the impression of evangelical voters as a homogeneous, monolithically conservative bloc.

It is misguided, however, to think in such broad terms. A critique of the effects of evangelicalism's growth in political life is possible without generalising about the evangelical segment per se. The problem is not that the evangelical community in Brazil is growing, nor even that this community has come to perceive itself as a political agent. The question is that, among evangelicals, this representation has so far been hegemonised by histrionic conservatives who are less interested in solving the real problems affecting their constituencies than in building political capital out of pursuing a reactionary agenda and

furthering their churches' (and their own) business interests. This does not mean that progressive evangelicals who support a secular state do not or could not exist. The image of the evangelical segment as politically homogeneous and uniformly conservative is at once an optical illusion caused by the fact that the conservative leaders within the community enjoy much greater visibility, and a real effect that follows from the fact that these leaders echo, select and reinforce the most regressive aspects of the constituencies they purport to represent. In other words, it is not a uniform constituency, but is increasingly galvanised politically and ideologically by the effect – also felt among Catholics and other religions – of the conservative politics pushed by some of its leaders.

Catholics and evangelicals in politics

In the course of this demographic transformation in Brazil, the Catholic Church has been losing its central position in society and its privileged access to politics while a large number of diverse and autonomous evangelical churches, mainly pentecostal, have been gaining ground. This process is partially due to the Vatican's efforts in the 1980s to suppress Liberation Theology, which had been key to the capillarisation of the Catholic Church in the poorest parts of Latin America since the 1960s. The organising work done by this current in ecclesial base communities dotted across the countryside, *favelas* and urban peripheries of Brazil, was essential to an explosion of new social movements witnessed around the end of the military regime. Its fingerprints can be found in the formation of the unions that led the autoworkers strikes of the late 1970s, the Landless Workers' Movement (MST), the Workers' Party and Chico Mendes' Alliance of the Peoples of the Forest. The persecution of prominent figures under the papacy of John Paul II, and a certain demobilisation resulting from the creation of new political outlets for the poor, caused the presence of Liberation Theology to decline. This left a void at once religious and socio-political, given the role ecclesial base communities played in coordinating community initiatives and welfare, which evangelical churches came to fill.

Evangelical participation in institutional politics began in a more systematic and organised manner with the Constitutional Assembly (1986-88) tasked with producing a new constitution after the end of the dictatorship established in 1964. The pentecostal denomination Assembly of God (*Assembleia de Deus*) was the one that made the most significant moves in this direction at the time, responding to rumours that the Catholic Church had plans to make Catholicism the official state religion once again. The growth of evangelical involvement in politics could thus be described as a reaction to Catholic influence.

In the first direct presidential elections after re-democratisation in 1989, some denominations and churches declared support for a candidate: Fernando Collor de Mello, who beat PT's Luis Inácio Lula da Silva in the second round. Some of the arguments used to justify that support – resistance to a supposed communist threat, the fight against corruption, the promise of an 'outsider' who would bring the political system in line with moral values – would resurface in 2018.[11] It was at that time that reactions within the evangelical segment began to appear, primarily among protestants, who started constituting the first groupings of an 'evangelical left'; in doing so, they were in fact reconnecting with an earlier history of protestant liberationist Christianity.[12]

Coincidence or not, the last decade of the 20th century was also marked by a growing engagement of members of the Catholic Church's more conservative movements in party politics and electoral disputes, especially those belonging to the Charismatic Renewal group. Catholics and evangelicals have gone back and forth between competition and cooperation in politics for a long time. They started coordinating more closely in Congress in order to 'defend family values' after the launch of the PT government-sponsored Third National Human Rights Programme (PNDH-3) in 2009. PNDH-3 stirred controversy by proposing a bill (later withdrawn) to fully decriminalise abortion 'on grounds of women's autonomy to decide on matters pertaining to their own bodies' and a number of bills and policies with the purpose of 'ensuring respect for free sexual orientation and gender identity'.[13] These two issues were the main rallying points for religious groups.

Two figures played an important part in Catholic and evangelical resistance against social movements: Damares Alves, the legislative advisor of the Evangelical Parliamentary Front (FPE) at the time, and Jair Bolsonaro, a federal representative chosen by the FPE to be its main speaker in public hearings against the PNDH-3, and who worked actively as a spokesperson for Catholics and evangelicals in Congress. Today, Damares Alves is not only one of Bolsonaro's main political operators but, as head of what used to be the Ministry for Human Rights – now Ministry of Women, Family and Human Rights – she is the most popular member of cabinet and increasingly discussed as a potential vice-presidential pick for the 2022 elections.

Resistance to the PNDH-3, particularly to the decriminalisation of abortion and the criminalisation of homophobia, became an important issue in the 2010 presidential campaign and, even though evangelical leaders had until then enjoyed a mutually beneficial working relationship with PT, would increasingly become a focal point for the opposition to Lula's replacement, Dilma Rousseff.[14] The most notable incident in this regard, which would mark an inflection in the relationship between religious leaders and the PT and become the first major victory for the religious right, was the Catholic and evangelical campaign against the Ministry of Education's guidelines for teachers on gay students and homophobia. Pejoratively nicknamed 'the government's Gay Kit', they became a source of a moral panic and numerous fanciful stories which have regularly recurred since then – not least the one about the 'penis-shaped milk bottle', which set WhatsApp ablaze in the run-up to the 2018 elections. Rather than standing its ground and dispelling myths, the government recalled it before it was ever distributed and, two years later, supported evangelical pastor Marcos Feliciano's bid for the presidency of the Human Rights Committee in the lower house.[15] Instead of being appeased, the religious right smelled blood and Catholic and evangelical collaboration in the 2014 elections extended to areas like education and public safety, even though their commonalities in these were smaller. Although many continued to be part of PT's coalition until after Rousseff's re-election, most would jump ship in time to support her impeachment. In 2018, many would support Bolsonaro against Fernando Haddad, Minister of Education at the time of the 'Gay Kit' scandal, relishing the opportunity to mobilise the same stories against him.

The Brazilian electorate's turn to the right, which had been sensed for the first time in the 2014 elections, continued to grow in the 2016 municipal elections and, in light of the collapse of the traditional right, turned to the far right in 2018.[16] Misogyny, punitivism, militarism and anti-Left sentiments were brought into different institutional arenas and combined. Under Bolsonaro, the link between religion and politics has become even more explicit. His cabinet is full of proactive Christian figures, both Catholic and evangelical, who promote a neoconservative religious agenda. 'The time has come for the church to occupy the nation' was how Damares Alves recently described the new conjuncture.[17] For Foreign Minister Ernesto Araújo, in turn, 'Christian values should be back at the core of how we see the world'.[18] In less than two years, the Ministry of Education has been fronted by three 'proud Christians' (two Catholic, one evangelical).

Yet a reaction to the conquest of rights by certain groups was not the only reason for the rightward turn in the last elections. The country that went to the polls in 2018 had the highest unemployment rate in recent history and one of highest homicide rates in the world, with the majority of victims being young, black, poor and living in urban peripheries.[19] It was also going through a moment of extreme institutional discredit, with 62% of the population believing 'the System' was broken beyond repair.[20]

Politicians – religious *and* non-religious – mobilised the language of religion to propose a response to the daily problems faced by the vast majority of the population amidst the worst crisis the country had faced in decades. It offered belonging and the prospect of a return to order, predictability, safety and unity. With this package were tied the interests – political and financial – of religious groups and their leaders. In this conjuncture, their message swayed millions who had voted for the Left in the recent past. For the Left to simplify this process by presuming a homogeneous religious vote or a uniformly conservative evangelical segment is not only analytically incorrect, but politically catastrophic. It disregards complex motivations and concrete realities, stigmatises a huge fraction of the working classes with whom it must communicate, pre-empts efforts to deepen our understanding of and engagement with this sector, and hands the language of religion entirely over to a conservatism that has thus far proved very adept at using it to build symbolic and affective ties with the poor.

Ana Carolina Evangelista is a political scientist and coordinator of the Religion and Public Space cluster at the Institute of Religion Studies (ISER) in Rio de Janeiro. She was a visiting researcher at Sciences Po (Paris) and is completing a PhD at the Centre for Research and Documentation of Contemporary Brazilian History at the Getúlio Vargas Foundation.

Notes

1. See Jairo Nicolau, *O Brasil Dobrou à Direita. Uma Radiografia da Eleição de Bolsonaro em 2018* (Rio de Janeiro: Zahar, 2020), 76.
2. Departamento Intersindical de Assesoria Parlamentar, *Novo Congresso Nacional em Números. 2019-2023* (2018).
3. Maria das Dores Campos Machado, 'Religião, Cultura e Política', *Religião e Sociedade*, 32(2), 2012, 29–56.
4. 'Protestant' here includes people who identify with historical mainline and evangelical protestant denominations, those who belong to pentecostal denominations such as the Assemblies of God and the Foursquare Church, and members of independent churches, thousands of which are neopentecostal, like Igreja Universal do Reino de Deus.
5. These appear in the Pew Research graph as 'unafilliated'. See Pew Research Center, 'Roman Catholics in Decline, Protestants on the Rise. Brazil's Changing Religious Landscape', 18 July 2013, 2.
6. Prosperity Theology is a fast-growing movement frequently

associated with Pentecostalism, Evangelicalism and Charismatic Christianity. It centres around the idea that believers are able to transcend poverty and/or illness through devotion and that material success is a sign of grace.

7. One of the several bestsellers penned by Igreja Universal's Bishop Edir Macedo was a 1997 book accusing Afro-Brazilian religions of being 'demonic sects'. According to the author, these religions are the source of diseases, disputes, addictions and other evils in people's lives. It is no coincidence that it was relaunched in 2019, when authoritarianism and religious intolerance gained space in public debate. In Bolsonaro's first six months in power, reported cases of religious intolerance were up by 56% in relation to the same period in 2018, the majority against Afro-Brazilian religions. See Maria Duarte de Souza, 'Denúncias de Intolerância Religiosa Aumentaram 56% no Brasil em 2019', Brasil de Fato, January 21 2020, https://www.brasilde-fato.com.br/2020/01/21/denuncias-de-intolerancia-religiosa-aumentaram-56-no-brasil-em-2019.

8. Edir Macedo, *Plano de Poder. Deus, os Cristãos e a Política* (São Paulo: Thomas Nelson, 2008), 18.

9. Andrea Dip, *Em Nome de Quem? A Bancada Evangélica e seu Projeto de Poder* (Rio de Janeiro: Civilização Brasileira, 2018), 28.

10. Ari Pedro, 'A Política da Igreja Universal e Seus Reflexos nos Campos Religioso e Político Brasileiros', *Revista Brasileira de Ciências Sociais* 53:18 (2003), 62.

11. See Ricardo Mariano and Antonio Flavio Pierucci, 'O Envolvimento dos Pentecostais na Eleição de Collor', *Novos Estudos Cebrap* 34:3 (1992), 92–106.

12. See Michael Löwy, *The War of Gods. Religion and Politics in Latin America* (London: Verso, 1996), 108ff.

13. See http://www.planalto.gov.br/ccivil_03/_Ato2007-2010/2009/Decreto/D7037.htm. In Brazil abortion is only legal (and freely available in the public health system) in case of rape, anencephaly or life-threatening risk for the mother.

14. Antônio Flávio Pierucci, 'Eleição 2010: Desmoralização Eleitoral do Moralismo Religioso', *Novos Estudos* (2011), 5–15.

15. Now a federal representative for the third time, Marco Feliciano is a pastor in one of the churches in the Assembleia de Deus denomination, the largest in Brazil, and one of the main spokespeople for the 'pro-life', 'pro-family' religious lobby.

16. See Nicolau, *O Brasil Virou à Direita*; Ronaldo Almeida, 'Bolsonaro Presidente'.

17. Karina Gomes, 'É o Momento de a Igreja Ocupar a Nação', diz Damares Alves', Deutsche Welle, February 28 2020.

18. 'Bolsonaro's foreign envoy says he favours Trump and Netanyahu', *Financial Times*, June 24 2019, https://www.ft.com/content/c0215762-9106-11e9-aea1-2b1d33ac3271.

19. See Instituto de Pesquisa Econômica Aplicada, *Atlas da Violência* (2019), https://www.ipea.gov.br/portal/images/stories/PDFs/relatorio_institucional/190605_atlas_da_violencia_2019.pdf. The World Health Organisation considers homicide rates above 10 per 100,000 inhabitants to be epidemic. In 2017, Brazil recorded 31.6 deaths per 100,000 thousand inhabitants – double the rate of Iraq in 2015, for example.

20. *Edelman TRUST BAROMETER Global Report* (2017), https://www.slideshare.net/EdelmanInsights/2017-edelman-trust-barometer-global-results-71035413.

Unnatural feelings

The affective life of 'anti-gender' mobilisations

Clare Hemmings

We had already clocked him pacing at the back. A latecomer, ill fitting in the book-lined library: white man in his forties, baggy clothes, shaved hair and prominent facial scar jarring with the 120 groomed young people in the room, all facing forward, rapt by Professor Kimberlé Crenshaw's invocations to think and act intersectionally.[1] He moves to lean on a pillar. My hackles rise, prickling down my spine. I tell myself that I have been working in an elite institution for too long and need to check my judgment; those hackles go down a bit. I am about to go and ask him if he would like to sit down and join us, when he starts to speak over Kimberlé. Both she and I know he is not going to stop; it's hardly our first encounter with attempted silencing. The man speaks louder and so does Kimberlé. His diatribe in Italian shows he isn't interested in dialogue; her American tones echo behind me. I walk straight up the aisle to about a foot away from him and raise my hands. *Please stop talking over our guest; please sit down.* Then, when he doesn't stop: *please leave.* He backs me up the way I have just come, and I keep the same distance – the two speakers now in discordant unison. *Please stop talking over our guest, please leave this workshop, please be respectful, please leave.* I manoeuvre him back up the aisle and he is shouting invective now, *dirty ugly feminist, shut up ugly bitch.* I don't really need the translation from Italian provided by students later. He is by the door he came in now, and as I back him up through the door, he grabs and twists my arm in a last ditch effort, then turns and shouts his way out, to be met by the security guards the PhD student stewards have already called. They wrestle him out of the building, and we can hear his echoes for minutes after we can no longer see him.

I am shaking. Kimberlé is shaking, students are shaking, some crying. Kimberlé breathes in her experience of decades and breathes out the last ninety minutes of an extraordinary workshop. She opens herself to the students' shock and anger and knits their experience back together with the intersectional theory they have read and thought they would simply be asked to say something clever about. One student tells us about her fear: that she would lose the hearing in her other ear, having lost it in one after being beaten by Hindu nationalists. Another whispers that she was looking for a table to hide under, as she had when that man came into the classroom and started shooting. We talk about our own privilege and this man's likely mental health issues, as well as the ways in which anti-feminism has always exploited subjective as well as collective vulnerabilities. We make the transnational connections across forms of anti-feminist, racist, homophobic and transphobic violence, and feel enraged at the possibility of our silence. We express feeling shame too, that we could not effectively interrupt this man without passing him over to security. What were we waiting for? An institutional response, perhaps, despite our collective schooling in the misogyny, classism and racism of institutions.

This article addresses the attacks on feminism and Gender Studies by an increasingly virulent anti-'gender ideology' movement, and asks after the best ways of grappling with the violence of these mobilisations at political, epistemic and collective levels. As is well documented, attacks on the concept of 'gender' and on feminist, anti-homophobic and intersectional social movements are a central part of how a right-wing populist agenda generates its appeal and furthers its aims.[2] 'Gender Ideology', or the concept of 'gender' itself, has been consistently set up as eroding family values, challenging the natural status of heterosexual gender roles, and promoting perversion. Sonia Corrêa, David Patternote and Roman Kuhar describe these right-wing movements as operating at a transnational level, but focusing on a national or local scale,[3] bringing together homophobic campaigns in France, Germany and Brazil,[4] the defence of sovereignty in Poland, Serbia and Hungary, and religious re-intrenchments in Costa Rica, Chile and Uganda.[5] While the demonisation of feminism by the Right is hardly new, I agree with Kuhar and Patternote's suggestion that there is an increased fervour within these national as well as transnational movements that targets 'gender ideology' as a particular threat to national and local security, providing the perfect confluence of misogyny, homophobia and racism.[6]

There have been consistent attacks on Gender Studies as a field in recent years, with the closure of the degree at Central European University (CEU) in Budapest,[7] the attempted bombing at the National Secretariat for Gender Research at the University of Göteborg,[8] and most recently the June 2020 legislative move to ban 'gender identity studies in schools and universities' in Romania.[9] It is not that such campaigns have a central architecture (or architects), but more that their reliance on anti-'gender ideology' is precisely what allows for a transnational response to bring together otherwise disparate interests. As Andrea Pető notes in her protest at the closure of Gender Studies at CEU, 'the concept of "gender" is used to mobilise very different political forces to construct one, united enemy to hate'.[10] Attempts to control the curriculum also characterised the mobilisation of divergent political strands in the Manif Pour Tous movement in France, which claimed that recognition of gay marriage would undermine complementary roles as the natural basis of marriage, and that the teaching of 'gender' to children was a politically motivated absurdity.[11] Efforts to stop teaching 'genderism' in Germany similarly drew on what Eva von Redecker describes as 'the resentful mobilisation against pluralism and "political correctness", which are perceived as instituted by "gender ideologues".'[12]

The aggression that characterises this hostility is not only directed at legislative or institutional contexts; the derision towards 'gender' as a category is also directed towards its proponents. In Germany, for example, complaints seeking to remove Gender Studies teachers from the university were and remain vitriolic. In Hungary, Pető was subject to extensive harassment. In Brazil, feminists on university campuses endure consistent personal abuse, accused not only of violating nature, but exhibiting national betrayal in their adopting of 'foreign' terms of reference. In November 2017, while she was visiting Rio, right-wing activists burned Judith Butler in effigy, marking 'gender', '(homo)sexuality' and 'Americanness' as equally vile (and subject to violence).[13]

Anti-'gender ideology' proponents frame their own project as a moderate, commonsense one that protects natural sex roles and the relationship between family and nation. It is always others who are the aggressors: feminists who want to pervert the course of natural childhood and adult roles; queers who relish the destruction of the family and have no allegiances or ties; and 'outsiders' who cannot be trusted and are the agents rather than objects of inequality. It is the 'gender ideologues' and the perverse foreigners who are the hysterics, the ones who always go too far, the ones who have no core values. These framings are important as a way of deflecting or projecting aggression onto the targets of violence, of course, and are essential to both inflame anti-'gender' feeling as legitimate, and its affective aggression as belonging to someone else.

This article explores the spatio-temporal tricks that present gender equality as needing to be tempered by that common sense in the face of the destructiveness of both feminism gone too far, and reactionary cultural patriarchalism of the interloper. The focus throughout is on the affective life of anti-'gender ideology' claims, precisely as a way of trying to short-circuit that displacement effort. I explore its logic of the privileging of 'sex' as natural and complementary as precisely the locus of aggression, and make a claim for the importance of rooting feminist, queer and transnational approaches in anti-white supremacist affect. Overall, I am interested in exploring feminist methods for undoing the misogynist, homophobic and racist fantasies of annihilation – their own and ours – as an urgent task for our troubled present.

Spatio-temporal logics

'Gender ideology' is described by feminist commentators as a convenient 'empty signifier' that constitutes a useful trope to unite resistance to a range of rights and equality claims, an insistence on closed borders, and a feeling of dissatisfaction as the global order shifts on its austere axis. Yet that emptiness should not mislead us into thinking that these attacks are only casually linked, or that the presence of anti-feminism at their heart is in any way accidental. Writing of anti-'gender ideology' in Brazil, Joseph Souza highlights ways in which 'sexism [provides] a framework to connect right-wing ideologies of corruption, subversion and family values' that form a 'cognitive and affective glue' between accusations against feminism that would otherwise not make sense.[14]

For a range of commentators, the anti-feminism that campaigns against the invented phenomenon of a global 'gender ideology' is a backlash against equality gains and a political mechanism to safeguard privilege or lament its perceived loss.[15] It trades in what the editors of the *Signs* special issue on 'Gender and the Rise of the Right' describe as a 'hostility to feminism' that masks and contributes to the 'very real inequalities and fears produced by neoliberalism and globalisation'.[16] Yet this anti-feminism is not entirely straightforward. In both its religious and political versions, anti-'gender ideology' activists cast themselves as on the side of women's equality, and only antagonistic to a feminism that takes things too far, is too aggressively anti-family or imposes itself on specific (often global south) contexts.[17] In making 'gender ideology' into the enemy of ordinary men and women, who want reasonable access to opportunity, relationships free from violence, or other improved conditions within conventional family frameworks, anti-'gender ideology' proponents claim the very ground feminism has called its own. Once it has been established that 'gender ideology' is what unites a range of challenges to the heteronormative modern family, claims for same-sex marriage, reproductive rights, sex education, trans* recognition or equal pay, being against it can be cast as a defence rather than an attack. In challenging the excesses of 'gender ideology' (the term itself casts 'gender' as form of political, propagandistic posturing), then, anti-feminists can be reassured that they are resisting affronts to natural sex roles, rather than refusing women's equality *per se*.[18]

Anti-gender discourse hinges on a utopian fantasy of a bankrupt present and future, one that can only be remedied by a return to the integrity of naturalised and complementary sexual difference as the conventional bedrock of the local and the national, but with a twist. If women's subordination can be framed as something that has already been addressed, then a return to sex difference within a heteronormative, nationalist imaginary can be framed as opening up a future that occupies a *sane middle ground*.[19] As Kapya Kaoma notes, the very 'future of the human family' relies on this complementarity.[20] A return to sex complementarity is thus cast as the foundation of a local, regional or national future at direct odds with the bankruptcy of current global hegemony.Those who continue to insist on *excessive denaturing* can be positioned as part of an apocalyptic drive to a non-reproductive, barren future, and can be belittled and discarded. Feminism joins anti-racism and anti-ablism in the bin marked 'political correctness', and thus can be dismissed as absurd even as it is framed as a serious threat.

There is a spatial dimension to this claiming of the modern ground of equality by anti-'gender-ideology' advocates which is overlaid on its temporality, and that contributes to the ability to align the ills of feminists, queer subjects and migrants. Anti-'gender ideology' positions 'gender' as a kind of import-export commodity and its misguided adherents as its cosmopolitan brokers. Key to the contrast made between the safety of heterosexual family and a corrupting 'gender ideology', is *where* these come from and settle, as well as *when* they can be said to be appropriate. Anti-'gender ideology' arguments consistently construct 'gender' itself as an import, a foreign interloper that challenges the *time and place* of family and nation. In France, 'gender' is at once the 'enemy within' that tears at the very fabric of the sexual-democratic contract, and an exterior threat to 'national security' in the form of transnational politics and language. Thus, as Eric Fassin argues, 'gender' is problematic both for its challenge to the sovereignty of heterosexual sex difference, *and because* it is perceived as coming from America rather than being 'home grown'.[21] It is foreign in the sense of both origin and its untranslatability. That 'foreignness' does not have to come from

a specific national context, however. It can also be positioned precisely as that 'empty signifier' of the unreasonable demands of a transnational elite, and the institutions that protect their interests.[22] Thus in Eastern Europe, 'gender' is constructed as an imposed transnational EU or neoliberal threat to national sovereignty, a threat that true Poles, Hungarians or Romanians can resist being subject to. In this respect anti-'gender ideology' arguments suture naturalised (hetero)sexual difference to nation both as a return to the sanity of pre-'political correctness' and as a way of resisting global forces in a post-industrial, post-welfare, securitised world.

To go back to the French context for a moment, if 'gender' and homosexuality are imports that threaten family and nation, then care must be taken to ensure that 'other' threat to Frenchness – Muslim religion or identity – is also kept on the outside. This is where the sane temporality of equality is so important, and why anti-'gender ideology' proponents need to claim a moderate ground. While 'gender ideology' goes too far on the one hand, the *patriarchal control* of Islam threatens to pull us back into an excessive past. Here of course, 'Frenchness' is always already neither Muslim, nor queer (and certainly not both).[23] The externalisation of 'gender' in this European context, then, ensures that heterosexual difference is always 'secular' and white, as well as quintessentially moderate within what Fassin terms 'sexual nationalism'.[24] For Kováts too, it is precisely the focus on *authentic womanhood* that ties anti-gender to anti-immigrant narratives of the national modern.[25] This modern woman is neither alienated from her true sex, nor patriarchally subordinated to perverse Muslim maleness, and thus she is free to take up her natural role as her (white, heterosexual, male) partner's democratic complement. Importantly, then, what we see consistently in right-wing anti-'gender ideology' arguments is an interweaving of naturalised gender with naturalised racial and religious difference. That right wing populist appeal to a newly 'modern woman' is not confined to the West, of course, as the Hindu framing of Muslims as pre-modern, excessive, and closely aligned with homosexuality also suggests.[26]

The claim that 'gender' is a foreign import or the preserve of a transnational elite class is a tactic that follows the time-honoured trick of blaming individuals or groups already viewed with suspicion or hostility for home grown ills and the economic and social difficulties that attend globalisation. And so it is perhaps not so surprising that it is the queer, the feminist, and the migrant that become over-associated with transnational elites and protection in anti 'gender ideology' discourse, while maleness, whiteness and heterosexuality are increasingly figured as bound to the local or the deflated national. So it is that white men emerge as under threat from progressive elites rather than imbued with power in their own right; they are the besieged, rather that the routine agents of misogynist, homophobic or racist violence.

A final externalising tactic that overlays space and time in anti-'gender ideology' discourse is the positioning of 'gender' as a colonial term, and its use as a continuation of lamentable imperialism. Citing Kováts, Corredor affirms that the 'language equating gender ideology with colonisation, imperialism, and unwarranted cultural imposition has been another prevalent strategy for the Global Right'.[27] Kaoma writes that 'anti-gender arguments circulate in sub-Saharan Africa within a frame that portrays 'gender' and homosexuality as neo-colonial imports', *and as* the contemporary imposition of transnational elites.[28] And in a rather different frame, 'gender ideology' is cast as 'Western European' in Poland or Turkey and thus corrupt or a-religious.[29] On this broader scale, then, sexual and gendered challenges to heterosexual family are positioned as a malign import expressly designed to prevent 'the nation' from reproducing itself, whether that nation is a Western one that struggles to retain its history, or a postcolonial one that struggles to assert its freedom.

The harnessing of a decolonial discourse by anti-'gender-ideology' commentators who remain otherwise resolutely uninterested in anti-racist or decolonial politics is, as Corrêa points out, cynical at best.[30] We might also want to point to the particular irony of critiquing feminists for their imposition of 'gender ideology' by those who seek to re-entrench those naturalised categories of sex and gender that are the hallmark of colonial endeavour. It is precisely those naturalised forms that are presented as the future, in other words, that have a violent and colonial past linked to colonial administrations and the suturing of sexed and gendered difference to whiteness. That future can only be rhetorically assured through displacement of its history onto contemporary feminist and queer subjects rather than the white

heterosexual men and women who continue to benefit from its legacy.[31] Disingenuous though it may be, this discursive framing of 'gender equality movements [as] powerful and foreign colonisers' does important political work.[32] As Elzbieta Korolczuk and Agnieszka Graff highlight, it enables anti-'gender ideology' advocates to position themselves as 'protectors of the world's colonised peoples, the disenfranchised and the economically disadvantaged'.[33] That mirroring of a colonial past with a global present thus allows for anti-'gender ideology' activists to link their nationalism and populism with decolonial resistance movements and anti-austerity activism rather than imperial projects in a profoundly ironic trick of the light.[34]

It is more straightforward to counter the argument that authentic national identity is rooted in heterosexual sex difference, than the one that positions 'gender' and 'homosexuality' as colonial impositions, however. That colonial history is very real and present. The violence of 'gender' as a binary colonial imposition that regulates sexed and sexual behaviour in moral and religious frames, and that marks 'womanhood' as white and either Christian or (later) secular, is a legacy that feminists need to continue to pay close attention to.[35] Indeed, the violence of Western concepts of 'gender' continues to delimit identity and perpetuate the epistemic violence of exclusion and inclusion.[36] It is a sober truth that this accusation (that 'gender' is colonial) is all the more available to the Right precisely because of that history, and indeed precisely because of the continued claims by some strands of feminism that women's freedom and equality are most compromised outside of 'the West', or by queer scholars that gay and lesbian rights in their familiar Western form are a sign of 'the modern' that others must play catch-up to emulate.[37]

It is feminist, queer and post- or decolonial thinkers who have pointed out how the flames of the fantasies of a specifically Western gendered and sexual 'modern' as guiding global progress narratives are fanned by national elites committed to maintaining established power relations. I am thinking here of the important work by Rahul Rao on the citation of colonial imposition of gender binaries as both an important part of the history and present of power relations, and as a way in which contemporary investments in national gender and sexual inequalities are managed.[38] Rao's work is exemplary, precisely because it weaves a complex picture of those in power always working with the resources that they have at their disposal.[39] In her intervention on anti-'gender ideology' and the Gulf region, Nour Almazidi writes in a similar vein of the ways in which national sovereignty is consistently imagined at the expense of sexual and gendered minorities within those contexts.[40] For Almazidi, to back away from supporting gendered and sexual rights in those contexts because of the anxiety of reimposing colonial or Western frames is to cede the terrain. For these theorists, as for Uma Narayan writing about India over twenty years ago, the externalisation of gendered and sexual equality as a perverse imperial effect is one of the key ways in which progressive politics are foreclosed.[41] We need then to wrestle gendered and sexual complexity back from right-wing anti-'gender ideology' advocates, insisting on the duplicity at the heart of their co-optation on the one hand, yet paying close attention to the multiple ways in which 'gender' travels with its historical and contemporary baggage of epistemological and deadly violence on the other.

Affective fictions

As we have seen, anti-'gender ideology' mobilisations are suffused with violence and a sense of entitlement, and yet their aggression is deflected through the logic of naturalised sex difference as under threat, as about to disappear without immediate action. That negative affect (and its deflection or re-routing) is central to how anti-'gender ideology' arguments work, and here I want to spend more time on how this works narratively. I refer to these political and intersubjective techniques as the 'affective fictions' of anti-'gender ideology' logics as a way of making clear that feelings do not need to be 'true' to be powerful. In fact, as Eve Sedgwick and Lauren Berlant both make abundantly clear in their work on the draw of heteronormativity, affective investments in a structure that promises more than it will deliver are the very motor of contemporary life.[42] Berlant brilliantly proposes 'cruel optimism' as the best way of explaining the hyperbolic investments in the futurity of naturalised kinship in the face of increased global austerity.[43] For her, this optimism is 'cruel' because it invests in the very promises that kinship cannot deliver on, and indeed is part of the way in which neoliberalism reproduces itself.

Reading anti-'gender ideology' movements as 'cruel' is to emphasise how investment in heterosexual kinship and its related gender roles as reliable, appealing and (most of all) natural, works to offer what Gabriela Arguedes-Ramirez characterises as 'some sort of ontological certainty' in the face of global uncertainty of a wide range of kinds.[44]

Yet if that optimism resides in the hyper-investment in sex difference and naturalised familial authority as a counter to the disappointments of austerity, its cruelty does not rest there. In anti-'gender ideology' discourse it locates the blame (and therefore the rage) firmly with those who are perceived to have gained from contemporary global shifts: the feminists, gay men and lesbians, whose rights seem to trump those of ordinary families; and migrants whose claims on a failing welfare state have produced economic insecurity for genuine citizens. The excavation of that terrible wound, which as discussed above centres a normative family as the subject of the future even as it laments its imagined displacement in the present, allows the Right to depict 'religious conservatives as a embattled minority'.[45] That loss, that heart-felt cry of pain by white heterosexual men at the perceived rolling back of their privileges: these are affects that only intensify with empirical information that counters the basis of that misery. It matters little, then, whether one can point to the ways in which racial, sexual and gendered minorities precisely do not experience austerity as a boon. Starting from affect and narrative requires an uncomfortable encounter with the aggression at the heart of attempts to recentre an authoritative (usually white) masculine subject, one *fantastically positioned* as though he had lost his place at the heart of power. Kimberlé Crenshaw and I both instinctively knew that when encountering the anti-feminism of the man who interrupted the workshop at LSE, we had to get him out of the room, not try to persuade him into our way of thinking. It is unlikely this was a privileged subject in respects other than gender and race, but of course this is precisely Berlant's point: his 'cruel optimism' requires an hyperbolic (aggressive) affirmation of gendered authority as an affective panacea.

That 'ontological certainty' relies on a further powerful affective fiction: that authenticity is always already sutured to sex difference and cannot be claimed otherwise or elsewhere. That is why in anti-'gender ideology' rhetoric, 'gender' itself is considered a fabrication, a foreign import or colonial imposition that has nothing to do with natural difference. Thus not only is 'gender' a disruptive force within and outside the family and nation, it is a lie that is peddled to distract ordinary men and women from the business of present and future citizenship and entitlement. 'Gender' is an abstraction, a *pure fiction* rather than a serious proposition: that is why it can be both dangerous and laughable. For Joni Cohen, this contrast between the naturalness of 'sex' and the abstraction of 'gender' lies at the heart of the ability to dismiss its politicisation of the family and nation: it can be mocked, even while it is constructed as all powerful.[46] Indeed, in her perceptive transfeminist analysis, Cohen theorises 'gender' itself not as 'empty signifier' but as a *sign* of a 'rootless cosmopolitanism' that precludes the possibility of a stable society. 'Gender ideology' is thus available to be linked to a range of other suspect ideologies and identities, through the casting of oppositions between rootedness and flux. For Cohen this is what links anti-'gender ideology' campaigns to anti-Semitism and nationalism. For Sarah Bracke and Patternotte, too, 'gender ideology' is 'separated from the sphere of reality' leaving only the truth of 'rooted' heterosexual gender roles, with their investment in that other 'real' of 'race' as national inheritance.[47]

In pitting 'real sex' against 'fake gender', anti-'gender ideology' advocates position feminists, queers and foreigners not only as misguided about intimacy and the importance of family as national bedrock, but also – and perhaps more importantly – as *inauthentic*. They represent everything that is bankrupt within the current social order, and thus their claims for rights are not only dangerous but also fundamentally false. Feminists not only peddle lies about 'gender', they actively deny women (and men) access to 'authentic' womanhood. Homosexuality is not only 'less' than heterosexuality, it makes a mockery of it, and is at heart a violent failure to embrace the real intimacy of heterosexual complementarity, as we have seen in the French case. In this sense, 'gender' itself is given the status of a *con*, one that tricks its proponents and others into devaluing their own bodies, stripping themselves of the possibility of real reciprocity, of masculinity and femininity. 'Gender ideology' is undignified and miserable, but it is also selfish and individualist – the opposite of communal social investment in kinship and

locale. It trades in sad shadows of relationships, providing no stable affective ties; resisting it is thus a national duty based in love and care rather than aggression.[48]

There is a similar logic at play in transphobic narratives that the reader will no doubt recognise. Anti-trans* arguments have long relied on the opposition between 'real sex' and 'fake gender' in order to underwrite the hostility towards trans* subjects as legitimate, and as you might expect, anti-'gender ideology' advocates are profoundly transphobic as well as homophobic, misogynist and racist. Self-identified feminists too can be virulently transphobic, reaffirming 'sex' as real and 'gender' as a duplicitous fiction in ways that echo the aggression of anti-'gender ideology' arguments. Indeed, the work of trans-exclusionary radical feminists (TERFS) always fails to take seriously trans* claims to dignity and self-determination, rendering trans* subjects similarly both unreal (and predatory) but also a joke.[49] Alyosxa Tudor's work intervenes here by linking the anti-'gender ideology' arguments of the Right, feminist transphobia and racism, stressing the importance of a decolonial perspective as a counter to the dehumanisation that recentres authentic binary 'sex' common to all three.[50] Their work is also important in its refusal to reduce feminist history to transphobic history, however, insisting that where feminism takes seriously the colonial history of 'sex', it will also see the links between lesbian feminism and transfeminisms as deeply resonant and value laden.[51]

Because 'gender ideology' is both unreal and a palpable threat, a mimic and mocker of authentic ties, the people who are its subjects do not have to be respected. And to continue to think of fictions, that inauthentic unreality of 'gender' is precisely how centuries of feminist, queer and anti-racist political work are established as a chimeras, figments, ghosts. Even its grammar is elusive in this right-wing discourse: 'gender ideology' appears to have both agency and no firm ground; its subjects are deluded and absurd yet powerful; it is everywhere and nowhere, and its advocates are mere proponents of a dangerous pseudo-science.[52] The 'affective fictions' of anti-'gender ideology' discourse thereby provide the rationale and alibi for what Elsa Dorlin (following Marilyn Frye) describes as its 'epistemics of obliteration'.[53] Dorlin positions anti-'gender ideology' movements as governed by the logic of 'semiotic extermination'. Once understood as inauthentic, Dorlin argues, queer lives can

be understood as permanently assault-able as well as immoral: they will always be fair game. These 'epistemics of obliteration' mean that anti-'gender ideology' mobilisations can be framed as responses to violence rather than its agents, and it means that aggression itself is attributed to those who are in fact its targets. Only those who are real, are human, in the first place can be assaulted. For Dorlin, the attribution of violence to those on the margins means they are steeped in it, and also that they can never escape being accused of it, with the result that any violence done to them is inevitably understood as self defence.[54]

In her recent book *Imperial Intimacies*, Hazel Carby represents the destructive modes of white supremacy that form these 'affective fictions' with searing accuracy, shifting the analytic and political direction from the history of 'blackness' to the question of the lived violence of whiteness.[55] Two examples strike me as particularly helpful for the discussion thus far. In the first, Carby tells us of her teacher who insists that the RAF does not

have any black people in it. Carby knows for a fact that it does (her black father was in the RAF), but this is irrelevant to her teacher's ignorant certainty. The teacher's knowledge that *it does not* trumps 'the girl's' that *it does*; evidence is neither here nor there. In the second, Carby's white poor family embrace superiority over the enslaved black people of the Jamaican plantation as 'white entitlement', enjoying vicious pleasure at the horror others have to endure.

Carby's point here is that the affective life of white supremacy is key to its appeal;[56] it provides a 'cruel' investment in the hierarchies that ultimately also diminish its white working class participants. As Carby's bewildered childhood encounter with her ignorant teacher makes plain, white supremacy cannot be argued with or defeated at the level of logic: it has already identified her as outside of an epistemic frame of intelligibility. Her girlhood knowledge is at once untrustworthy, aggressive and absurd.

Affective reckonings

To conclude, I want to take forward Dorlin's and Carby's understandings of the 'epistemics of obliteration' and the affects of white supremacy to think through how to challenge the personal and political violence of anti-'gender ideology'.[57] How might I do justice to these authors' understanding that histories of gender and race are a battle for survival not an exchange of views, are a struggle to outlive the murderous gaze that imagines itself vulnerable, not a desire for recognition? And finally, how might the question of 'affective fictions' be helpful for a political response that does not cede the terrain of sex/gender, race and sexuality to the Right?

To do so I reconsider Gayle Rubin's analysis of the 'sex/gender' system, reading it as an early analysis of the violent effects of naturalising 'sex' and 'gender', but also as an unfinished account of affect and violence.[58] Rubin's 1975 intervention, 'The Traffic in Women: Notes on the "Political Economy" of Sex' establishes 'sex/gender' not as a relationship between the body and the social, or between origin and endpoint, but as a coupling designed to obscure power relations within a patriarchal system.[59] For Rubin, it is the collapse of 'gender' into 'sex', the naturalisation of their relationship *as no relationship at all*, that secures inequality as a fact of life rather than as a regime that systematically benefits men over women.

In 'Traffic', Rubin is concerned both with that naturalisation mechanism (the collapse of 'gender' into 'sex') and with its impact on those who fall outside of its norms or refuse them. While 'sex/gender' as a system is universal for Rubin, so too are the ruptures and fissures in its logic that mean 'oppression is not inevitable'.[60] We have to make visible that 'sex/gender system', Rubin says, if we are to challenge the naturalisation process that reduces human life to 'exchange' and if we are to value the lives of those who cannot (or refuse) to be thus contained.[61]

I read Rubin as an early theorist of the relationship between 'sex' and 'gender' as a *pernicious fiction*, one that all gendered subjects must accept in order to be legible as 'men' or 'women' within patriarchal regimes. This is an affective regime too, of course, precisely because of that naturalisation as the central technique of power. If 'sex' is understood as pure and unadulterated, as without the corrupting presence of 'gender', its violence is obscured

and can no longer be rationalised as violence. Following Rubin, this is one reason that anti-'gender ideology' is so central to the Right: to admit to 'gender' is to disrupt the relationship between family and nation so crucial to anti-immigration and racist agendas that underpin it. Instead, as we have seen, violence 'sticks' to those who appear disruptive of a system whose workings have already been smoothed over. It is a 'sex/gender system', in other words, that allows for the aggression of anti-'gender ideology' mobilisations to be displaced, and for *vulnerability* to remain the preserve of the privileged. This is also an 'affective fiction', then, in that the cloaking of the mechanisms of authority enable anger at its exposure to be righteous, and disgust at those who refuse its terms to be justified. Rubin's account also goes some way to explaining why both agency and abjection stick to those at the margins: within a 'sex/gender system', legitimate affect can only belong to those who occupy its naturalised positions. Challenging the contemporary Right's campaign to renaturalise power, then, has to start from both debunking that legitimacy, and insisting on the value of those lives whose affects bubble up in excess of that regime.

Rubin has been critiqued for privileging 'sex/gender' over 'race/gender' as the determining system of patriarchal societies,[62] and thereby naturalising colonial or imperial regimes in turn rather than opening them up to scrutiny. And indeed, as Hortense Spillers and Gail Lewis have laid out, in Western contexts only white women can historically and contemporarily lay claim to womanhood and its affects without ambivalence at best and often deadly violence.[63] Not only are black women and women of colour more likely to be understood as aggressive than white women (*because of* rather than *despite* being more likely to be the targets of violence, this analysis has shown), they are also denied access to womanhood within a 'sex/gender system'. For Carby, however, the racialisation of a 'sex/gender system' is part of how it works. If 'womanhood' is naturalised through rather than in parallel to whiteness, then its impact is to demonise all those who 'fail' to allow that naturalisation to remain invisible, and punish all those who refuse that demonisation.[64]

In 'White Woman Listen!', Carby provides a generous reading of Rubin's 'Traffic' as an important spur to denaturalising the 'sex/gender system' as one that pushes all those who would challenge its obscuring logic to the edges of 'the human'. Here Carby not only provides a useful extension of Rubin's analysis of a 'sex/gender system' to centre the colonial logics of racism, she also provides a basis for thinking about the political and affective marginalisation of black people, people of colour, queer, trans* and feminist subjects together (and those who might be all the above). Thinking with Rubin via Carby, then, allows us to explore the affective as well as political and social work that naturalisation does, but it also cracks open the links between different political responses as part of how we might imagine solidarity across different denaturalising positions.

In an interview for the 'Haunting Feminism' special issue of *Feminist Theory*, Lewis reflects on her decades of political work as a black feminist in the UK.[65] Echoing Dorlin's insistence on understanding right-wing anti-'gender ideology' as a confrontation with 'epistemic obliteration', Lewis is clear that the Right has her and others in its deadly sights. 'They're going to kill us. They are killing us' she says as a matter of fact.[66] For Lewis, the violence of white male supremacy is not only an external force, but also one that shapes what it means to be oneself in the world. Lewis tells us that 'it was hard for me to come out as a black woman as a lesbian', remarking wryly that 'I suppose when you're excised from full humanity that's one of its consequences.'[67] Lewis is not making a case for being 'recognised' or granted entry to womanhood on authoritarian terms, though. She sees the problem as precisely rooted in the binary oppositions that anti-'gender ideology' movements propose as the basis of a rosy future, insisting that it 'kills us to occupy these position as "men" and "women"'.[68] Here Lewis connects black, trans*, queer and feminist exclusions through their continuous failure to be counted as full women or men, but importantly sees the costs of seeking entry into those as just as damaging.

In an extended discussion of the racial dynamics that shape feminism, Lewis continues to explore the affective costs of occupying or being excluded from womanhood. Starting from her own experience on feminist collectives, Lewis describes 'how unbearable it is... when you're with some white women and the question of race comes up and the white women will collapse into tears, like a classic performance of the fey little woman, who's not strong enough, like a little bird ... she might faint.'[69] In her trenchant analysis, Lewis points precisely to the 'sex/gender system' as always already racialised. As a black woman she is not able to retreat into femininity, and is marked instead and predictably as the aggressor. White femininity for Lewis is constituted through the 'threat of an assault' whether by (white or black) men or by black women; it is constituted by the displacement of racist violence and exclusion onto the other and as a black feminist that is simply 'unbearable'.

For Lewis, the confrontation with fantasies of victimhood as part of how a 'sex/gender system' maintains itself must be the first thing we undo as part of a creative politics of freedom (though this will be a different project for white and black feminists). Otherwise, one continues to see oneself through the eyes of the white male supremacist. A refusal to accept the 'affective fictions' that underpin anti-'gender ideology' requires a leap of affective faith in its own right.

Yet of course we are not starting from scratch. There is, and always has been excess and resistance and 'our lives are never fully encompassed and limited by all of these processes and structures.'[70] As Lewis notes, it '*is* frightening', but 'that's the project. Isn't it? We have to.'[71] Here Lewis joins Rubin and Carby in returning us to the scene of 'sex/gender' as both an important political focus with respect to structures of violence, and as a way of understanding affective lives that separate and connect those it excludes. Her call is to refuse the empty ('cruel' perhaps) promises of sex/gender, refuse it as a devastating fiction, and align with affects rooted in histories of political action and affirmation.

At the end of the interrupted 'Intersectionality and Politics' workshop, Kimberlé Crenshaw asks us to breathe, to pause, to feel our bodies. To inhabit that space and no other space. To be real. She asks us to go back and to remember what happened step by step and to finish it, leave it alone, pay it no more mind. And then to imagine something else. To replay the scene of being silenced, rewriting it as we would have liked it to unfold, and to take that with us into the world. We know authentic intimacy because it is hard won; we can feel it in our encounters with others. We know the sham in which violence is passed off as kinship, and we do not accept its terms. We see each other, and we already bask in the pleasure of a new world.

Clare Hemmings is Professor of Feminist Theory in the Department of Gender Studies, LSE, where she has taught for over 20 years. She works on the overlaps among feminist, queer and postcolonial studies, and is particularly interested in how stories of these fields are narrated, felt and institutionalised.

Notes

1. Crenshaw gave this cross-departmental workshop on 'Intersectionality and Politics: An Interactive Workshop with Professor Kimberlé Crenshaw', on Monday 21st January 2019 hosted by the Gender Studies Department at the LSE.
2. Elizabeth S. Corredor, 'Unpacking "Gender Ideology" and the Global Right's Antigender Countermovement', *Signs: Journal of Women in Culture and Society* 44:3 (Spring 2019).
3. Sonia Corrêa, David Patternote and Roman Kuhar, 'The Globalisation of Anti-Gender Campaigns: Transnational Anti-Gender Movements in Europe and Latin America Create Unlikely Alliances', *International Politics and Society*, 31 May 2018, https://www.ips-journal.eu/topics/human-rights/article/show/the-globalisation-of-anti-gender-campaigns-2761
4. See Eva von Redecker, 'Anti-Genderismus and Right-wing Hegemony', *Radical Philosophy* 198 (Jul/Aug 2016) and Joseph Jay Sosa, 'Subversive, Mother, Killjoy: Sexism Against Dilma Rousseff and the Social Imaginary of Brazil's Rightward Turn', *Signs: Journal of Women in Culture and Society* 44:3 (Spring 2019).
5. A 2019 special issue in *Signs* provides a useful collection of articles from different locations that demonstrate both national and transnational right-wing attacks on 'gender ideology': Agnieszka Graff, Ratna Kapur and Suzanne Walters, 'Introduction: Gender and the Rise of the Global Right', *Signs: Journal of Women in Culture and Society* 44:3 (Spring 2019).
6. Roman Kuhar and David Patternote, eds, *Anti-Gender Campaigns in Europe: Mobilizing Against Equality* (London: Roman and Littlefield, 2017).
7. Andrea Pető, 'Attack on Freedom of Education in Hungary: the Case of Gender Studies', *Engenderings*, 24 September 2018, blogs.lse.ac.uk/gender/2018/09/24/attack-on-freedom-of-education-in-hungary-the-case-of-gender-studies
8. Jennifer Evans, 'The New War on Gender Studies', *The Conversation*, 6 Jan 2019, https://theconversation.com/the-new-war-on-gender-studies-109109
9. euronews.com/2020/06/17/romania-gender-studies-ban-students-slam-new-law-as-going-back-to-the-middle-ages. The case is now awaiting constitutional review, after President Iohannis submitted an appeal after pressure from within and outside of Romania: https://eua.eu/news/536:romanian-president-moves-to-reject-ban-on-gender-studies.html
10. Pető, 'Attack on Freedom of Education in Hungary'.
11. Ilana Eloit, 'American Lesbians are not French Women: Heterosexual French Feminism and the Americanisation of Lesbianism in the 1970s', *Feminist Theory* 20:4 (2019), 381–404. See also: Éric Fassin, 'Gender Is/In French', *Differences: a Journal of Feminist Cultural Studies* 27:2 (2016), 178–97.
12. Von Redecker, 'Anti-Genderismus and Right-wing Hegemony'.
13. Sonia Corrêa, 'Gender Ideology: Tracking Its Origins and Meanings in Current Gender Politics', *Engenderings*, 11 December 2019, https://blogs.lse.ac.uk/gender/2017/12/11/gender-ideology-tracking-its-origins-and-meanings-in-current-gender-politics
14. Sosa, 'Subversive, Mother, Killjoy', 738, 724.
15. Corredor, 'Unpacking "Gender Ideology"', 614.
16. Graff, Kapur and Walters, 'Introduction: Gender and the Rise of the Global Right', 550.
17. Sara Garbagnoli and Massimo Prearo, *La Croisade Anti-Genre: du Vatican au Manif Pour Tous* [The Anti-Gender Crusade] (Paris, Textuel: 2017); Weronica Grzebalska, Eszter Kováts and Andrea Pető, 'Gender as Symbolic Glue: How "Gender" Became an Umbrella Term for the Rejection of the (Neo)liberal Order', *Krytyka Polityczna [Political Critique] and European Alternatives*, 13 January 2017, http://politicalcritique.org/long-read/2017/-gender-as-symbolic-glue-how-gender-became-an-umbrella-term-for-the-rejection-of-the-neoliberal-order
18. Erica Millar makes a related argument concerning anti-abortion activists' claims to be the real feminists, on the side of women's happiness and well-being. Millar, *Happy Abortions: Our Bodies in the Era of Choice*, (London: Zed Books, 2017). Thanks to Victoria Browne for pointing to this important intervention.
19. Gabriele Dietze and Julia Roth, eds, *Right-Wing Populism and Gender: European Perspectives and Beyond* (Verlag: Bielefeld, 2020). See also Lynn Berg, 'Between Anti-Feminism and Ethnicized Sexism: Far-Right Gender Politics in Germany', in *Post-Digital Cultures of the Far Right*, eds. Mark Fielitz and Nick Thurston (Verlag: Bielefeld, 2020), 79–91, on the links between anti-feminism and anti-migration arguments in contemporary Germany.
20. Kapya Kaoma, 'The Vatican Anti-Gender Theory and Sexual Politics: an African Response', *Religion & Gender* 6:2 (2016), 282–292.
21. Fassin, 'Gender Is/In French'.
22. Eszter Kováts, 'Questioning Consensuses: Right-Wing Populism, Anti-Populism, and the Threat of "Gender Ideology"', *Sociological Research Online* 23:2 (2018), 528–38.
23. See Fatima El-Tayeb for an analysis of the construction of Europeanness more broadly against both Muslim and queer subjectivities: El-Tayeb, '"Gays Who Cannot Properly be Gay": Queer Muslims in the Neo-liberal European City', *European Journal of Women's Studies* 19:1 (2012), 79–95.
24. Éric Fassin, 'Sexual Democracy and the New Racialisation of Europe', *Journal of Civil Society* 8:3 (2012), 285–88. And in my own work on this context, I focus on the ways in which French anxiety about 'Americanness' allows for the promulgation of a nationalism stripped of its (displaced) racism. Clare Hemmings, 'Is "Gender Studies" Singular? Stories of Queer/Feminist Difference and Displacement', *Differences: a Journal of Feminist Cultural Studies* 27:2 (2016), 79–102.
25. Kováts, 'Questioning Consensuses', 531.
26. Graff, Kapur and Walters, 'Introduction', 554.
27. Corredor, 'Unpacking "Gender Ideology"', 628.
28. Kaoma, 'The Vatican Anti-Gender Theory'. The term 'sub-Saharan Africa' is Kaoma's, and while general, is intended to link

the significant gains of anti-'gender ideology' mobilisations in a range of countries.

29. Michelle Gallo, *Anti-Gender Movements: Comparing Poland and Colombia*, Gender Centre Research Brief, Geneva Centre, Graduate Institute of International Development Studies (2020); Selin Çağatay, 'Varieties of Anti-Gender Mobilisation: Is Turkey a Case?' *Engenderings*, 2 April 2019, https://blogs.lse.ac.uk/gender/2019/01/09/varieties-of-anti-gender-mobilizations-is-turkey-a-case

30. Corrêa, 'Gender Ideology'.

31. See Catherine Hall, Nicholas Draper, Keith McClelland, Katie Donington and Rachel Lang, *Legacies of British Slave-Ownership: Colonial Slavery and the Formation of Victorian Britain* (Cambridge: Cambridge University Press, 2014), for examples of these material and economic legacies.

32. Elżbieta Korolczuk and Agnieszka Graff, 'Gender as "Ebola from Brussels:" the Anticolonial Frame and the Rise of Illiberal Populism', *Signs: Journal of Women in Culture and Society* 43:4 (Summer 2018), 799.

33. Korolczuk and Graff, 'Gender as "Ebola from Brussels"', 807–8.

34. Alyosxa Tudor, *Transgender Studies Quarterly* (2021) Decolonising Trans/Gender Studies: Teaching Race, Sexuality and Migration in Times of the Rise of the Global Right', *TSQ: Transgender Studies Quarterly* 8:2.

35. See María Lugones, 'Heterosexualism and the Colonial/Modern Gender System', *Hypatia: a Journal of Feminist Philosophy* 22:1 (February 2007), 186–219, on the colonial history of modern oppositional 'gender'.

36. Hortense Spillers and Gail Lewis write beautifully of the consequences of this imposition and history on black women in the US and the UK respectively. Spillers, 'Mama's Baby, Papa's Maybe: An American Grammar Book', *Diacritics* 17:2 (1987), 64–81; Lewis, 'Questions of Presence.' *Feminist Review* 117 (2017): 1–19.

37. This critique has been very firmly established by writers including: Jin Haritaworn, 'Women's Rights, Gay Rights and Anti-Muslim Racism in Europe', *European Journal of Women's Studies* 19:1 (2012), 73–78; Joseph Massad, *Desiring Arabs* (Chicago: University of Chicago Press, 2007); Jasbir Puar, 'Mapping US Homonormativities', *Gender, Place & Culture* 13:1 (2006), 67–88; Mitra Rastegar, 'Emotional Attachments and Secular Imaginings: Western LGBTQ Activism on Iran', *GLQ* 19:1 (2013): 1–29.

38. Rahul Rao, 'The Locations of Homophobia', *London Review of International Law* 2:2 (September 2014), 169–99.

39. See Rahul Rao, *Out of Time: The Queer Politics of Postcolonality* (Oxford: Oxford University Press, 2020).

40. Nour Almazidi, 'The Institutional and Epistemic Marginality of Gender Studies in the Gulf Region', *Engenderings*, 14 January 2019, https://blogs.lse.ac.uk/gender/2019/01/14/the-institutional-and-epistemic-marginality-of-gender-studiesin-the-gulf-region

41. Uma Narayan, *Dislocating Cultures: Identities, Traditions and Third Word Feminism* (New York: Routledge, 1997).

42. Eve Kosofsky Sedgwick, *Epistemology of the Closet* (Berkeley, CA: University of California Press, 1990); Lauren Berlant, 'Cruel Optimism', *Differences: A Journal of Feminist Cultural Studies* 17:3 (2006), 20–36.

43. Berlant, 'Cruel Optimism'.

44. Gabriela Arguedas-Ramirez, 'Gender Ideology, Religious Fundamentalism and the Electoral Campaign (2017-2018) in Costa Rica', *Engenderings*, 7 November 2018, https://blogs.lse.ac.uk/gender/2018/11/07/gender-ideology-religious-fundamentalism-and-the-electoralcampaign-2017-2018-in-costa-rica

45. Korolczuk and Graff, 'Gender as "Ebola from Brussels"', 798.

46. Joni Alizah Cohen, 'The Eradication of "Talmudic Abstractions": Anti-Semitism, Transmisogyny and the National Socialist Project', Verso Blog, 19 December 2018, https://www.versobooks.com/blogs/4188-the-eradication-of-talmudic-abstractions-anti-semitism-transmisogyny-and-the-national-socialist-project

47. Sarah Bracke and David Paternotte, 'Unpacking the Sin of Gender', *Religion and Gender* 6:2 (2016), 143–54.

48. Sara Ahmed, 'Affective Economies', *Social Text* 22:2 (2004), 117–39.

49. Most recently JK Rowling has used this familiar mockery, positioning trans* claims to authentic womanhood or manhood as a farce any sensible man or woman would laugh at. This has a long history, with Germaine Greer famously mocking transwomen's failed attempts to pass as women, echoing Janice Raymond's similarly dismissive tone. I am not keen to provide citations to these three interventions, because it gives more authority to them than I would like. So let me point you to Alyosxa Tudor's acerbic riposte to Rowling that turns this mockery right around: 'Terfism is White Distraction: On BLM, Decolonising the Curriculum, Anti Gender Attacks and Feminist Transphobia', *Engenderings*, 19 June 2020, https://blogs.lse.ac.uk/gender/2020/06/19/terfism-is-white-distraction-on-blm-decolonisingthe-curriculum-anti-gender-attacks-and-feminist-transphobia/

50. Tudor, 'Decolonising Trans/Gender Studies'.

51. Alyosxa Tudor, 'Im/possibilities of Refusing and Choosing Gender', *Feminist Theory* 20:4 (2019), 361–80. I take my cue from Tudor's work here, in that it offers a transfeminist perspective that reclaims decolonial approaches from the disingenuous right-wing claim that 'gender ideology' trades (exclusively) in colonial categories. See also D-M Withers' article on the overlapping histories of lesbian and transfeminist critiques of 'gender': Withers, 'Laboratories of Gender: Women's Liberation and the Transfeminist Present', *Radical Philosophy* 2.04 (Spring 2019).

52. There are echoes of this idea of pseudo science in the 'culture wars' mocking of what are perceived to be fake disciplines (including media studies, cultural studies, and of course ethnic, queer and gender studies) through 'hoaxes'. See Emma Spruce, Jacob Breslow and Tomás Ojeda, 'Study Your Grievances', *Engenderings*, 29 October 2018, https://blogs.lse.ac.uk/gender/2018/10/29/study-your-grievances

53. Elsa Dorlin, 'Unreal: Catholic Ideology as Epistemological War', *Religion and Gender* 6:2 (2016), 264–67.

54. In her more recent work, Dorlin further contends that 'self defence' as a political and epistemic possibility is denied to those on the margins; they are always primary agents of violence,

never its mistreated objects. Dorlin, 'What a Body Can Do', *Radical Philosophy* 2.05 (Autumn 2019).

55. Hazel Carby, *Imperial Intimacies: a Tale of Two Islands* (London: Verso, 2020).

56. In related vein, Sharon P. Holland explores the ordinary life of racism as a sequence of investments and affective ties one can never be distant from. Holland, *The Erotic Life of Racism* (Durham: Duke University Press, 2012).

57. Dorlin, 'Unreal'; Carby, *Imperial Intimacies*.

58. Gayle Rubin, 'The Traffic in Women: Notes on the "Political Economy" of Sex', in *Toward an Anthropology of Women*, ed. Rayna Reiter (New York: Monthly Review Press, 1975), 157–210.

59. Ibid.

60. Ibid., 168.

61. It is that impetus to value the bravery of lives and choices deemed 'perverse' that underwrites Rubin's second major intervention some ten years later: Gayle Rubin, 'Thinking Sex: Notes for a Radical Theory of the Politics of Sexuality [1984]', in *Devi-*ations: A Gayle Rubin Reader* (Durham: Duke University Press, 2012).

62. Donna Haraway proposes this alternative conceptualisation in Haraway, "'Gender" for a Marxist Dictionary: the Sexual Politics of a Word', *Simians, Cyborgs and Women: the Reinvention of Nature* (London, Free Association Books: 1991), 127–48.

63. See footnote 35.

64. Hazel Carby, 'White Woman Listen! Black Feminism and the Boundaries of Sisterhood', in *The Empire Strikes back: Race and Racism in 70s Britain*, eds. Centre for Contemporary Cultural Studies (London: Hutchinson, 1982), 212–235.

65. Lewis and Hemmings, '"Where Might We Go if We Dare"'.

66. Ibid., 419.

67. Ibid., 419.

68. Ibid., 416.

69. Ibid., 412.

70. Ibid., 415.

71. Ibid., 416, 419.

Always trouble

Gender before and after *Gender Trouble*

Isabell Dahms

This article investigates how the concept of gender might be located within a broader history of the medicalisation and policing of a binary concept of sexual difference and of reproductive knowledge and control. It begins by tracing the origins of gender as a clinical and behavioural category, which was first introduced to medicalise intersex and trans bodies. It then looks at the reappropriation of the concept for feminist purposes, first in sociology and thereafter – through the notion of performativity – as a philosophical concept. I argue that Judith Butler's redefinition in *Gender Trouble* (1990) of gender as performativity marks a decisive change in the meaning of this term: after her intervention, gender is no longer primarily a clinical or sociological category, but one that asks questions about ontology. However, Butler herself does not engage with the concept's complicated history. While her belated recognition of trans and intersex concerns in the second edition of *Gender Trouble* and in subsequent works demonstrates Butler's political investment in addressing these issues, the question of what centring trans and intersex might do to our notion of gender ontology remains unaddressed.[1]

The ontological status of gender, as defined by Butler, is also brought into question in Hortense Spillers's and Saidiya Hartman's accounts of how race operates to undo gender. Spillers and Hartman complicate Butler's notion of the normativity and performativity of gender by questioning the types of histories and range of performances that are deemed normative in the constitution of gender categories. While this article accepts Butler's redefinition of gender as primarily an ontological category, one that is constituted performatively within a normative framework, it demonstrates how transgender, intersex and Black feminist theories complicate this no-

tion of gender ontology, expanding Butler's proposition of gender ontology beyond the limited scope of *Gender Trouble*. Given the omission of intersex, transness and Blackness as integral to Butler's conception of gender, how can recuperating these histories transform our understanding of the performativity of gender? The aim of this analysis is not to affirm gender once more as the most pertinent category for feminist analysis and critique or to reopen tired debates about whether gender remains a useful category of analysis, but to reframe gender through an engagement with its complicated history and, in so doing, expand our understanding of how gender categories operate.

The biopolitical origins of 'gender'

The conceptual use of gender to name and describe the social dimension of human sexed bodily life was not invented by Butler but was first proposed in a clinical context. Gender emerged not in feminist discourse but in post-World War II psychological and sexological studies of intersexuality and transsexualism in the US.[2] Nonetheless, Butler's reframing of gender through the concept of performativity marks a critical intervention in the use and understanding of gender, subversively transforming what was a highly problematic term into a philosophical concept and critical feminist tool.

The child psychologist John Money, who treated intersex babies, was the first to use the linguistic category of gender as a clinical and diagnostic tool.[3] In Money's own words, gender was given 'a new lease on life' with the 1955 publication 'Hermaphroditism, Gender and Precocity in Hyperadrenocorticism' in the *Bulletin of the Johns Hopkins Hospital*.[4] Money employed gender not in its common sense usage but as a clinical category to describe one aspect of sexual differentiation in the human body. Gender, as Money conceived of it, names the ways in which people comport themselves in their roles as boys or girls, men or women.[5] As Money remarks, '(i)n this paper the word *gender* made its first appearance in English as a human attribute, but it was not simply a synonym for *sex*'.[6]

In the 1995 *Gendermaps*, Money observes that this initially medical usage quickly spread into the vernacular, though not without misunderstandings.[7] Money, in this later text, demarcates his 'invention' from its use in feminist and queer studies, but also sociological and cultural studies more broadly. Money himself notes that the concept quickly took on a life of its own as it became an analytic category in the social sciences, demography and public policy. Though a somewhat different concept in each of these fields, for scientists, governments and feminists alike, the question posed by 'gender', as Jemima Repo notes, revolves around the problem of not only how to understand sex but also how to govern it.[8]

The question of governing sex was at the centre of Money's research, which was mainly focused on the treatment of what used to be called 'hermaphroditism' and is more appropriately understood as intersex. 'Hermaphroditism', according to Money, demonstrates that the unitary definition of sex as either male or female has to be abandoned.[9] Money argues that the term 'sex', as it is commonly used, is too narrow to cover the masculinity or femininity of 'hermaphrodites'.[10] Characterised as a 'genital birth defect', 'hermaphroditism' is construed as the medical anomaly or problem to which Money proposes gender as both an explanatory response and a clinical solution.[11] In view of this 'defect', which means that the sex of the baby cannot be specified within the binary frame of male and female, gender, according to Money, comes to signify 'the overall degree of masculinity and/or femininity that is privately experienced and publicly manifested in infancy, childhood, and adulthood, and which usually though not invariably correlates with the anatomy of the organs of procreation.'[12]

While gender is not disassociated from the biological aspects of sex, in his 1955 article Money argues that gender is more connected to early life experience than to chromosomal or gonadal sex.[13] It is this proposition that was enthusiastically taken up by psychoanalyst and psy-chiatrist Robert Stoller, who popularised the term gender identity, as well as by feminists in the 1960s and 1970s, often in isolation from Money's other claims.

Money not only proposes the category of gender in addition to sex, he also redefines the latter. Instead of a unitary notion, Money proposes a list of five prenatally-determined variables of sex which can be independent of one another: chromosomal sex, gonadal sex, internal and external morphological sex, and hormonal sex (prenatal and pubertal).[14] According to Money, two postnatal determinants have to be added to this list. First, the sex of assignment or rearing; and, second, what Money terms 'gender role' – that is, the private imagery and ideation, and the public manifestation and expression, of masculinity and femininity.[15] For Money, as this list indicates, gender is part of sex, one of its seven variables. It is not to be understood as a psychological term opposed to somatic sex. It is Stoller who makes this distinction in the first volume of his *Sex and Gender*, owing to the overdetermination of the concept of sex.[16] As a consequence, it is Stoller, rather than Money, who is generally cited in the second-wave feminist literature on gender.

Though not conceived as opposites, gender nonetheless marks a radical intervention in the thinking of sex. Money reverses the categorial order of importance. While all variables of sex are important, they are not all equally decisive. In Money's work, what is projected as stable or enduring is no longer what was previously known as sex – the five prenatally determined variables – but rather the potential of every human being to achieve a stable gender identity and role.

For Money, the putative importance of a strong binary gender role and identity justifies early infantile correction surgery and pubertal or life-long hormonal intervention. It is in this sense that the invention of gender, as a variable of sex and as potential overall organising principle, allows for the appearance and development of a series of new biopolitical techniques for the normalisation and transformation of living beings.[17] Thus, while Money does not precisely split off gender from sex, he reverses the order of stability and, with it, the order of importance. Gender is proposed as a response to the question of how to govern sex. As such, gender is not simply an explanatory concept but a strategic response, invented above all to rationalise and 'correct' those bodies which appear not to conform to medical norms. Given this origin, as Repo argues, gender has been a site of political struggle from its inception.[18]

Gender is transgender

While Money's research is focused on establishing a treatment protocol for intersex children, his writings on intersex often make mention of and include an analysis of transness.[19] According to Money, research on intersex and trans – as well as homosexuality – are interconnected, though primarily by way of their negative denomination as gender identity anomalies. Transness in particular is deemed pathological. Transgender people, according to Money, impersonate the opposite sex, while cisgender men and women are referred to throughout his works as 'the normal male' and 'the normal female'.[20] Money nonetheless comes to the conclusion that transgender people should receive surgery if they request it. Recognising that transgender people cannot be convinced that their gender 'contradiction' is a delusion, Money concludes that the only responsible medical reaction is to offer transgender people hormones and surgery.[21]

Although Money is an early advocate for the kind of transgender medical rights that are increasingly, if unevenly, recognised today, this comes at the same time as a more problematic promotion of early infantile surgery in intersex children. In 1966, under Money's influence, the Johns Hopkins Hospital became the first research institution in the US to perform gender-affirming surgeries.[22] Prior to this, the Institute for Sexual Science in Berlin, founded by the German physician Magnus Hirschfeld in 1919, had performed the first such surgeries in the 1930s. However, the Institute was taken over and dissolved by the Nazis in 1933 when Hirschfeld, a gay Jew, emigrated to New York. In a sense, the Johns Hopkins Hospital followed in the footsteps of the Institute for Sexual Science, but the knowledge of how to perform gender-affirming surgeries and administer hormonal treatment was gained from Money's research on intersex children. As such, Money's legacy of problematic medicalisation reveals some of the commonalities and differences in the medicalisation of intersex and trans people.

Since Money's concept of gender intends to provide a theoretical explanation as well as a standardised treatment protocol for intersex and trans people, it can be concluded that gender was from the start a discourse about intersex and trans bodies and a site of their medicalisation. As Talia Mae Bettcher points out, '(b)oth transgender and intersex politics arose in reaction to the problematic medicalisation of, respectively, transsexual and intersex people'.[23] The oppressive dynamics of identity invalidation, undermining a person's chosen gender, and the medical, political and cultural enforcement of a gender, provide a further basis for coalition among intersex and trans activists and suggest possibilities for understanding the intersections of intersex, trans and sexist oppression.[24]

At the same time, despite raising similar issues, intersex and trans experiences are not identical. For example, while protection from discrimination in employment, housing and public accommodation is vital for trans people, as activist and writer Emi Koyama points out, it is inadequate as a strategy for intersex people since much of the violation of their rights takes place in other areas.[25] Thus, recognition of the common generative contexts for intersex and trans politics in John Money's work and conceptualisation of gender should not diminish the distinctness of these struggles.

As will be shown in more detail later on, Butler only engages with Money once in her 2004 publication *Undoing Gender,* in the context of an essay on the Reimer case – Money's most prominent study. But Butler offers no analysis here of Money's role in conceptualising 'gender' more broadly. This omission is significant as it obscures how the term gender was, from the start, a discourse about intersex and trans bodies, albeit with the intention to normalise them. Circumventing a more thorough confrontation with Money, Butler finds herself in search of theoretical tools to adequately address trans and intersex concerns, but what remains missing is the theoretical acknowledgement that trans and intersex theory and activism are foundational to, not simply exemplary of, the very concept of gender itself.

While *Gender Trouble* does not directly address transness, it argues that drag exposes the imaginary relations of compulsory heterosexuality and the contingent nature of gender and identity. The use of drag as illustration and example has been criticised in trans scholarship. Vivienne Namaste contextualises Butler's use of drag as example by complicating queer culture's relations to drag, gender and gender performance. Namaste points to the paradox that 'at precisely the moment that it underlines the constructed nature of gendered performance, drag is contained as a performance in itself. Gay male identity, in contrast, established itself as something prior to performance.'[26] The relegation of drag queens and the containment of gender transgression to the stage works against transgender people in a variety of ways and is, Namaste argues, a move that excludes transgender people even as it seeks to include them.[27]

With gender being a key category of feminist thought, trans and intersex issues should take centre stage. While her work facilitates a philosophical rethinking of gender, this aspect in particular is not spelled out by Butler. If she had conceded Money's role in coining and circulating the concept of gender, trans and intersex issues might have been foregrounded and not, as in the second preface to *Gender Trouble*, acknowledged in retrospect, as an addendum to the text. By contrast, looking at the history of the concept of gender provides an opportunity to raise intersex concerns and to challenge transphobic claims within feminism. While taking a stance against transphobic feminism and politics – exemplified for instance in the works of Sheila Jeffreys and Janice Raymond[28]

and contemporary trans-exclusionary radical feminists (TERFs) such as UK philosopher Kathleen Stock – it must be acknowledged that trans and intersex theory and activism are always already at the heart of the concept of gender that most feminists appeal to and, as such, are at the heart of feminism itself. Recalling the clinical origin of gender might therefore offer a productive and timely intervention in contemporary debates.

Cybernetics and post-World War II surgery

Money's publications were singularly influential from the mid-1950s to the 1970s and, until recently, have been the main point of reference for medical theory and practice.[29] The concept of gender identity/role introduced psychological principles into the medical treatment of intersexuality, and in so doing provided a link between the fields of psychology, endocrinology and surgery in gender affirmation.[30] Establishing a point of convergence, gender, Repo argues, became the major sexual discourse of the mid-twentieth and early twenty-first centuries, just as sexuality had been the subject of scientific and biopolitical discourse in the nineteenth century.[31] Yet to fully understand this shift, we need to move beyond Money to attend to the historical context more broadly.

The medical interest in intersex people that gave birth to the notion of gender occurred at a time when the West was rebuilding the social, political and economic order after the Second World War.[32] While the management of sex was an integral part of post-War order, military technology in turn was a condition of possibility for new approaches to intersex treatment. Plastic and cosmetic surgery, which had advanced in the First World War, set out not only to reconstruct broken bodies but also shell-shocked minds by means of operations.[33] Surgeons emphasised the positive psychological impact of their operations, which came to justify surgical intervention more broadly. As Iain Morland notes, the symmetries between these interwar treatments and Money's advocacy of gender reassignment surgery are striking.[34]

Until Money's publications in the mid-twentieth century, medical intervention in intersex conditions remained uncommon, partly due to a lack of technological capacity.[35] As Katrina Karkazis explains in *Fixing Sex,* rather than thinking about ways of intervening, the medical establishment had previously focused on how to understand and classify intersex bodies.[36] Advancement in surgical techniques, the discovery of sex hormones, new understandings of sex differentiation in embryology, and the ability to test for sex chromosomes, all shaped Money's understanding of sex as a differential term and his proposed protocol and intervention.[37]

However, there was another important if unexpected influence. Money was motivated in his work not only by surgical and psychological innovation but also by cybernetics, the study of communication and control that was first conceived in military research during the 1940s.[38] If understood as part of the general postwar US scientific context, this influence on his work will be less surprising. Cybernetics gave Money new theoretical tools and concepts with which to rethink sex and define gender.

As Morland demonstrates in 'Cybernetic Sexology', Money uses a cybernetic vocabulary of 'variables', 'thresholds', and 'feedback systems' to replace central psychological concepts such as those of motivation and drive.[39] The use of a cybernetic vocabulary was meant to offer a more up-to-date sexology and to provide an alternative to both psychoanalytic and biological explanations of sex, gender and sexuality.[40] Money had read and, in a 1949 paper, cited Norbert Wiener, who is considered the originator of cybernetics. In particular, Money referred to Wiener's analysis of systems and it is noticeable that Money's definition of sex as a list of five prenatally-determined variables follows the cybernetic definition of a system.

According to cybernetics, a system is not a thing but a list of variables chosen by an observer. As Morland outlines, '(t)he definition of systems as sets of observer-selected variables allowed cybernetics to recognise a world of boundless complexity, but also to constrain it, much like Money's multivariate definition of sex'.[41] For Money, cybernetics offered a precedent in its creative use of language to define a new discipline and to set up a new research institute.[42]

However, as Morland argues, 'Money did not merely borrow cybernetic rhetoric in articulating gender. For Money, gender was cybernetic, directly.'[43] What this means is that Money recognises sex difference as having a complexity that can nonetheless be contained by defining certain key variables by which sex can be understood and governed. If gender has cybernetic roots, then the discourse of gender must be understood as being shaped by contexts of communication, warfare and control. Even as Money deployed new surgical and hormonal technologies as well as cybernetic ideas of communication, feedback and control to modify intersex bodies, effectively questioning the fictitious unity of sex and acknowledging the malleability of sex difference and anatomy, his conception of gender did nothing to unsettle older nineteenth century *Naturphilosophie* ideas of sexual difference as being rooted in nature and structuring all of human life.

The philosophers Friedrich Schelling and G.W.F. Hegel, among others, as well as medical practitioners such as Carl Gustav Carus, proposed a theory of sexual complementarity according to which men and women are not physical and moral equals but complementary opposites whose complementarity underpins the notions of species, nature and reproduction as expressed in the concept of sexual difference.[44] It followed that if sexual difference, defined as complementary dualism, was the general principle of the species, then no individual existence could, according to Hegel, Schelling and Carus escape it.

Money's theory of gender did not question the *naturphilosophische* conception of sexual difference as a complementary dualism that structures all of human life, but rather envisaged those clinical, medical and surgical procedures that would implement sexual duality. In other words, even though the possibility of a straightforward revelation of sex was no longer conceivable in Money's framework, he did not conceive of a new understanding of sex/gender that escaped binarism.

Gender, accordingly, became the terrain on which *Naturphilosophie* met biotechnological medical care. Once sexual dimorphism was no longer tenable as a universal description of human nature and biology, it was gender that implemented the promise of nineteenth-century sexual difference and sex dimorphism through technological, surgical and psychological means. What emerged was a new sex/gender regime produced by the unexpected alliance between a nineteenth-century naturalist metaphysics of sexual dimorphism that focused on heterosexual reproduction and the rise of cybernetics and a medical biotech industry that acknowledged that gender roles and identities could be artificially redesigned.[45]

Gender in feminist theory

Money's work gained not only medical but also a wider public recognition. In the 1970s and 1980s, he was interviewed in mainstream magazines, appeared frequently on television and was often quoted in newspapers.[46] While feminists in this period seized on the concept of gender as a means to oppose biological determinism and its control over women's bodies and capacities, and while this uptake has resulted in the radical rethinking of sex, gender and reproduction, Money's influence on feminist theory has remained largely implicit.

It is in the works of second-wave feminists that the concept of gender is first rethought, most importantly as a sociological category. Ann Oakley's influential book *Sex, Gender and Society* has often been credited with initiating a new use of the term gender and specifically with introducing this use into the lexicon of social science.[47] According to Oakley, who refers to the work of Money and Stoller as well as anthropologists like Margaret Mead, gender is 'the cultural construction of femininity and masculinity'.[48] Splitting gender from sex, Oakley aligns herself with Stoller more than Money. For Oakley, the purpose of affirming a sex-gender distinction is, first, to argue that the physical effects of biological differences between men and women are exaggerated and employed to maintain a patriarchal system of power[49] and, second, to introduce gender as a new analytical category into the social sciences in order to illuminate how all fields of life are shaped by patriarchal relations.

Money, Oakley argues, 'has done important research on the social-sexual identity of people, who are biologically intersexual.'[50] While rethinking gender and claiming it as a feminist sociological concept that departs in important ways from Money's as well as Stoller's use of the term, Oakley does not problematise Money's work. With the exception of her 2015 introduction to the new edition of *Sex, Gender and Society*, Oakley uncritically refers to Money's research, using it as scientific proof to support her own claim that culture plays an important part in the shaping of male and female identity.[51] By not engaging rigorously with Money, using his work primarily as scientific confirmation and evidence of her own claims, trans and intersex considerations are marginalised in Oakley's research. It is therefore not surprising that they do not find their way into mainstream feminism and into the majority of writings that come out of second-wave feminist scholarship. As a result, gender comes to be disassociated from intersex and trans concerns.

In the introduction to the 2011 volume *Deviations* that anthologises her work, Gayle Rubin remarks on the impact of Money's analytic framework on her early work.[52] In her influential 1975 essay 'The Traffic in Women', Rubin introduced the concept sex/gender system, which she defined as 'a set of arrangements by which a society transforms biological sexuality into products of human activity'.[53] In *Deviations*, Rubin acknowledges that while she did not cite Money in her early work, she was indeed influenced by him and had absorbed aspects of his analytic framework without grasping its novelty.[54] Rubin writes that Money's 'gender' 'was one of the resources at hand with which to build feminist frameworks' that together with Karl Marx's discussion of reproduction, Claude Lévi-Strauss's analysis of kinship, and Sigmund Freud and Jacques Lacan's discourse on femininity, contributed to her own choice of terminology.[55] Money's concept of gender draws attention to the social production of sex and gender identity. But while for Money, this proposition establishes 'gender' as a clinical and behavioural term with implications for the medical 'treatment' and normalisation of intersex children, Rubin reads the social construction of gender through a Marxist psychoanalytic framework, concluding that the social and historical production of gender roles and norms is a site of political struggle. Contrary to Money who sees the reorganisation of sex/gender as a clinical issue, Rubin advocates the reorganisation of the sex/gender system through political action.

A similar pattern of Money's unacknowledged influence can also be observed in Butler's work. It is in *Undoing Gender* – Butler's re-elaboration in 2004 of the question of gender performativity – rather than the earlier *Gender Trouble* or *Bodies That Matter* – that Butler first mentions and engages with Money's work and acknowledges trans and intersex discourses as inherent to the question of gender performativity. Until *Undoing Gender*, Butler, in line with feminist theory more generally, ignored the medical and biotechnological dimensions of gender production.[56] In this book, moreover, the definition of gender performativity is elaborated as both a doing and an undoing. Accordingly, the work brings together the two separate but related discourses that are of interest here: namely, an analysis of gender that includes its historical origin as a term meant to answer questions regarding the status and medical treatment of intersex and trans persons, as well as a philosophical account of gender ontology.

From gender to gender performativity

Butler's discussion of intersex and transgender activism and theory demonstrates her political and theoretical commitment to challenging mainstream feminist discourses. Intended, like *Gender Trouble*, as a critical intervention in contemporary feminism by highlighting how 'its own practice sets up exclusionary gender norms',[57] *Undoing Gender* shows Butler's continued investment in opening up feminist theory and practice. As she states at the outset, it was intended to investigate 'what it might mean to undo restrictively normative conceptions of sexual and gendered life'.[58] While also dependent on other social factors such as class, race and age, this normative pressure affects not only women but queer, trans and intersex people who may or may not identify as women but who have a shared interest in challenging the violence of gender norms.

Although Butler emphasises that she wants to understand gender historically and biopolitically, there are limits to her approach. She writes that '[t]o understand gender as a historical category [...] is to accept that gender, understood as one way of culturally configuring the body, is open to a continual remaking, and that "anatomy" and "sex" are not without cultural framing.'[59] Butler argues that the concept of gender, if understood through the concept of performativity, contains a reference to history by definition, both historicising ontology and presenting this as an historical account of gender. Her project, in other words, is to construct a concept of being that is open to change and that in its definition includes an understanding of social temporality and of the cultural shaping of what 'is'. Defined as such, the concept of gender stands in tension with some versions of sexual difference as defined in French psychoanalytic theory, for instance in the works of Lacan, Luce Irigaray and Julia Kristeva, but also as taken up by Slavoj Žižek and Joan Copjec among others. In *Undoing Gender*, Butler argues that the sexual difference framework is unable

to respond to the following questions: 'What is the history of this category? Where are we in its history at this time?'[60] Yet when it comes to the concept of gender, she does not seem to have an answer to these questions either.

When Butler emphasises that gender as a concept is inherently historical, she makes a convincing philosophical claim regarding the nature of conceptual form and its ontological instantiation. However, this does not translate into a retelling of the particular history of gender. While this does not invalidate her critique of the sexual difference paradigm of French psychoanalytic thought, I would like to suggest that Butler needs to specify what kind of history she is talking about. There are at least two histories of gender at stake: one at the level of conceptual form and ontology, which is about the nature of ontology itself; and one that traces the history and politics of gender as a social category and notes its changing meanings over time. While both accounts are necessary, Butler largely addresses only the former.

Repo criticises Butler's emphasis on rethinking ontology, which, she argues, comes at the expense of a Foucauldian analysis of the operations of power that are necessary to understand the historical origin and workings of the concept of gender. According to Repo, 'Butler's gender theory evades these questions of biopolitical strategies and tactics that are central to Foucault's analysis of the apparatus of sexuality/sex'.[61] Repo argues that instead of a Foucauldian analysis of power, there is in Butler's work an overemphasis on 'the rules of the dialectical production of meaning that serves to satisfy the subject's laborious desire for recognition'.[62] Here Butler is critiqued for being too Hegelian in her analysis. While Repo is justified in arguing that Butler does not sufficiently engage with Money and the clinical protocols out of which the discourse of gender emerges as well as with the sociology of gender, Butler's interventions into ontology are nonetheless vital and should not be underestimated. Moreover, they do not preclude an analysis of power and do not imply that her findings are politically irrelevant.

In *Gender Trouble*, Butler describes her project as not simply a genealogy of gender but as 'a genealogy of gender *ontology*'.[63] Butler's enquiry seeks to demonstrate that there is no pre-established ontology of gender because ontology in general does not constitute a foundation. Rather, Butler argues, ontology should be understood in terms of a series of normative injunctions that operate by installing themselves into political discourse as its necessary ground.[64] Among these normative injunctions are, for instance, ideal dimorphism, heterosexual complementarity of bodies, and ideals and rules of proper and improper masculinity and femininity, all of which are also underwritten by racial codes.[65] Political discourse, according to Butler, establishes an 'ontological field' in which bodies can be given legitimate expression.[66] Ontology, thus understood, will always ask questions about power, violence, resistance and freedom. Inherently political, ontology is open to transformation. For feminist philosophy this means, on the one hand the possibility of change, but on the other, that no pre-established and stable category of 'woman' exists on which to build a politics. What these conclusions mean for philosophy more broadly remains to be investigated, but in Butler's work the understanding of ontology is elaborated through her conception of performativity. While there has been a lot of work in recent years on linguistics and performativity and the relation between performance studies and philosophy, the question of performativity as social ontology, already hinted at in Butler's work, has not been widely addressed.

While Butler's notion of performativity explains a very specific doing, namely that of gender, a more general notion, even if not explicitly addressed, is still at work in Butler and allows her to transpose her concept of performativity onto other contexts, for instance in *Excitable Speech: A Politics of the Performative* and *Notes Toward a Performative Theory of Assembly*.[67] What is thought through in all these instances is a concept of activity that does not start from or rely upon an already-given idea of subjectivity. Although sceptical of traditional ontology, Butler's work nonetheless interrogates the conditions of possibility for ontological claims, since these are decisive for subjectivity and agency and thus for any feminist and emancipatory project. Thus, despite her thoroughgoing critique of ontology, it is becoming increasingly clear, as Stephen K. White points out, that Butler is herself affirming an alternative ontology.[68] Unmasking the essentialism at work in various conceptualisations of masculinity and femininity, and thus of subjectivity, gender and the body,[69] Butler also develops alongside this critique a concept of 'performativity' that is mobilised to describe not only linguistic acts and theatrical performances but more generally the processes through which ontological claims come to manifest on or in the body or even as body.

Though Butler does not propose it explicitly in these terms, I want to suggest that her concept of performativity is better understood as performative ontology. Gender, according to Butler, is performative in that it is a doing that constitutes the identity it is purported to be.[70] It follows that the gendered body 'has no ontological status apart from the various acts which constitute its reality.'[71] In other words, by means of her concept of performativity, Butler develops a new language of ontology, a new discourse describing how selves come to body forth – what Gerhard Thonhauser has recently characterised as 'a theory that could be called a social ontology.'[72] This is an attempt to move away from ontological essentialism towards a speculative ontology that is neither voluntaristic nor entirely structurally constrained. What might such an ontology look like?

Reading Butler as a thinker of ontology means understanding her project not only as discourse analysis, as a discussion of Derridean iterability or a Foucauldian analysis of power, but as an attempt to construct a speculative social ontology. Given that for Butler, ontology is inherently unstable and works through a series of normative injunctions and within a field of constraint, this is not to break with either Derrida or Foucault. Nor is the question of ontology superimposed onto them, since iterability and the discursive production of meaning are always, as Butler also shows, linked to their bodily instantiation as ritual and habit. Moreover, thinking about or in terms of ontology does not mean that all other questions are bracketed. Rather, the question of being is dispersed and is shown to be often as much a question of language, power, identity and discourse.

The question of ontology comes to the fore at different moments in Butler's work. It is implied in the conceptualisation of gender performativity through statements such as the following: 'There is no gender identity behind the expressions of gender; that identity is performatively constituted by the very "expressions" that are said to be its result.'[73] Statements such as these could be interpreted as saying that gender is constructed and therefore is completely individually produced. Recognising that performativity is to be understood as social ontology, however, complicates this claim. Norms, institutions, history and culture performatively create the context out of which individuals' genders are produced. Butler's performativity is a doing and undoing that is not the wilful act of an already-determined subject. Reframing performativity as a form of speculative social ontology offers an avenue out of the oft-repeated criticism that Butler's account of gender performativity is overly voluntaristic.

Gender ideals 'work', according to Butler, because 'performativity is not a singular act, but a repetition and a ritual, which achieves its effects through its naturalisation in the context of a body'.[74] In other words, through their performative repetition, gender norms come to be experienced and lived as a second nature. What seems to be instinctive, such as masculine and feminine gender norms, is a habitual production. In this sense, gender is produced '*on the surface* of the body' and comes to have 'the effect of an internal core or substance.'[75] Gender, then, has an ontological 'effect', but, since performative, 'it has no ontological status apart from the various acts which constitute its reality.'[76] Gender, in other words, is produced habitually. However, this is not just a personal habit but institutional, and the result is that rather than being produced, gender becomes enforced. Is gender then a 'bad habit'? According to Butler, the question is 'not whether to repeat, but how to repeat'[77] – that is, not how to break out of habit as such but how to break out of a bad habit. In this way, Money's intervention in sexual difference by way of gender is pursued further by Butler, though under radically different premises. While Money wants to fix trouble, Butler asks 'how best to make it, what best way to be in it.'[78] It is therefore telling that in the preface to the second edition of *Gender Trouble*, Butler remarks that if she were to rewrite the book under present circumstances she 'would include a discussion of transgender and intersexuality, the way that ideal gender dimorphism works in both sorts of discourses, the different relations to surgical intervention that these related concerns sustain.'[79] The discussion of gender would, thereby, come full circle.

The Reimer case

The 'John/Joan' case, as it was first referred to for reasons of anonymity,[80] details the childhood and adolescence of David Reimer, an identical twin, who in 1965 had his penis burned off in a circumcision accident and who was subsequently raised as a girl under Money's medical care.[81] While this case was central to changing beliefs about the relationship between the social construction of gender and biological sex, Money failed to mention that Reimer rejected his female gender assignment as an adult and lived the rest of his life, until his suicide in 2004, as a man.[82] In 2000, John Colapinto published a book on the case that was critical of Money's intervention, eliciting a number of responses raising concerns about the ethics of Money's practice but also vindicating biological explanations of gender.[83] According to the latter critiques, Money's writing and experiments had done violence to the unassailable nature of man and woman.[84]

Butler's retelling of the Reimer case is commendable for the way that she enables his story to be heard while questioning Money's clinical framework for its enforcement of gender stereotypes and sexual dimorphism, without however using Reimer's story for her own theoretical and political purposes. What Butler shows is that Reimer's experiences at home, in school and in the medical establishment shed light on the experiences of non-binary and trans people more broadly. Reimer's experience and double 'transition' is presented in its complexity by Butler, who makes no final judgement on whether Reimer is trans or not.

Reimer functions, for Money, as an exemplar of his own theoretical beliefs. Butler rightly observes that in Money's work, Reimer's body becomes a point of reference for a narrative that is not about this body, but seizes upon the body, as it were, in order to inaugurate a particular narrative about what it means to be human.[85] For Money, gender describes the social dimension of sexed bodily life as noncausal and yet as utterly predictable and controllable. By means of the concept of gender, bodies are 'normalised' and governed under Money's care. But why could Reimer not be a man without a penis? Or decide for himself, as he later did, whether and how to identify in gender terms? Money's emphasis on 'looking normal' not only reinforced gender norms, it also encouraged early infancy surgery, which risked permanently depriving a person of sexual function and pleasure.[86] The surgery, ostensibly for the patient's sake, is in fact performed for society's sake, a society which, as Butler observes, demands a 'normal-looking' body.[87]

For Butler, the better imperative is 'to imagine a world in which individuals with mixed genital attributes might be accepted and loved without having to transform them into a more socially coherent or normative version of gender.'[88] In *Lessons from the Intersexed*, Suzanne J. Kessler makes a similar point: 'Why are unusually sized and shaped genitals not accepted as reasonable markers of gender – gender either as we know it in the two-option scheme or as we could know it in a new gender system?'[89] Kessler, moreover, points to the heteronormative bias that underlies Money's clinical protocol. When Money argues that Reimer, because of the loss of his penis, should not be raised as a boy but be assigned the female gender, one of the justifications for this decision is that Reimer will not be able to have heterosexual intercourse. This supports Butler's claim that gender dimorphism is inherently linked to heterosexism in what she refers to as a heterosexual matrix or hegemony.

A critique of idealised gender dimorphism, as put forward by Butler and Kessler among others, does not, however, lead to the conclusion that transgender people should not be allowed the right to surgery. The difference between intersex and transsexual surgery is that in the first case, physicians typically practice gender upon others – often, as in the case of intersex surgery, without the explicit knowledge and permission of the patient because it tends to be done in early infancy. In contrast, in claiming gender-affirming surgery, trans persons practice gender on themselves – they 'do' their own gender.[90] This is not an attempt to violently implement a norm, although this practice does not take place outside of a normative framework. Transness can illustrate the malleability of anatomy, gender identity and role but, as Butler points out, unlike in the Reimer case, malleability is not imposed here.[91]

Tame the white middle class!

When considering the history of 'gender', it is imperative to reflect on the race and class of the intersex bodies that were of concern to the medical establishment. We must ask whose children the medical establishment was invested in when defining the category of intersex. As Repo outlines, gender was primarily 'an apparatus designed to tame, normalise, and regulate White, middle-class children and parents into harmonious, reproductive, and productive nuclear units.'[92] But who goes without health insurance and never enters the hospital in the first place? Who is from the start not meant to ever form a part of the harmonious, reproductive nuclear family unit? If the medical category of gender was in the 1950s predominantly concerned with white, middle-class families, is this concern maintained by feminists who take up the category for use as a feminist analytical tool? According to Repo, the answer is yes. This, however, is not because gender could be a better and more critical term but because the entanglement of feminist thought with the biopolitical practices of the postwar US medical establishment have never been sufficiently interrogated.

The unacknowledged origin of the concept of gender in medical, psychological and anthropological scholarship and in post-World War II nation building in the US continues also to trouble Butler's work. Moreover, while Butler explains that gender and sexuality are not immediately self-explanatory, by and large race and class remain abstract terms in her work, truths taken to be self-evident. Butler states that all social markers are inherently related, but the nature of their relation is never explicitly explored. This is surprising given that performativity is a term that – like the prefix 'trans', in which Butler seems especially invested in her more recent work – implies a movement across or beyond given states of affairs.[93] However, even though 'performativity', 'trans' and 'queer' are terms that speak to each other as they try to address a processual, anti-essentialist notion of being and being-with, they can also at times end up obscuring the specific and complicated histories of social and political categories.

The ontological status of gender, as defined by Butler, is brought into question in Hortense Spillers's and Saidiya Hartman's accounts of how race operates to undo gender. Looking at the transatlantic slave trade and its legacy, Spillers introduces the notion of the ungendering of the Black body. What is at stake in this concept is the exact status of an ontology of gender in relation to both its historicity and to its performative and normative character. This analysis forms part of Spillers's broader theoretical work on the distinction between captive and liberated subject positions. In her landmark essay 'Mama's Baby, Papa's Maybe: An American Grammar Book' (1987), Spillers proposes a distinction between 'body' and 'flesh'. According to Spillers, before the 'body' there is 'flesh', a zero degree of social conceptualisation.[94] Spillers argues that the transatlantic slave trade

> marked a *theft of the body* – a wilful and violent (and unimaginable from this distance) severing of the captive body from its motive will, its active desire. Under these conditions, we lose at least *gender* difference *in the outcome*, and the female body and the male body become a territory of cultural and political maneuver, not at all gender-related, gender-specific. But this body, at least from the point of view of the captive community, focuses a private and particular space, at which point of convergence biological, sexual, social, cultural, linguistic, ritualistic, and psychological fortunes join'.[95]

As Alexander Weheliye explains, Spillers's notion of the flesh does not demarcate an abject zone of exclusion that culminates in death but a zone in which kinship and social structures that are determining of Western society are suspended.[96] Most notable is the suspension of gender and sex-role assignation, which, with the exception of the reproductive labour of birthing, do not emerge for enslaved African-Americans in this historic instance.[97] Because Black women's sexual and reproductive capacities were used to reinforce the existing relations of production and the continuation of slavery, it might be argued that slavery in this way bears a gendered aspect. But despite Black women's sexual and reproductive capacities being essential to slavery, Hartman and Spillers argue that gender and sexual differentiation are unimportant, or matter only indirectly, as categories in this historical context. In her essay 'The Belly of the World: A Note on Black Women's Labors' (2016), Hartman explains that this is because these categories are absent whenever the productive labour of the enslaved comes into view.[98] Kinship and gender relations lose meaning because they can be obliterated by property relations at any given moment.[99] For this reason, reproductive labour, including birthing, and not gender, is the central category for understanding slavery and its afterlife in global capitalism.

The reproductive labour of birthing is also a driving force for nineteenth century gynaecological innovation in the US South. It is not surprising that one of the first specialised US medical journals is an obstetrical journal.[100] As Deleso Alford Washington outlines, '[s]lavery, medicine, and medical publishing formed a synergistic partnership in which Southern medicine could

emerge as regionally distinctive, at least through its representation in medical literature, and especially with regard to gynaecology.'[101] Since gynaecology and women's health contribute to the maintenance of slavery, the concern for women's health is here primarily driven by a desire to maintain and reproduce existing property relations. Moreover, these innovations illustrate that conceptions of sex, gender and sexual difference are inseparable from race. The experimental surgical treatment of Black enslaved women, as conducted for instance by James Marion Sims – once considered to be the 'father' of American gynaecology – 'othered' the women he experimented on based upon a construction of race but also 'samed' their bodies for purposes of extracting reproductive knowledge and surgical innovations that could benefit all women.[102] In other words, while Black female bodies are othered for the duration of surgical experimentation, once a cure is found it applies not only to all women but, as Sims once remarked, to the entirety of humanity.[103]

Spillers argues that the marking of the Black body as flesh is passed on from one generation to another. According to her, the naming, valuation and relegation of Black bodies to the status of dispensable commodities is effective today through various symbolic substitutes, such as skin colour and ethnicity. In Spillers's words, 'the flesh is the concentration of "ethnicity"'.[104] It follows that with racism and structural discrimination, ungendering of Black and ethnic bodies continues too. This in turn raises questions about the types of histories and range of performances that are deemed normative in the constitution of gender categories today. What is at stake in Spillers's and Hartman's writings is the status of an ontology of gender.

According to Spillers, 'gendering' takes place within the confines of the domestic only to spread over a wider ground of human and social purposes. By contrast, the human cargo of a slave vessel offers a counternarrative to notions of the domestic.[105] The effacement of African family and proper names under conditions of enslavement leads to the creation of an alternate domestic sphere. Spillers writes:

> It seems clear, however, that 'Family', as we practice and understand it 'in the West' – the *vertical* transfer of a bloodline, of a patronymic, of titles and entitlements, of real estate and the prerogatives of 'cold cash', from

fathers to *sons* and in the supposedly free exchange of affectional ties between a male and a female of *his* choice – becomes the mythically revered privilege of a free and freed community.[106]

Spillers demonstrates that the kinship models of Black communities are unintelligible within the terms of a white American grammar of gender and family relations. The loss of gender differentiation becomes a critical part of Blackness in the US, while the notion of the ungendering of the Black body demonstrates that gender and sex differences are also racial arrangements.[107]

Hartman makes a similar point when she argues that the suspension of gender norms under slavery has led to the emergence of gender nonconforming Black communities in the US and to forms of domesticity distinct from those that obtain in the majority of white households.[108] Spillers and Hartman accordingly identify a queerness within Black gender and kinship relations, which creates a social subject position that is ungendered. Spillers urges us 'to make a place for this different social subject', ungendered and insurgent.[109]

While Butler understands gender to be both performative and normative and intrinsically linked to heteronormative kinship ideals, she does not question its historical origins in the imperial slave-holding nation state. Spillers and Hartman, by contrast, explain that race and ethnicity, not only heterosexuality, are defining normative elements that determine whether a person can establish normative gender relations and whether their recognition by others might be foreclosed. It is in this sense that they question Butler's notion of the normativity and performativity of gender.

Butler rightly claims that gender performativity is a practice of improvisation within a scene of constraint. But while she identifies heteronormativity and cisgender as normatively constraining, she does not address racial capitalism as a scene of constraint for gender relations. Gender, according to Butler, is a social law that 'subsumes' everyone; yet as Spillers and Hartman argue, only certain populations are subsumed into a realm of domesticity supported by state institutions, in which gender relations are formed. The normativity of whiteness as integral to gender performativity remains unanalysed in Butler's work.

Conclusion

In this article, I have attempted to further Butler's emphasis on the role and power of state institutions by looking, first, at the deployment of gender as a tool of medicalisation and enforcement of sex dimorphism and, second, albeit more briefly, at the white middle class nuclear family as the dominant form of domesticity which enforces a specific ideal of civil society. What remains to be addressed beyond this article, is how to think the relation between Blackness, transness and intersex in relation to the undoing of gender. In his book *Black on Both Sides: A Racial History of Trans Identity*, C. Riley Snorton gives an insightful account of this question. Snorton proposes that the notion of captive flesh, as defined by Spillers, figures a critical genealogy for modern transness.[110] This, Snorton writes, is because Blackness like transness articulates the paradox of nonbeing that is expressed in Spillers's notion of the flesh.[111] In this sense, the ungendering of the Black body gives rise to an understanding of gender as mutable and as an amendable form of being, a context for imagining gender as subject to rearrangement.[112] If therefore the notion of female flesh ungendered 'offers a praxis and a theory, a text for living and dying',[113] could this be a transfeminist theory and praxis?

Emphasising the importance of being precise in recounting the connections between and within Blackness and transness, Snorton remarks on the difficulty of giving an exhaustive account or a full explanation of their relation. One reason for this is that some of these connections are a question of the future, of not yet known but possible alliances against a very violent history. Thinking these connections, as Snorton suggests, is an exercise in 'seeking to understand the conditions of emergence of things and beings that may not yet exist'.[114] What this means for the conception of gender is that though gender has a history which forms the conditions of possibility for normative gender identities and relations, interrogating gender is at the same time a theorising of what might be possible, an attempt at thinking and living gender otherwise. As Spillers emphasises, the aim is not to join the ranks of gendered femaleness but to gain an insurgent ground for a different social subject position, which might be female, nonbinary or other.[115] By illuminating the violence and exclusion in the birth of gender as a concept, alternative futures and trajectories may be forged.

Gender without history is a generic concept that has become an emancipatory tool as much as a core category of governmentality, where it is often used against those whom it should help by impeding access to resources and services such as healthcare, housing, employment and refuge from violence. This article aims to revive gender as a critical feminist tool by offering an account of how trans, intersex and Black feminist concerns, although foundational to its history, slipped out of its early conceptualisation in feminist theory. If gender is to remain a critical and useful concept for feminist analysis, then its problematic past and present need to be addressed. Butler's intervention is still helpful in this regard as it outlines a speculative social ontology of how the markers of sex and sexuality gain meaning and come to be embodied. Nonetheless, the omission of intersex, trans and Blackness from her initial conceptualisation of gender ontology necessitates a recuperation of these histories with a view to grasping how they might transform our understanding of gender ontology.

Isabell Dahms recently completed a PhD on the history of concepts of speculation and performativity at the Centre for Research in Modern European Philosophy at Kingston University London.

Notes

1. Judith Butler, *Undoing Gender* (New York: Routledge, 2004); Cristan Williams 'Gender Performance: The TransAdvocate interviews Judith Butler', *The TransAdvocate*, 1 May 2014; Sara Ahmed, 'Interview with Judith Butler', *Sexualities* 19:4 (2016).
2. Jemima Repo, *The Biopolitics of Gender* (New York: Oxford University Press), 75.
3. Paul B. Preciado, *Testo Junkie: Sex, Drugs, and Biopolitics in the Pharmacopornographic Era* (New York: The Feminist Press, 2013), 99.
4. John Money, *Gendermaps: Social Constructionism, Feminism and Sexosophical History* (London: Bloomsbury 2016), 11.
5. Ibid., 11.
6. Ibid., 18–19.
7. Ibid., 18–19.
8. Repo, *The Biopolitics of Gender*, 4.
9. Money, *Gendermaps*, 21.
10. Ines Orobio de Castro, *Made to Order: Sex/Gender in a Transsexual Perspective* (Amsterdam: Spinhuis, 1993), 24.
11. Money, *Gendermaps*, 18–19.
12. Ibid., 18–19.
13. Terry Goldie, *The Man Who Invented Gender: Engaging the Ideas of John Money* (Vancouver: UBC Press, 2014), 39.
14. Money, *Gendermaps*, 21.
15. Ibid., 21.
16. Robert Stoller, *Sex and Gender (Volume 1): The Development of Masculinity and Femininity* (London: Maresfield, 1984), vi: '... the word *sexuality* usually does not communicate much, for it covers so much. Trying to be more precise, we have split off "gender" as a distinguishable part of "sexuality"'.
17. Preciado, *Testo Junkie*, 111.
18. Repo, *The Biopolitics of Gender*, 4.
19. John Money and Anke A. Erhardt, *Man and Woman, Boy and Girl* (Baltimore: The Johns Hopkins University Press, 1972).
20. Ibid., 244.
21. Goldie, *The Man Who Invented Gender*, 207.
22. Talia Mae Bettcher, 'Intersexuality, Transgender, and Transsexuality' in *The Oxford Handbook of Feminist Theory*, eds. Lisa Disch and Mary Hawkesworth (Oxford: Oxford University Press, 2016), 409. Johns Hopkins halted gender affirming surgeries in 1979 and only formally reopened its transgender health service, including a surgical program, in 2017.
23. Ibid., 408.
24. Ibid., 420.
25. Emi Koyama, 'Interrogating the Politics of Commonality: Building a Bisexual, Trans and Intersex Alliance', in *Introduction to Intersex Activism: A Guide for Allies* (Portland, Oregon: Intersex Initiative Portland, 2003), 18.
26. Viviane Namaste, *Sex Change, Social Change: Reflections on Identity, Institutions, and Imperialism* (Toronto: Women's Press Toronto, 2005), 13.
27. Ibid., 11.
28. Janice G. Raymond, *The Transsexual Empire* (London: Women's Press, 1980) and critical response by Sandy Stone, 'The Empire Strikes Back: A Posttranssexual Manifesto', *Camera Obscura* 29 (1992), who was personally attacked by Raymond.
29. Iain Morland, 'Gender, Genitals, and the Meaning of Being Human', in *Fuckology: Critical Essays on John Money's Diagnostic Concepts*, eds. Lisa Downing, Iain Morland and Nikki Sullivan (Chicago, IL: The University of Chicago Press, 2015), 69.
30. Katrina Karkazis, *Fixing Sex: Intersex, Medical Authority and Lived Experience* (Durham, NC: Duke University Press, 2008), 48.
31. Repo, *The Biopolitics of Gender*, 1.
32. Ibid., 47.
33. Morland, 'Gender, Genitals, and the Meaning of Being Human', 83.
34. Ibid., 83.
35. Karkazis, *Fixing Sex*, 31.
36. Ibid.
37. Ibid., 31–32.
38. Iain Morland, 'Cybernetic Sexology', in *Fuckology: Critical Essays on John Money's Diagnostic Concepts*, 101.
39. Ibid., 101. Morland's essay is to this day the only text on this subject.
40. Ibid., 101.
41. Ibid., 111.

42. Ibid., 105.

43. Ibid., 105.

44. Susanne Lettow, 'Population, Race and Gender: On the Genealogy of the Modern Politics of Reproduction', *Distinktion: Scandinavian Journal of Social Theory* 16:3 (2015), 2.

45. Preciado, *Testo Junkie*, 103.

46. Goldie, *The Man Who Invented Gender*, 3.

47. Ann Oakley, *The Ann Oakley Reader: Gender, Women, and Social Science* (Bristol: Policy Press, 2005), 2.

48. Ann Oakley, *Experiments in Knowing: Gender and Method in the Social Sciences* (Cambridge: Polity Press, 2000), 3.

49. Jane Pilcher and Imelda Whelehan, *50 Key Concepts in Gender Studies* (London: Sage Publications, 2004), 56.

50. Ann Oakley, *Sex, Gender and Society* (Farnham, Surrey: Ashgate, 2015), 61.

51. See especially Oakley, *Sex, Gender and Society*, chapter 6.

52. Gayle Rubin, *Deviations: A Gayle Rubin Reader* (Durham, NC and London: Duke University Press, 2011), 14.

53. Ibid., 178.

54. Ibid., 14.

55. Ibid., 15.

56. Preciado, *Testo Junkie*, 106.

57. Judith Butler, *Gender Trouble: Feminism and the Subversion of Identity* (New York: Routledge, 1999), viii.

58. Butler, *Undoing Gender*, 1.

59. Ibid., 10.

60. Ibid., 38.

61. Repo, *The Biopolitics of Gender*, 6.

62. Ibid., 6.

63. Butler, *Gender Trouble*, 43, my emphasis.

64. Ibid., 189.

65. Ibid., xxiii.

66. Ibid., xxiii.

67. Judith Butler, *Excitable Speech: A Politics of the Performative* (New York and London: Routledge, 1997); Judith Butler, *Notes Toward a Performative Theory of Assembly* (Cambridge, MA: Harvard University Press, 2015).

68. Stephen K. White, 'As the World Turns: Ontology and Politics in Judith Butler', *Polity* 32:2 (1999), 156.

69. Ibid., 158.

70. Butler, *Gender Trouble*, 34.

71. Ibid., 185.

72. Gerhard Thonhauser, 'Butler's Social Ontology of the Subject and its Agency', in *Frei sein, frei handeln: Freiheit zwischen theoretischer und praktischer Philosophie*, eds. Diego D'Angelo et al. (Freiburg: Alber Karl, 2013), 144.

73. Butler, *Gender Trouble*, 34.

74. Ibid., xv.

75. Ibid., 185, emphasis in original.

76. Ibid., 185.

77. Ibid., 202.

78. Ibid., xxvii.

79. Ibid., xxvi.

80. The case was initially discussed anonymously to protect Reimer's privacy and that of his family. Reimer's identity only became known when he went public with his story to help discuss Money's medical practices.

81. Goldie, *The Man who Invented Gender*, 4.

82. Ibid., 4.

83. Lisa Downing, Iain Morland, and Nikki Sullivan, 'Introduction: On the "Duke of Dysfunction"', in *Fuckology: Critical Essays on John Money's Diagnostic Concepts*, 6.

84. Ibid., 6.

85. Butler, *Undoing Gender*, 65.

86. Ibid., 63.

87. Ibid., 64.

88. Ibid., 65–66.

89. Suzanne J. Kessler, *Lessons from the Intersexed* (New Brunswick, NJ: Rutgers University Press, 1998), 105.

90. Ibid., 121.

91. Butler, *Undoing Gender*, 66.

92. Repo, *The Biopolitics of Gender*, 74.

93. Tawny Andersen, 'An Object that Belongs to No One', *Performance Research* 21:5 (2016), 12.

94. Hortense Spillers, 'Mama's Baby, Papa's Maybe: An American Grammar Book', *Diacritics* 17:2 (1987), 67.

95. Ibid.

96. Alexander G. Weheliye, *Habeas Viscus: Racializing Assemblages, Biopolitics and Black Feminist Theories of the Human* (Durham, NC: Duke University Press, 2014), 43.

97. Spillers, 'Mama's Baby', 79.

98. Saidiya Hartman, 'The Belly of the World: A Note on Black Women's Labors', *Souls: A Critical Journal on Black Politics, Culture and Society* 18:1 (2016), 166.

99. Spillers, 'Mama's Baby', 74.

100. G. J. Barker-Benfield, *The Horrors of the Half-Known Life: Male Attitudes Toward Women and Sexuality in Nineteenth-Century America* (New York: Routledge, 2000), 82.

101. Deirdre Cooper Owens, *Medical Bondage: Race, Gender, and the Origins of American Gynecology* (Athens: The University of Georgia Press, 2017), 18.

102. Deleso Alford Washington, 'Critical Race Feminist Bioethics: Telling Stories in Law School and Medical School in Pursuit of "Cultural Competency"', *Albany Law Review* 72:4 (2009), 964–65.

103. When Sims finally discovered a cure to treat vesicovaginal fistulas, he remarked that he had made 'perhaps, one of the most important discoveries of the age for the relief of suffering humanity.' James Marion Sims, *The Story of My Life* (New York: D. Appleton and Company, 1885).

104. Spillers, 'Mama's Baby', 68.

105. Ibid., 72.

106. Ibid., 74.

107. C. Riley Snorton, *Black on Both Sides: A Racial History of Trans Identity* (Minneapolis and London: University of Minnesota Press, 2017), 12.

108. Hartman, 'The Belly of the World', 169.

109. Spillers, 'Mama's Baby', 80.

110. Snorton, *Black on Both Sides*, 57.

111. Ibid., 5.

112. Ibid., 56.

113. Spillers, 'Mama's Baby', 68.

114. Snorton, *Black on Both Sides*, xiv.

115. Spillers, 'Mama's Baby', 80.

Uncaptured desires

What affirms our political imaginaries?

Demet Sahende Dinler

1.

As a younger activist I used to find it puzzling that some people who suffer the most from inequalities in capitalist society had little interest in radical egalitarian imaginaries, in the form of, for example, communal solidarity economies.[1] Certain individuals were attracted to groups defending those ideas only temporarily in crisis situations, when their access to jobs, land, housing, resources was at risk. Others found them unrealistic or unattractive. Given their frequency, I also found it odd that interpersonal rejections and break-ups in the mundane life of organising did not receive more attention. The risks of ascribing a romanticised homogenous agency to subaltern groups who might have different priorities and preferences were perhaps revealed[2], but reflections on these differences and their implications for activism and critical theory were limited. The poor reception of egalitarian ideas could be attributed to the hegemony of neoliberalism that prevents people from imagining a life beyond it or to the failure of social movements to make those ideas palpable to broader audiences. Therefore, one should work harder and wait for the right political and social conditions to make radical visions heard and seen. But this attitude put these visions in a privileged position, offering them exemption from critical scrutiny.

In this essay, I take seriously the moments of mismatch between political ideals and the people they appeal to for change. Rather than reading such moments as another notch on the long list of defeats feeding our left-wing melancholia or as missed opportunities to be seized again under correct circumstances, I propose to analyse them on their own terms, as a reality to acknowledge with humility, whose investigation can speak back to the very roots of radical imaginaries. I examine various groups' engagements and dis-engagements with particular visions and practices by using ethnographic, historical evidence from secondary literature as well as my past experience as an activist and engaged researcher. Experiments on collective property and cooperatives serve as ethnographic vignettes opening up to broader issues on the contradictions of political imaginaries, whose desirability is often taken for granted. I pay self-reflexive attention to my own failures in grasping the complexity of life forms, with the hope that the lessons I derive go beyond my immediate experience and become relatable for others. The overarching question which I attempt to answer is this: When people who are invited to defend and implement a political ideal have little interest in its promises, how should the ideal cope with refusal?[3]

2.

Two great ethnographers of urban and rural Brazil, Kathleen Millar and Wendy Wolford, took seriously the question of abandonment in the context of two cooperative projects. In one of the chapters of Millar's ethnography, we see a group of *catadores* (reclaimers) who build a cooperative called ACAMJG (Associação dos Catadores do Aterro Metropolitano de Jardim Gramacho / Association of Collectors of the Metropolitan Landfill of Jardim Gramacho) with its own recycling facility, trucks and customers. What starts as a therapeutic group conversation led by Tiao, one of the reclaimers working on the garbage dump in Jardim Gramacho, Rio de Janeiro, on how to improve reclaimers' conditions over a drink turns, by 2004, into an institutionalised system of waste management. In order to make the cooperative viable within the broader recycling economy, the leading activists oblige all members to accept weekly payments due to lack of reserves, to wear the cooperative uniforms while collecting waste, to schedule in advance when the truck will pick up the collected material and to make a discount on materials deemed dirty. They prohibit advance payments, use of drugs at the recycling facility and side-selling of recyclables to scrap dealers. Many *catadores* who are used to selling their waste to any dealers in exchange for immediate cash, demand advance money when they need it and go to work only when they want to, find it hard to adhere to these disciplinary measures. Most of them had returned to the dump after they had worked in formal jobs to avoid the coercive discipline of wage work and have a more fluid life rhythm. The freedom to choose when to work, how to work and when to get paid has a higher worth than better prices offered by the cooperative. Those who prefer a more stable and regular life stay, others leave. As Tiao's sister, Gloria, the manager of the cooperative, says 'The ones who withdrew from ACAMJG withdrew because they were not able to live under the rules. They were not able to adapt'.[4]

Cautious of facile interpretations which could see in this fall-out a tension between a solidarity economy and individualistic attitudes, Millar explores different forms of solidarity hidden in the fabric of everyday life on the dump: *truta*, a work partnership to share earnings between two *catadores*, helps to encourage, motivate, help each other by making garbage work an uplifting experience. Made up of workers who live on the dump rather than travelling back and forth to their remote towns, *unions* accept members who share the daily work of bringing water, cooking and cleaning. They emerge, disappear, re-emerge and persist in some form on the dump to support people who need a place to live. Collective mobilisations are not rare, either to protest against dealers who reduce prices or about the unfair practices of the company which manages the dump. They emerge occasionally when people feel there is an injustice to resist. The dump is generative of different forms of living, sharing and resisting of which the ACAMJG is only one example. Leaving the cooperative indicates less an incapacity for collective organisation than a choice to mobilise other forms of self-organising.[5]

15 years before ACAMJG, an agricultural production cooperative named Copagro was being established on a Vento settlement in Santa Caterina, southern Brazil, by the members of the Landless Workers' Movement, MST (Movimento dos Trabalhadores Rurais Sem Terra). The cooperative had a fate similar to ACAMJG, gradually losing many of its member families. MST leaders who are very successful in mobilising landless people for occupations, explained these failures as the incapacity of certain individualistic peasant groups to adapt to the 'New Society' the movement is building. Wolford disagrees: Farming families had a strong egalitarian ethic praising hard work. They embraced the cooperative at the beginning due to their long-standing experience of cooperation and mutual aid. They also liked the idea of making investment in machinery which would upgrade the value of their work and which they could never afford on their own. However, the rules brought about by the MST leadership contradicted the customs and rhythms of communities, similar to what happened in Jardin Gramacho as depicted by Millar: families were forced to buy subsistence food from the cooperative market rather than producing for themselves, children were not allowed to work and be remunerated, cooperative leaders were appointed by MST leadership rather than from the community ranks and they did little physical work. Specialisation of tasks was incompatible with diversification and rotation, generating feelings of boredom, unfairness and the comparison of those who worked more with those who worked less.[6]

Despite the failure of this initial cooperative, most families in the South who used to migrate wherever land was available still represented MST's ethos of small family farmers as the backbone of a more egalitarian society. Successful MST occupations appealed to these families in a period of land shortage caused by powerful landlords and environmental degradation. The reality in the Pernambuco state of the North-East, however, was strikingly different. Communities lacked strong ties, children left home to seek work at a young age, most individuals worked in sugar plantations and changed employer when conditions worsened. They joined the MST mostly for pragmatic reasons, due to the crisis in the sugarcane industry. Once these rural workers accustomed to working independently were turned into settlers, their reservations about collective work persisted. In one case, settlers resisted the plans to work for a large fish pond that would be managed by the whole settlement, funded by the government. Traditional understandings of community and compensation contradicted their perception of the need to remunerate individual work with wages. These groups were reluctant to plant alternative crops dictated by the MST and left the movement once the sugar cane industry revitalised.[7]

Neither Wolford nor Millar impose a moral judgement on decisions to join or leave a collective project. Instead, they pay close attention to differences in meanings attached to individual, family and community rhythms of work, as well as to perceptions about what constitutes a good and desirable life. They reflect on how these differences lend support to or challenge the validity of a particular imaginary in a particular time and place. Theirs is a rare call to relativise political mobilisations which are sometimes frozen in their moments of glory rather than examined through everyday fractures.

3.

Some of the waste pickers I met in Ankara for the first time in 2007 had little interest in the idea of a recycling cooperative that some activists and workers from the waste pickers' movement were testing the waters for. The movement had gained momentum as a response to rising violence towards waste pickers. The municipal police were forcing waste pickers, who worked over the public bins in thousands of urban streets, to sell their waste at a lower price to a multinational investor who had bought the management rights of the largest dump and confiscated the metal carriers used to gather and manually transport waste. By the time I met them, they were selling the second issue of their magazine, consisting of the poems, stories and short articles written by waste pickers themselves. With its unique focus on the emotions and aspirations of waste pickers, the magazine became a big hit in a short period of time, mobilising large public support for the protection of waste pickers.

Having followed one of the organisers to warehouses to satisfy my curiosity about this story, I quickly found myself doing more activism than research. While spending my days in recycling warehouses, public bins and squatter settlements, I joined the discussions around the possibility of building a recycling cooperative. At the time waste pickers' movements were growing in the Global South, with the shared demand to be recognised

as recycling workers rather than informal scavengers. They were building associations, unions and cooperatives, increasing their bargaining power in the market and entering public bids for waste collection in municipal districts. Like some organisers, waste pickers and informal warehouse owners, I was dreaming of seeing similar collective enterprises in Turkey. Recycling traders were reaping the fruit of waste pickers' hard work. It only made sense to join forces to alter power relations and have a more formal representation at the municipal level.

I would soon realise that the desires, interests and ambitions around a simple warehouse were stronger than I could imagine. It was still two years before the price of recyclable materials would plummet with the world financial crisis and the informal recycling economy was growing to satisfy local and foreign investors. A warehouse was very easy to build in a shanty town, to rent at a cheap price in an abandoned industrial zone and to replace in case of evacuation. Some of those who ran a warehouse wanted to expand it by hiring new workers or buying from smaller warehouses lacking transport means. The ones who worked for a warehouse wanted to open one. Some received advance money from large warehouse owners to open their own place in exchange for regular waste supply. There were also those who simply wanted to continue working with family members for a regular income. Owning one's own small business mattered to people. The city was enclosed by a web of warehouses, some of which were barely surviving in conditions of poverty, while others pursued fantasies to grow. Despite the love and respect I had for waste pickers who were becoming my friends, I was coming to the conclusion that in economic matters, some of them were too cautious and individualistic to act together.

At the beginning, I was unable to grasp forms of solidarity within waste picking communities properly, since they were not framed within grander narratives of egalitarianism. Millar would have known how to appreciate them: one of the largest migrant communities who had come to Ankara and started collecting wastepaper, had divided the city centre according to a type of customary rights, which were not equally distributed, yet allowed every family to have a particular spot to collect waste. When new communities arrived, they found new routes and neighbourhoods to work over public bins and this process of sharing the urban space evolved without centralised planning and conflict. In the summer period young seasonal migrant workers came to the capital city to earn some money for school expenditures or family. Settled waste pickers would open various spots for these young migrants and share their own workspace. More dangerous, risky and physically demanding, scrap metal collection pushed some waste pickers to work in pairs or groups who would carry heavy materials together, protect each other against possible risks in the late evenings and share earnings.

Solidarity was not confined to spatial organisation. Financial contributions were also common within settled waste picking communities connected via kinship bonds. Jonathan Parry and Maurice Bloch show how the relationship between short term individual gain and long-term social order is one of the fundamental questions that societies seek to answer.[8] Communities in very different geo-political spaces perform special rituals to transform polluted individual money gained in the market into a morally acceptable form without a social purpose. In the case of waste pickers, money was desirable and legitimate as an end in itself. Moral justification lay in the obligation to give some part of this individual money to the community during wedding and funeral rituals. The long-term survival of the community and their family components relied on these monetary contributions.

Waste pickers did not have to speak my language of solidarity and egalitarianism in order to practice those values. Some warehouses in the inner city hosted the unemployed, migrant individuals with past convictions, young kids who escaped violence at home or school, workers who sought freedom from atrocities of sweatshops and factories. Similar to them, I enjoyed stories told around the fire in the yard, pouring tea into dozens of cups on a big tray and sharing them, observing care and compassion for newcomers; a home without kinship and blood ties, everyone being the elder brother of another, no one being judged. Experiments led by certain organisers to turn some warehouses into a collective sharing income, food, books and debates on alternative futures refused to be captivated by the economic logic of recycling units.

That individualism and solidarity do not have to be mutually exclusive is further qualified by Harry Walker's ethnography of Urarina community in the Peruvian Amazon. Walker suggests that Urarina are obsessed with individual autonomy and ownership. Each person in the community aspires to own at least one item as a material possession, which embodies self-sufficiency. The rules, institutions and corporate custodianship required by collective ownership are entirely antithetical to their way of thinking.[9] However sharing remains the paramount moral virtue as can be seen in eating rituals. Although hunting is a solitary act, people expect the hunter to share the food widely. How the meat will be allocated depends on the hunter's distribution rights.[10]

The prerequisite of this collective act is the separation of the giver from the receiver. This was antithetical to my thinking, which considered collective ownership as a precondition for common good, solidarity in egalitarian terms. To complicate things further, there were communities which did not feel that they had to stick to one particular organisation. Depending on their needs, they could shift between social orders, moving, for instance, from egalitarian forms of decision-making in the winter months to disciplining hierarchical forms during the summer hunting season.[11]

The more my own thinking was pushed by encountering other life forms, the more I was able to catch the nuances pertaining to the meanings of ownership and property in waste pickers' everyday lives. The search for individual gain and property ownership was gradually losing its pejorative connotation in my mind. I was able to make new connections between my previous observations. For example, I was deeply sensitive about the forced migration of Kurdish waste pickers in the 1990s. They had been forced to leave behind all their land, cattle, houses, a whole history. But it would take time for me to comprehend that one reason behind the attachment to their individual economic property in the city was this memory of violence and dispossession. In fact, in 2004, when the local authorities wanted to demolish informal recycling warehouses they had built, these waste pickers refused to live the same traumatic history twice and burnt their own warehouses in a moment of collective rage. As with a piece of land to cultivate or cattle to graze, a warehouse or a truck were not regarded simply as material property: they were the anchor by which those communities were building new roots and histories.

Replacing the narrow lens of individualism with a wide angle one, I began to think that the association of individual desire for growth and prosperity solely with the capitalist motive for accumulation or profit-making might also be inaccurate. In her long-term ethnography of Indonesian Highlanders, Tania Murray Li argues that the initial impulse of the community to enclose land for cocoa production was a mundane desire to have a better life for future generations, since years of hard work had not substantially changed their conditions.[12] In a similar spirit, warehouse owners who wanted to expand recycling business did not explain this only in individualistic terms; they believed that to generate wealth for others, one needed to be better off in the first place. A small individual property was a first step to gain autonomy from the obligation to sell labour power and build an independent life. Evan Killick's critical engagement with the recent discourses around *Buen Vivir* (Living Well) in South America, calling for alternative non-capitalist sustainable communal life forms based on indigenous cultures makes a similar point: the Amazonian Ashaninka with whom Evan Killick worked in Peru for over two decades engaged with the timber industry to offer a better life for their families and children, even if extraction contradicts an idealised notion of indigeneity. Rather than trying to make people fit those ideals, 'Buen Vivir needs

to move from associating indigenous lives with a specific idea of communality and sociality to a more general one of self-determination.'[13]

There was another reason why the complexities of the informal economy in and around warehouses could be easily ignored while targeting the waste picker as a labourer to organise, as the precursor of an egalitarian cooperative. The waste picker who wants to expand their business seemed to be incompatible with the disheartening and beautiful photographs of young waste pickers represented in the media that depict solitary faces of hard work and dignity, reflecting the pride to make a life out of waste in poverty. Where capitalism saw the disposable, the abject, the bare lives, we saw the subject of an emerging and enticing social movement. We were moved by their stories of exclusion, their desire to be visible. We were touched by their poems deploying metaphors of waste to describe their love for young women who they could not to speak to. Researchers, journalists and activists wrote stories of those lives at the margins. The broader economy of emotions around warehouses did not fit the romantic story we had invested in.

Wolford discusses a similar romanticisation of the reality of landless peasants in Brazil, depicted by the wonderful, disheartening, yet ultimately misleading photographs by Sebastiao Salgado. She discusses how the so-called scandalous stories about those MST members who rarely live on encampments, do additional wage work, use several land plots to initiate capital-intensive technological farming are only scandalous because we would like to see them as depicted in those pictures: desperate, half-naked, attached fully to the land they occupy and share. Why can't we accept, she rightly asks, that there may be all sorts of people with different preferences within a movement? Why shouldn't dignity and livelihoods rather than the sharing of land be a movement's unifying principle?[14] I could engage in a similar questioning in my case: neither the concepts of disposable/bare lives nor of angry/conscious subjects were able to fully explain the agency of waste pickers, although they corresponded to different modes of their existence. Many might have preferred independent autonomous work over a collective enterprise, decent secure work over a constant fight for dignity in the garbage. A common metaphor they used in their poems, 'stolen dreams', suggests that they probably had many desires and aspirations which would remain unknown to us. Our efforts to explain their subjectivities would inevitably leave something out.

This is not to deny the intrinsic and intricate relationship between the informal waste economy and the broader circuits of accumulation. Waste pickers did not need to be told how little they got by working so much. Their desire for a better life did not preclude their critical sensibilities regarding systemic economic inequalities which they experienced first hand. Tens of thousands of simple acts of collecting, sorting and storing waste nourished the appetite of global recycling capital. Some warehouse owners were growing by hiring wage labour via kinship networks, investing in transport and even, in certain limited cases, a press machine to upgrade the value of waste in the supply chain. But even in those cases, there was more value than capital could fully capture. An economy of care was enmeshed within the circuit of accumulation and it was not always possible to reduce the former to the needs of the latter. Large warehouse owners were expected to provide for their community to handle multiple challenges of urban life. Some of them were supporting the waste pickers' movement, letting organisers visit their warehouses.

The life and work rhythm of waste picking communities was not homogenous. Some collected and sold scrap metal on a daily basis, worked as temporary labourers for recycling factories. Others had much more rigid work discipline, sought to increase their waste supply and preferred saving money for the future. Those migrants who were settled in the squatter settlements in the city and those who worked as seasonal workers staying in warehouses had a different relationship to the waste economy. For seasonal migrants, waste picking was one of the many jobs they did in a range of on-farm and off-farm activities. They could easily leave for another city if municipal authorities evacuated warehouses in a specific area. For the settled groups, it was their essential job to look after their families. What kind of rules and principles of common ownership would appeal to different individuals and groups if they were to work under the same roof? Also, did they really want to be under the same roof?

Waste pickers achieved a lot during and after my time with them. A retrospective look might see the actualisation of another kind of political imaginary: a heterogeneous, fragmented, powerful mobilisation, which obtained the legitimacy to negotiate solutions to their problems with local governments and altered significantly the dominant representation of waste pickers. The informal waste picker was now a recycling worker whose contribution to environmental sustainability and dignity was recognised, whose complex forms of personhood reflected in their writings on everyday emotions and metaphysical questions about life were appreciated. The vision that organisers articulated was a world where no one would be obliged to pick waste. While fighting for the immediate improvement of their conditions and recognition of their rights as labourers, they never gave up this vision which bonded them to all other dominated classes in diverse geographies: 'We want to eliminate the conditions which reproduce us as waste pickers.'[15]

This reflection gives a partial explanation about why people may choose not to engage with particular visions. It shows how other imaginaries, such as the dignity restored to waste pickers, emerge gradually from the dialogical spaces of organising. It reminds us that a desire for a better life does not preclude a critique of capitalism, that movements include multiple voices converging and diverging over time, whose irreducibility to a singular voice should be welcomed rather than feared. However, this understanding still maintains my own vision as pure, intact, flawless, while endowing the communities that I am observing, in a subtly arrogant way, with the right to refuse it. It fails to consider the very possibility that my initial puzzle might have been ill-defined. This is what Saba Mahmood asks in her ethnography of the women's mosque movement in Egypt: In the process of translating other life worlds (in her case an illiberal movement) can one's own certainty about how the world should proceed (in her case progressive secular feminism) remain stable? She proposes proceeding with humility, with 'a sense that one does not always know what one opposes and that a political vision at times has to admit its own finitude in order to even comprehend what it has sought to oppose.'[16]

What if I were to re-phrase my puzzle, then, by problematising the nature, rather than the target of my ideal: why should my political imaginary be superior or more desirable than other life forms? To address this question, I will turn to debates on the roots of collective ownership.

4.

In *Communal Luxury, Political Imaginary of the Paris Commune*, Kristin Ross mines the rich residues and afterlives of the Commune,[17] following the paths of Communards in exile in Europe, engaging with philosophers, revolutionaries and scientists who found in the Commune a prolific source of ideas. Pyotr Kropotkin collaborates with the former Communard Elisée Reclus to write a volume of *Géographie Universelle* and uses his observations and findings in Scandinavia and Siberia as a state geographer to write *Mutual Aid: A Factor of Evolution*, demonstrating the natural and social basis of cooperation informing anarchist visions. Kropotkin rethinks the possibilities of the Paris Commune for agricultural self-sufficiency as part of a revolutionary strategy. In his imagination Paris solves its supply problems by using intensive horticultural methods and experimental gardening. The Commune's ideas also penetrate Marx's mind, first through his conversations with a Communard in exile, Elisabeth Dimitrieff. In these debates, historical examples of communal forms are re-discovered as potential alternatives to alienated forms of capitalist production.

Why does the Paris Commune continue to excite activists today? Following William Morris' interpretation of pre-capitalist forms of solidarity and using his expression that the 'tale of the past [i]s a parable of the days to come', Ross argues that a parable is not about reversing time but opening up a web of possibilities, a way of 'recruiting past hopes to serve present needs.'[18] If the Communards recruited the hopes of pre-capitalist forms for the nineteenth century, contemporary activists recruit the hopes of the Commune for today. J.K. Gibson-Graham engages in a similar enterprise, but they seek potentials also at the heart of contemporary capitalism. They cite numerous alternative activities within past and existing economic

structures, presented as marginal or peripheral: workers' cooperatives, complementary currencies, local trading systems, peer-to-peer lending regimes, mutual aid societies, housing cooperatives. The performative ontology they defend is to make visible, credible and more real all these collaborative practices.[19] Since nothing is built in a vacuum, it is to this catalogue of tools that activists turn when they experiment with alternatives. They pick up materials, depending on their political socialisation and organisation, from the garbage dump of history and present, recycle and re-assemble them for new purposes, similar to the rag picker as described by Walter Benjamin.[20] And because capitalism is usually understood in terms of private ownership, self-interest and impersonal market exchange, we tend to select materials which represent the opposite of these features: collective ownership, mutual aid, reciprocity, amongst others, as the basis of an alternative economy.

The 'parable', the 'performative', the 'recyclable' may not shine at first glance. They may be rusty broken keys that we need to polish and repair with the hope of unlocking doors to a different future. Not everyone passes through these doors with a clear post-capitalist vision. Many people are thrown into them, into barter exchange when financial crisis evaporates monetary transactions, into occupied factories when employers abandon factories, into housing cooperatives when financial speculation eliminates the security of citizens. From these unintended origins, new experiments flourish, evolve or evaporate.

In June 2013, when an attempt at protecting a park in the centre of Istanbul by a small group of activists turned into a nation-wide protest, a unique opportunity to test the political currency of collective imaginaries came into being. The Gezi protests were an abrupt fissure in people's long-standing feelings of impotence. The communal space in Taksim Square was governed by spontaneous cooperation, with all needs met immediately by self-organising local groups. People were curious, eager to learn, participate, improvise. Former antagonisms ceded their place to a new safe space of collaboration. The desire for reciprocity and mutual aid, thought to have been eroded from the public sphere, was realised. It was truly the most memorable and beautiful June of a lifetime. Although it lasted only two weeks, this almost effortless, horizontal exchange of goods, services, relationships and ideas became a source of inspiration. Perhaps that is why the interest in cooperatives and communal forms increased in its aftermath.[21]

It was in those years, long after my first encounter with waste pickers, that I had a chance to engage with cooperatives in different roles, as a trainer, activist and researcher. This experience altered my earlier ungrounded perception about cooperatives by qualifying it in diverse, contradictory ways. Similar to a warehouse, the meaning and impact of a cooperative was much richer and more complex than I had imagined, depending on the broader social relations in which it was embedded. A women's cooperative in a patriarchal culture is a chance for women to go out of their house, gain independence and new skills, attach a new purpose to their life. When tied to grassroots community organising, its transformative power for gender relations goes beyond its economic function. People see different benefits in the same cooperative: A farmers' cooperative means simple price security and protection against middlemen for some members, affordable innovative production techniques for others. A worker's cooperative liberates workers from despotic labour regimes, blurs the boundaries between work and leisure time, yields new forms of social bonds and ethical subjectivities. Discussions on how to spend the surplus/common value – in individual remuneration, social care, new investment, solidarity funds – help members to reflect on what is valuable to them as individuals and members of the broader society. Engagement with other cooperatives, activists and local governments generate new sources of skills, mutual learning and collaboration.

Problems and conflicts can be equally complex. The everyday life of a collective offers as much tension as joy and hope. Organising a fair division of labour, making decisions on day-to-day activities at long meetings, fixing problems can consume productive energies. There can be disagreements between incumbent members who share a collective identity and new members. Conflicts may be caused by people's sentiment of unfairness regarding the allocation of work, responsibility, power and remuneration. If open conflict resolution mechanisms are not in place, these feelings evolve into frustration and resentment. Economic instabilities can exert further pressures on the ethical economic enterprise which has to handle rising costs and market competition while also cultivating its own values.

My certitude about the superiority of my imaginary was already unsettled, I knew the particular type of economic and social organisation I was defending did not represent an inherent good, that there were various positive and negative energies it could unleash. Instruments available to cooperatives could be used to democratise and empower as well as to create new hierarchies.[22] But I also knew that no form was immune to conflict. Although I cannot do full justice to the merits of the cooperative movement in this essay, their historical trajectory suggests how cooperatives worked hard to design methods for the fair allocation of work, remuneration of labour and distribution of surplus. They learned, by trial and error, how to create dispute resolution systems, enhance participation, collaborate with other cooperatives, develop their own finance system, reduce working hours and increase leisure time. They moved from fading to flourishing, reproducing to overcoming crises, being a simple economic enterprise for income to implementing a radical vision. The tensions I found difficult to come to terms with were the grim realities of collective life that one has to face honestly in order to turn experiments into a rewarding experience.

Communal life forms are likely to haunt passionate minds seeking to build alternative futures. But I now would like to turn my eyes to another less appreciated possibility. I will ask whether there is a potential in individual property that we might be missing, which its portrayal as either a petty bourgeois attitude or understandable cultural desire is unable to capture, something powerful and emancipatory, worth integrating into the very design of our visions. To see this potential will require changing our road map and breaking the intrinsic relationship between capitalist relations and individual private property.

5.

There is a very strong reason why the common, communal, collective have been the unifying principles of many social struggles in the last few decades. Commodification of natural resources, massive expropriations and privatisations deprived thousands of communities of their right to water, energy, land and multiple livelihoods. Resistance to these processes was framed by a defense of the common against the private, collective against the individual, because the latter spheres have consolidated the power of oligarchs, giant contractors, mining and energy companies, political elites. In the fight against neoliberal capitalism, the reclaiming of the commons and people's power represents a truly radical critique of the profit-driven hierarchical opaque markets.

Studies on the value of self-organising, rule-based common governance structures as theorised by Elinor Ostrom[23] offer geographically and historically rich evidence to sustain movements' claims. One side effect of this approach is to formulate intrinsically positive principles for common property regimes, as if they are insulated from relations of power and oppression, as Duncan Law and Nicole Pepperell point out.[24] Ostrom, say Law and Pepperell, was well aware of the perils of domination by leaders who might alter the rules to their advantage, but her assumptions on the need for consensus on rules by community members defining an institution (as a corollary of her rational choice apparatus) fell short of accommodating these reflections. Pauline Peters expresses a similar concern with regard to the increasing emphasis on the community as a means for land redistribution in Africa. Her anthropological studies underline historical forms of inequities and exclusion within the communities, which turned into deeper conflict and class formations in contemporary capitalism.[25] Daniel Curtis adds to this cautionary tale in his survey of Medieval and early modern Europe, which interrupts romanticised narratives on pre-capitalist forms of property. Commons were not fully inclusive and free for all; their benefit depended on social contexts, negotiations of power, as well as demographic and commercial pressures. Subsistence offered to the poor – the right to hunt, fish, take wood – did not compensate for deeper inequalities and for better rights (such as access to grazing) enjoyed by the more powerful.[26] Similarly, Jose Lana Berasain shows how the use and benefits from the commons were very unequal in the case of Navarro, Spain. It was only against the background of great transformations changing property relations that those practices were retrospectively tied to a discourse of equity.[27]

How to re-think, then, the relationship between various property forms, without demonising or overrating their features, without disregarding their complex, context-specific meanings and effects? In an intervention on post-capitalist property, Paddy Ireland and Gaofeng Meng offer useful insights to address this question by a close reading of Marx and Hegel. According to Hegel, private individual property was progressive, because it enabled self-development, pushing individuals to behave rationally and responsibly.[28] As Andrew Chitty points out, Marx also agreed that private property had a positive essence, because it liberated individual energies and creativity from communal constraints.[29] He also believed that one of the features of communism would be to restore property to individual workers. Nevertheless, while supporting human capacities, private property in capitalist society generated estranged forms.[30] The right to enjoy property came at the expense of others. A whole history of enclosures and dispossessions made this process unequal and brutally violent. That is why truly socialised forms of property were needed, according to Marx, so that human need for autonomy and connectedness could be reconciled.

Indonesian Highlanders whom I discussed earlier in this article, with their mundane desire to have a better life, seemed to fully agree with Hegel on the value of individual property for self-growth. Families allocated to their children, as early as the age of ten, pieces of land to cultivate. This led them to take their own responsibility for it. Highlanders considered individuals to be the owners of their capacity to work and the property they created through their sweat. They thought attempts by men to control the labour of their wives and children were unnatural and unfair. Yet this went hand in hand with cooperation: exchange of labour within families and work parties for the community members to support each other. As long as land was abundant this system continued. It was only after the enclosure of land for cocoa production and its subjugation to the market imperative that private property took an estranged form, leading to differentiation and entrapping many individuals in wage-labour. [31]

To resolve the tension between the liberating and alienating aspects of private property and unleash its further possibilities, Ireland and Meng deploy the 'bundles of rights' approach to property ownership, according to which ownership consists of various categories such as right to possess, right to use, right to manage, right to transmit, right to alienate, right to income, right to capital and so on. In a given context these individual rights can be grouped and configured differently, yielding different results. The question is no longer whether we should totally abolish private property or enforce collective property by ascribing an intrinsically positive value to the latter, but to ask instead how to re-configure new permutations and combinations of property rights which will not reproduce discriminatory, alienated forms of ownership and inequalities. It is then possible to divide and sub-divide those rights and allocate them to different actors and institutions. Perhaps there are some housing cooperatives which acknowledge the individual right to use and inherit, restrict the individual right to transfer and alienate in order to prevent concentration of property and profit in that way.

It is possible to pursue the traces of these questions in the minds and experiments of policy makers, intellectuals and communities who lived in socialist countries. In China, Ireland and Meng explore the opportunities offered by the Household Responsibility System (HRS), which can be thought as a hybrid property regime. The right to use, possess, manage and receive income are allocated to individual households but for specified time periods and under restrictions. This gives autonomy to households which increase productivity and economic gains, while enabling the state to maintain control.[32] Initiated by a group of households seeking to resolve their economic problems in the late 1970s and then implemented by state officials in the 1980s, HRS could be seen at first glance as a proof of individual preference against collectives. Huaiyin Li disagrees: HRS emerged in a region where collectivisation had detrimental effects due to context-specific reasons such as low access to technology, enforcement of supra village communes inhibiting group solidarity, remunerations based on household size rather than rewarding individual contributions, heavy extractive policies by the state. In those regions and periods where collectives worked in small teams, individuals were rewarded for hard work, state taxation was less restrictive and there was higher technology and productivity, collectivisation was welcome.[33] Thus, the success or failure of collectives depended on broader economic and social conditions.

The long-term ethnographic fieldwork conducted by Chris Hann in Tázlár, Hungary offers further evidence on the potentials of hybrid property regimes and the multiple conditions to make them beneficial. During the 1960s and 70s, as part of broader plans to reform state socialism, cooperative farms established extra units in addition to farming activities and introduced an institution called household plot to 'harness the labour of their members'.[34] Households were allowed to move from self-sufficiency to market-oriented production for hogs, milk, grapes and wine. These could be sold either independently in nearby towns, or to the specialist cooperative which offered specific purchase prices and had themselves contracts with state enterprises. The state has also gradually expanded entitlements and social benefits to the countryside. Consumption goods were sold in the countryside where residents built and furnished their own houses. Those were the things enjoyed by Tázlár farmers until the synergies between various sectors disappeared quickly with neoliberalism and farmers lost against large corporations.

Hann's thoughts are in conversation with the socialist Minister of Agriculture, Ferenc Erdei, who did not live long enough to see all the positive effects of these reforms and their eventual decline. Erdei believed that the patriotic attachment of farmers to the soil did not need to be registered to a conservative ideology, it could be compatible with socialist emancipatory goals. That is why what he called 'embourgeoisement' of the village, which the Hungarian reforms achieved, could be thought as a positive step for socialism.[35] I wonder whether his ideas could be read as a critical response to some of the negative consequences of forced collectivisation in Soviet Russia after a brief period of New Economic Policy allowing individual property and market oriented production.

While Tázlár villagers were engaging with new economic experiments, a socialist intellectual in former Yugoslavia, Tibor Liska, was also thinking about alternative forms of socialist property.[36] According to Liska, once the motive of private profit and exploitation of wage-labour were abolished, everyone could be an entrepreneur in a society without having to own means of production. Individuals could be offered a 'socialist inheritance' to bid on the market for leasing or starting new business. The people who would work with these entrepreneurs would not be wage labourers but work teams who were themselves entrepreneurs.[37] On the death of their possessors, social inheritance would return to society. This idea of return is not new; it resonates with anthropological rituals to avoid the excesses of individual gain and to reconcile them with the social order. For the Merina of Madagascar, for instance, all goods acquired in trade and war called *harena* have to be disposed of before death, because they belong to a transient world which stands in contrast to collective ancestors in the tomb.[38]

The way Gibson-Graham read Mondragon Cooperative, the world's largest and most known cooperative, underlines how successful alternatives are the ones which took seriously some of the themes recurring in these debates: the relationship between individual autonomy and collective responsibility, the synergies between various actors and institutions within the broader ecology of economic relations. Founded in 1956 by the priest José Maria Arizmendiarrieta and his students in the Basque region of Spain, Mondragon owes its remarkable expansion to a focus on social connection and interdependence between workers and citizens, according to Gibson-Graham.

Apart from specific policies on wages and zero unemployment, the cooperative made a crucial decision for individual members to delegate the power to determine the redistribution of surplus to the Working People's Bank (*Caja Laboral Popular*). The bank which acts also as a development agency took responsibility for allocating investments to advance cooperativist ideas by offering business and financial support to start-up cooperatives. The surpluses deposited were used to establish second degree cooperatives serving primary producer cooperatives: social insurance, training and education, research and development.[39] Thus, Mondragon supported new entrepreneurial ideas in society if compatible with cooperative principles; it redistributed surplus to provide care, education, health for its members and expected them to reconcile individual interest with the broader social order. Even though the cooperative went through several challenges after its international expansion including the bankruptcy of one of its subsidiaries and clashes between new acquisitions and its own structure, it remains a significant case of what it means to not only imagine, but also perform, succeed and fail in alternatives. My search for blueprints was now over. Instead I was able to fully appreciate 'practical engagements with existing institutions' and 'experiments with alternatives'[40] as the basis of post-capitalist visions. In problem solving and learning, I was coming to realise, that radical imaginaries would be nourished and thrive.

6.

It is time for my own political imaginary to take a new shape in the light of multiple institutional configurations linking autonomy and connectedness, individual and collective property, difference and alliance.

At the beginning, perhaps, the small group of activists and waste pickers committed to egalitarianism could start a cooperative by getting some funding to support their enterprise. They could start thinking about the rules on decision-making, membership and about how to express and handle conflicts. They could explore the conditions of a fair division of labour for the spheres of production and social reproduction, how to use 'common' value for the future. They could continue the publication of their magazine and bring some of the ideas in their writings to the core of the discussions at the cooperative. Then, aware of the complexity of social relations in the informal recycling economy, they could start opening the cooperative to multiple levels of engagements for different waste picking communities. Individuals and families could maintain their warehouses and sell waste to the cooperative at an agreed price, whereas regular members could have additional advantages of benefiting from investments such as a new press machine to upgrade the value of waste or education benefits offered by sister cooperatives.

The cooperative could tap the skills and networks of some small middlemen in order to reach out to small warehouses in and outside of the region by offering incentives. Some waste pickers could perceive this space solely as an income-generating activity; more ambitious ones could use it to incubate new ideas. Grassroots innovators were no exceptions in the informal economy as I had witnessed on various occasions. Some of these could be invited to use existing space and resources to develop new recycling technologies connecting the cooperative to broader global projects of environmental sustainability. Some entrepreneurial minded people who are more interested in new revenue streams could take the lead for the production of waste picker carriers in house on the condition that this would benefit the collective and those who cannot afford them.

Such forms of moral economy could be further expanded by the introduction of an innovative physical scrap auction to trade scrap metals. This could attract, for instance, those waste pickers who might not want to formally join the cooperative yet wish to use its trading platforms. The auction could regulate prices for collectors against global market fluctuations and enhance interaction between communities and traders who are isolated from each other. As a result of these interactions, the cooperative could consider starting up or supporting a new logistics cooperative to expand its operations to other cities. Whereas the initial core group would maintain its egalitarian vision in basic operations, this evolution would make fairness rather than pure egalitarianism the regulating principle of the institution, because many people I worked with believed that every individual differed in motivation, resilience and rhythm and should thus be rewarded according to their specific contributions. They also believed that those who are less capable of looking after themselves or contributing to the collective should be supported when needed. For such forms of support, the cooperative could refer to the catalogue of communities' own practices of reciprocity and solidarity.

This jigsaw includes pieces of my imagination and examples I collected over the years. I can see how much more alluring this particular configuration might look to some people who were indifferent to my original ideas. I also see how it could be a failure, although a better one. Aren't the mundane banalities and lessons of a comprehensible failure preferable to an enigmatic romantic defeat or a missed opportunity with no chance to be tested?

Accommodating the desire for individual property, recognised with its anthropological roots and emancipatory potentials, balancing it with collective management and ownership of resources may provide the solid legitimate ground that my political imaginary seeks. This new enriched form refutes the dichotomy between individual and collective, relativises the virtues and vices of each side, speaks to people's real concerns, accommodates different interests and aspirations. Without compelling people to have an egalitarian vision, it invites them to contribute to its making, albeit in a different form.

What is still disturbing, what still does not feel right in this exercise is my relentless attempt to accommodate everything I had not anticipated in the first place. I might be right in making my vision the target of criticism and learning from its own weaknesses and others'

strengths. However, while avoiding the Charybdis of purity, I am now caught by the Scylla of vanity, the illusion that a political imaginary should be able to contain all differences and desires.

I think once again of the lives and aspirations of different waste pickers, like those who lost their jobs and families and found a refuge in a warehouse welcoming them. Would they really find comfort in a cooperative with new rules? Are they obliged to renounce their loyalty to their crew, to sometimes difficult but understanding family ready to accept them as they are, in exchange for more regular work in a cooperative? Or those children whose families work so hard to give them a chance for higher education so that they do not become waste pickers. Don't their eyes tell the desire to leave the garbage forever to build new imaginaries on their own rather than being the subject of others, who reconstruct them as cooperative members?

In whatever form we attempt to organise economic and social life, something will look amorphous because its shape is not familiar to us; something will remain unsatisfied because the object of its desire is not within our sight; something will remain irrational because the immanent grounds of its rationality have not touched our feet. It is from their incompleteness that radical visions take their strength. And as I would learn, despite the stubbornness of my faith in our ability to change everything towards the greater good as I define it, the best thing an activist can do sometimes is to respect other life forms, rather than seeking to encroach on them.

Acknowledging the impossibility of capturing all desires, can help create the conditions for the humility by which our political projects have to be subdued. Admitting that one can be unwanted and rejected gives maturity to the ardent activists. It replaces the self-referential criteria of the ideal with a recognition of multiple meanings of what makes a good desirable life. More painfully, it helps them to confront the mortality of their own projects. New needs and aspirations are yet to be borne in the womb of their experiments, which may be advanced, transformed or destroyed. To take seriously decay and oblivion means taking life more seriously, here and now, in its messy, contradictory forms, rather than waiting for the sudden awakening of the ember in people, which will finally lead to an understanding of where their 'real interest' lies and affirm our political imaginaries.

After explaining to Millar how some *catadores'* life style was not adaptable to the rules of the recycling co-operative, the manager Gloria added one final sentence: '… and I'm telling you there are some who will *never* be able to adapt'.[41] She was right. Some people will never be able to adapt to the rules. We should be glad they won't.

7.

Given the amount of words spent to prove the contrary, it might seem rather odd to defend, in the final part of this essay, the initial audacity of my political imaginary. Hoping that the risk of incoherence will be superseded by the value of a dialectical twist, I state that it is not only understandable but necessary for a radical imaginary to be considered as incompatible or unacceptable by those who encounter it for the first time. If a radical proposal were to be subdued by the exigencies of its new context, if it were to understand and accept all the reasons behind the reproduction of a particular life form, its raison d'etre would be nullified. There *must* be a pre-supposed misfit in this original encounter; why would anyone embrace something which promises nothing but the same? It is the novel, different, wild voice of unusual ideas which attracts individuals who seek change. This voice can belong to an outsider or someone from within the community, who struggles with the contradictions of their own life form. As Steven Lukes reminds us, communities are porous and heterogeneous, hosting identifiers, quasi-identifiers, non-identifiers, anti-identifiers, multi-identifiers who interpret and relate to local norms differently. Some of these individuals may be open to the infiltration of new ideas which may expose internal discontent or dare to utter unnamed desires. If each answer were to be true in its own place for everyone in strong cultural relativist terms, there would be no conflict, no clash, no change.[42]

The ideas introduced by Tiao in Rio emerged out of his conversations with other *catadores* at the meetings of Brazilian National Movement of Catadores (MNCR). Landless settlements owe their origin to MST leaders in Brazil, Mondragon to a priest and his students in Spain. The Chinese Household Responsibility System started as a conversation between a small group of farmers who wanted to resolve a problem. The movement of

waste pickers was initiated by a group of activists and waste pickers who wanted to organise informal precarious workers. Exposure to new interactions generates cross-pollinations. Thus, the weakness of a new vision lies less in its initial awkwardness than the arrogance to blame reality when its glamour is not praised by others, reluctance to develop self-reflexivity, to learn and transform.

The convoluted route I have taken now leads to a partial answer to my preamble: what validates a political imaginary is not its promises (for practical implementation can deviate from anticipation), is not its particular form (for different contexts can generate unexpected shapes), is not its content (for people may have very different accounts of worth in life), but is the dialectical process by which the imaginary's complex moments of truth and negation unfold. It cannot thrive without experimenting, succeeding, failing, learning and aging. It gets stronger only by admitting that the norms of the life form it seeks to build should not escape critical gaze.[43] That is why validation claims are almost always pragmatic, immanent and retrospective. After all, no alternative is to be found at an Archimedean point: by recognising their debt to their multiple ancestors, wrestling with and occasionally superseding them, our radical visions offer a grounded hope.

Demet S. Dinler is a Lecturer in International Development at the School of Global Studies, University of Sussex. She sits on the editorial board of the journal Historical Materialism.

Notes

1. This piece owes to discussions with beloved intellectual companion Ulus Atayurt. Special thanks to Alice Wilson, Anke Schwittay, Ebru Deniz Ozan, Meike Fechter, Nico Pizzolato, Paul Reynolds for commenting generously on an early version; to the Editorial Collective of *Radical Philosophy* and especially Hannah Proctor, whose thoughtful feedback and editorial suggestions helped to improve my arguments. I am grateful to all my friends – activists, organisers, waste pickers – whose wisdom continues to shape my life. All errors are mine.
2. Ilan Kapoor, 'Hyper Self-reflexive Development? Spivak on Representing the Third World 'Other', *Third World Quarterly* 25:4 (2006), 627–47.
3. One could ask a similar related question regarding the disappointment of communities when some organisers and activists give up their initial impulse and abandon collective projects. But this would be the subject of another essay.
4. Kathleen Millar, *Reclaiming the Discarded: Life and Labour on*

Rio's Garbage Dump (Durham, NC: Duke University Press, 2018), 164–67.

5. Ibid., 171–75.

6. Wendy Wolford, *This Land is Ours Now: Social Mobilisation and the Meanings of Land in Brazil* (Durham, NC: Duke University Press, 2010), 109–11.

7. Ibid., 188–92.

8. Jonathan Parry and Maurice Bloch, eds., *Money and the Morality of Exchange* (Cambridge: Cambridge University Press, 1989).

9. Harry Walker, *Under a Watchful Eye: Self, Power and Intimacy in Amazonia* (Berkeley: University of California Press, 2013), 120–21.

10. Ibid., 116–17.

11. Ilana Gershon, 'Porous Social Orders', *American Ethnologist* 46:4 (2019), 407–08.

12. Tania Li, *Land's End: Capitalist Relations on an Indigenous Frontier* (Durham, NC: Duke University Press, 2014).

13. Evan Killick, 'Extractive Relations: Natural Resource Use, Indigenous Peoples and Environmental Protection in Peru', *Bulletin of Latin American Research* 39:3 (2020), 292.

14. Wolford, *This Land is Ours*, 13.

15. For a detailed analysis of the writings and subjectivities of waste pickers and organisers, see Demet S. Dinler, *İşçinin Varlık Problemi: Sınıf, Erkeklik ve Duygular Üzerine Denemeler (Ontological Problem of the Worker: Essays on Class, Masculinity and Emotions)* (Istanbul: Metis, 2014).

16. Saba Mahmood, *Politics of Piety: The Islamic Revival and the Feminist Subject* (Princeton: Princeton University Press, 2012), 199.

17. Kristin Ross, *Communal Luxury: The Political Imaginary of the Paris Commune* (London: Verso, 2016).

18. Ibid., 75.

19. J.K. Gibson-Graham, 'Diverse Economies: Performative Practices for "Other Worlds"', *Progress in Human Geography* 32:5 (2008), 616.

20. Frederik Le Roy, 'Ragpickers and Leftover Performances', *Performance Research* 22:8 (2017), 128.

21. A rich variety of cooperative cases can be found in the thematic series 'Solidarity Economies' on the independent journalism website produced by 1+1 Express Collective in Turkey. Pieces in Turkish and English include interviews conducted with local and international activists, members and leaders of cooperatives as well as articles on this theme. https://www.birartibir.org/dayanisma-ekonomileri.

22. For an analysis of how accounting can be used as a bureaucratic tool to restrain social goals or to promote social responsibility and empowerment in the comparative study of two workers' cooperatives, see Alice Bryer, 'Beyond Bureaucracies, The Struggle for Social Responsibility in the Argentine Workers' Cooperatives', *Critique of Anthropology* 30:1 (2010), 41–61.

23. Elinor Ostrom, *Governing the Commons: The Evolution of Institutions for Collective Action* (Cambridge: Cambridge University Press, 1990).

24. Duncan Law and Nicole Pepperell, 'Oppression in the Commons: Cautionary Notes on Elinor Ostrom's Concept of Self-governance', in *Proceedings of the Australian Sociological Association Conference*, ed. G. Zajdow, Deakin University, Melbourne, 19-22 November 2018.

25. Pauline Peters, 'Challenges in Land Tenure and Land Reform in Africa: Anthropological Contributions', *World Development* 37:1 (2009), 1319.

26. Daniel Curtis, 'Did the Commons Make Medieval and Early Modern Rural Societies more Equitable? A Survey of Evidence from Across Western Europe, 1300-1800', *Journal of Agrarian Change* 16:4 (2016), 658.

27. Jose Miguel Lana Berasain, 'From Equilibrium to Equity, The Survival of the Commons in the Ebro Basin. Navarra from 15th to the 20th Centuries', *International Journal of the Commons* 2:2 (2008), 186.

28. Paddy Ireland and Geafong Meng, 'Post-capitalist Property', *Economy and Society* 46:3-4 (2017), 374.

29. Andrew Chitty (2013) 'Recognition and Property in Hegel and Early Marx', *Ethical Theory and Moral Practice* 16:4 (2013), 685–97.

30. Sharon Hutchinson highlights a similar duality for Simmel's approach to money in her ethnography of forms of exchange among the Nuer of Sudan. Money emancipates individuals from their dependence on specific ties and possessions by offering the freedom to take up business relations and cooperation anywhere. Concomitantly, it leads to avarice, possessive individualism, alienation. See Sharon Hutchinson, 'The Cattle of Money and the Cattle of Girls among the Nuer, 1930-83', *American Ethnologist* 19:2 (1992), 294.

31. Murray Li, *Land's End*.

32. Ireland and Meng, 'Post-capitalist Property', 391.

33. Huaiyin Li, 'Institutions and Work Incentives in Collective Farming in Maoist China', *Journal of Agrarian Change* 18:1 (2018), 84–5.

34. Chris Hann, 'Marketisation and Development on a European Periphery: From Peasant Oikos to Socialism and Neoliberal Capitalism on the Danube-Tisza Interfluve', *EPA, Economy and Space* 52:1 (2020), 212.

35. Ibid., 206.

36. Johanna Bockman, *Markets in the Name of Socialism: The Left Wing Origins of Neoliberalism* (Stanford: Stanford University Press, 2020), 162–63.

37. For further details, possibilities and problems of Liska's model, see J. Borsany, 'Tibor Liska's Concept of Socialist Entrepreneurship', *Acta Oeconomica* 28:4 (1982).

38. Parry and Bloch, *Money and Morality*, 24.

39. J. K. Gibson-Graham, 'Enabling Ethical Economies: Cooperativism and Class', *Critical Sociology* 29:2 (2003), 145, 156.

40. Ireland and Meng, 'Post-Capitalist Property', 390.

41. Millar, *Reclaiming the Discarded*, 167.

42. Steven Lukes, *Liberals and Cannibals: The Implications of Diversity* (London: Verso, 2017), 8.

43. I refer to Rahel Jaeggi's call for an immanent critique of life forms, which would reveal the contradictions of the very norms constitutive of these life forms and transform them in the process of critique. See Rahel Jaeggi, *Critique of Forms of Life*, trans. Ciaran Cronin (Cambridge, MA: Belknap Press, 2019).

Dossier: Universal Basic Income

From forced labour to creative work

Guy Standing with Martina Tazzioli

Martina Tazzioli: I would like to start with a general question about your work: how does your theorisation of basic income connect with your reflections on precarity and on the emergence of 'the precariat' as a class?*

Guy Standing: Well, I've been working on both subjects for many years. When we set up BIEN, the Basic Income Earth Network, in September 1986, of course that was a period when Thatcherism and neoliberal economics were coming into the fore. They were pushing for flexible labour markets. And what flexible labour markets meant to me, when I was working in the International Labour Organisation, was increasing insecurity for workers. I was convinced that the whole strategy of neo-liberalism would increase inequality and increase economic insecurity. So I initially favoured a basic income, way back then, for moral reasons, for ethical reasons, and as a way of giving people security and freedom.

So I had this philosophical approach to basic income, but at the same time I was working on labour markets, as I'm a labour economist. And I was convinced that what would happen is that a more fragmented society would develop, as a result of neoliberal policies. And while I didn't call it 'the precariat' back in the 1980s, by the 1990s, and since then, I've been thinking that what's been happening is a fragmentation of the old class structures of the nineteenth and twentieth centuries, as understood in Marxian terms. What's happened is that we now have a plutocracy at the top, then a salariat with employment security, in the middle; but below these two strata, the old proletariat (the industrial proletariat that people analysed in the nineteenth and twentieth centuries) was shrinking, while the precariat was growing. This was clearly going to increase insecurities for many people.

I wrote the book *The Precariat* in 2011, but actually I'd been discussing the growth of the precariat for many years before that. And it seemed to me that this growth was one of the major reasons for expecting that more and more people would come to support a basic income. If you've got a growing precariat, with all the insecurities and problems that come with that, then you should come to realise that the only way forward is to have some sort of basic income system that *guarantees* income security. So the two come together, as an integrated approach.

MT: In your book you argue that basic income should be unconditional – it is not just for precarious, impoverished people, it's for everyone, right?

---

* This interview was recorded in June 2019.

GS: Yes. But the difference is that members of the old working class enjoyed some degree of labour security. They had full-time stable jobs, they had pensions, relatively stable wages, and so on. Therefore to get *them* to support a basic income was harder than it is with the precariat. With the precariat you have volatile wages, you have insecure jobs, you don't get access to state benefits that give you some security, and so on. For these reasons the precariat will be inclined to support a basic income more than the old proletariat ever was, and I think that this prediction is coming true.

MT: As you argue in your book, basic income should be unconditional and should not depend on citizenship status. Does this mean that someone who arrives as a migrant and is in the country temporarily could get access to basic income payments?

GS: The payments should be unconditional in behavioural terms. In other words you shouldn't have to do X or Y or Z in order to get the benefit. I think for pragmatic reasons we have to say that we can give the basic income to usual resident citizens and to migrants who come into the country legally and who have been in the country for some time. That's a pragmatic criterion, not a philosophically grounded one, but if we don't have some sort of rule like that, we will never get the political support for introducing a basic income because the neo-fascists will play the standard xenophobic alien/stranger anti-migrant arguments. This does not mean that we should neglect the needs and aspirations of migrants. I believe in an open society and that people should be treated with dignity and support. I just think that when migrants come to a country they shouldn't automatically and immediately start to get the basic income; they should be treated well and given support, but other forms of support, not the basic income system.

MT: How do you see the role of the state in relation to basic income? And how do you respond to the criticism that has been raised by some people towards basic income theory, regarding the central role played by the state and citizens' dependency on the state?

GS: Philosophically, and from an economist's point of view, I think we need to re-examine what we mean by the state. And that means obviously more than government, it means the institutions in our society that govern the processes of life. What has happened in the neoliberal era is that the state has been turned into an instrument for creating a general neoliberal environment, and among many other terrible things this has involved the privatisation of the commons, of all amenities, our land, our water. Every part of life has been privatised. This has all intensified the sense of insecurity. The irony is of course that as a result the state has become far more coercive. It dominates life through institutions that favour capital, that favour profit making, that favour the privatisation of everything. So I think we need a different type of state.

Now a basic income is a way of giving people a sense of justice, sharing in the proceeds of society, from inherited wealth to everything else. It's an instrument for giving people a sense of personal freedom and particularly republican freedom – the sense that you're not dominated by authorities and by people in unaccountable positions of power. It doesn't do it totally, but it moves in the right direction: it gives people some sense of republican freedom. And it also gives security, which we need as human beings to function. By giving out a basic income, I don't think we'd be creating what is derided as a 'nanny state'. What we've got at the moment is a sort of punishing paternalistic state, and that is certainly something to be afraid of. The state is presuming to tell you what you need and to look after your needs, and if you don't accept that paternalism then it becomes punitive and coercive. We need to move away from that, away from behavioural economics, away from state paternalism to having a state that enables people to have a sense of freedom, where they can create or recreate real communities and recreate social solidarity.

And I think that we all ought to be looking at basic income not as a panacea, not as something that is a standalone policy, but as part of a new progressive politics, a new progressive way of saying we need to recreate society because the neoliberal project has been to atomise society, to break society, to reject society. I have just written a book called *Plunder of the Commons*, which came out in August 2019. It's an attempt to complete the circle of my analysis of the precariat and of basic income, by showing how the commons have been taken by commodification and privatisation, how they have been colonised by financial capital in particular. We need to recapture the commons for society if we are to have a new progressive politics.

MT: How do you engage with theories of cognitive capitalism and with authors who argue that in a post-Fordist economy we are all productive, we all produce, even if we don't work? I'm thinking of economists such as Christian Marazzi or Andrea Fumagalli, who approach the question of basic income slightly differently. They justify it by saying that, in reality, we all produce value, value which results from social cooperation, even if we aren't paid for waged work. They justify basic income by insisting that we are all productive, even if they conceptualise production more broadly.

GS: I've discussed this whole subject with Andrea Fumagalli many times over many years. He is an old friend and I think that you will find that his view and my view are very close. In our discussions we have sometimes used the word *common*-fare instead of welfare. But I think that the idea of cognitive capitalism is probably too abstract for most people to engage with, and I believe that the word productivist is also problematic. You can go back to the Marxian distinction between exchange value and use value. I think that what the technological revolution is doing is increasing the amount of unremunerated work, i.e. that has no exchange value. Take what we're doing right now, you and me, for example: you're not paying me of course, I'm not earning anything. We're doing more and more unpaid work in relation to paid labour. We're working more and more outside of workplaces, outside of formal labour-time, and though we cannot easily distinguish work and paid labour we know that many forms of work we're obliged to do are not remunerated.

So for me the whole essence of a basic income, or, if you like, common dividends – paying people out of the common fund that we should create, along the lines that I've proposed in my new book – is a way of merging this sense of common-fare and the nature of modern capitalism, where particularly if you're in the precariat you have to do a lot of work that is not labour, a lot of work that has use value but no exchange value. At the same time, if you had a basic income *system*, you would enable people to spend more time doing community work, care work, the sort of work we're doing right now. You would enable people to have a greater sense of control over their work, and that would therefore strengthen social solidarity, and strengthen the sense of society, because it would give you that basic sense of security. If we have no security and no distribution system then a lot of people are more vulnerable to exploitation and oppression.

MT: What do you think about the proposition advanced by feminist groups – such as Ni Una Menos in Argentina and Non Una di Meno in Italy – to introduce a self-determination income that expands the idea of basic income by including social reproduction? More broadly do you think that there is a need today to expand the meaning of 'production' in the sense of social reproduction?

GS: I don't know where I stand on that particular issue. I'm obviously a feminist because one has to stand for equality in every sense and one has to enable everybody to realise their potential. My position is that the wealth of our society is very largely being created by the past and by our commons, and we all have an equal right to share in the production of history. The sense of social justice is what motivates me in supporting the building of a common fund from which dividends are paid out equally to everybody. This would enable people to spend more time looking after each other, on all the dimensions of care and social reproduction, and it would give us all more creative and productive time too. It would also help us pursue the ecological objectives we want to set. I think that this is consistent with what you've just said about radical feminism, so I feel quite comfortable with it.

MT: Do you see any difference in the way in which basic income is understood and implemented in wealthy countries and in the so-called developing countries, i.e. in countries that have a more or less functioning welfare state and those that do not, or that don't yet have one?

GS: In a sense it's easier to introduce a basic income in a developing country because you don't have all the complex institutions at play in social welfare states. I recently produced a report on this for the Labour Party and we're proposing pilots in various parts of the country – and to do a pilot where you introduce a basic income you have to replace some other things. In the British context, in 2012 the Tories introduced their 'universal credit', which is a disgrace, a terrible system, and it makes implementation of a basic income more complicated. It's difficult to phase it in and you need quite a lot of institutional support from a central government to make it possible. We've done pilot projects in India where we introduced a modest basic income without replacing existing welfare systems. We found improvements in nutrition and health and schooling and women's status, the status of the disabled and so on. I'm sure that if we had a system introduced in Calabria or in Manchester it would have very similar effects.

My report for Labour took some of its inspiration from William Beveridge and the Welfare report he drafted in 1942. Beveridge justified the system that he wanted to introduce by saying that it would defeat a number of big diseases: idleness, ignorance and squalor. He thought that the Social Security system he was promoting would help overcome those giants, as he called them. I'm also trying to link the idea of a basic income to the idea of a good society. The giants that we have to defeat today are inequality, insecurity and huge private debt, all of which create enormous amounts of stress. Technological changes, automation and artificial intelligence are also increasing inequalities and insecurities. I don't think that any of these things are reducing or replacing work. I think we're having to do more work rather than less, and for many people it's unsustainable.

The next thing that may help us win the public debate on basic income is the threat of extinction. The extinction that stems from the ecological crisis is going to require us to move away from a production-based future of endless economic growth, commodification, the manipulation of desires, and so on. I think that we will need to impose eco taxes, and we will only be able to implement them if we distribute fairly the revenue they generate. The further danger that may prove equally important among politicians and social elites is the threat of neo-fascism. In situations dominated by figures like Boris Johnson in Britain or Donald Trump in the United States, progressive politicians should offer people some security through a basic income. If they don't have security more people may turn to fascism, and this is an argument that we should be using more effectively on the Left.

MT: You have spoken of the emancipatory effects of UBI schemes. But is this emancipation anti-capitalist, or does it ultimately serve to oil the wheels of capitalism? Wouldn't the provision of a basic income on its own simply preserve the class system as it is?

GS: I do think a basic income is emancipatory. It means that anybody whose position makes them more vulnerable to being oppressed or exploited or both has a greater ability to say no, to refuse to be subjected, to be dominated. I think no particular policy can by itself enable full emancipation, of course, but I think a UBI is far more emancipatory than any other social policy that exists. I would say to those people who are critical of basic income, please name another policy that is more emancipatory, rather than more paternalistic. I think that the essence of a basic income is to oppose paternalism of all sorts, whereas many forms of workfare or Social Security that are more directly contribution-based are in fact more paternalistic – the central argument being that if you behave in a certain way then we will provide you with something and you will be grateful. By contrast, I think the whole philosophical tradition behind the thrust of basic income is emancipatory and non-paternalistic.

MT: Do you think that the idea of basic income might appeal both to the right and the left wings of the political spectrum? And, if so, does basic income preserve the class system or might it be used for fighting unemployment?

GS: I think that a meaningful right to work – and I agree with Marx on this – is a bourgeois impossibility. A right to work only means something if you have the right to say 'no', the right to refuse a job that you don't want. And therefore you must have a basic income in order to have the right to work. These two are not in contradiction to each other, they are both necessary components. The duty to labour is not the right to work. The obligation to go out and get a job that you don't like but that you have to do because you're desperate is not the right to work. I also don't believe that there is a risk of mass unemployment now or in the near future because there's plenty of work to be done. We have more people in jobs now than at any time in history, at a time when technologies are also more advanced than at any time in history. So I don't believe that suddenly we're going to have no work to do.

There's an infinite number of things we might genuinely want to do: caring for each other, caring for society, caring for ourselves, doing things that help rather than deplete the environment, and so on. So I don't buy the argument that we're all going to become redundant. As human beings, we should reduce the amount of labour, of necessary or imposed labour, I'm all in favour of that; and that should allow us to increase the amount of time we can use for genuine work and leisure as creative activities.

Guy Standing is Professor of Development Studies at the School of Oriental and African Studies (SOAS), and co-founder of the Basic Income Earth Network. His books include Beyond the New Paternalism: Basic Security as Equality *(2002),* The Precariat: The New Dangerous Class *(2011),* A Precariat Charter: From Denizens to Citizens *(2014) and* Basic Income, and How We Can Make it Happen *(2017).*

Life is mine

Feminism, self-determination and basic income

Cristina Morini

In this intervention I investigate the relationships between feminist practices, basic income and the notion of 'self-determination income', focusing on the Italian feminist movement Non Una di Meno. The piece contends that self-determination income might foster a society of care and help to address the social and economic transformations occurring over the past three decades, which have been driven by neoliberal hegemony. Relatedly, it argues that the outbreak of Covid-19 has demonstrated the necessity to develop a model of welfare which matches our needs, as highlighted by feminist movements.

What is self-determination income ? Non Una di Meno defines it as a 'basic income which is self-determined, universal and unconditional and which does not depend on job activity, on citizenship status or a permit to stay. This kind of basic income will be a guarantee of economic independence and, therefore, it will constitute a concrete form of support for women who are coming out from situations of violence (domestic violence or violence in the work place). More broadly, it is an instrument for everyone – both women and men – for preventing gender violence and for providing autonomy and freedom from exploitation, labour and precarity.[1] The idea of self-determination income thus does not refer only to specific social categories, as it is unconditional and universal. It claims for women and for everyone an autonomous and livable life, without being blackmailed due to escalating existential precarity. Moreover, 'self-determination' is understood by Non Una di Meno not only as the result or goal of the income but also as its means, in that self-determination and emancipation stem from the very act of claiming it. In this feminist movement, the claim for a basic income is the keystone of a new deal that puts at its core different desires and life patterns. Indeed, self-determination income is pre-dicated upon the politicisation of care and social relationships, networks of proximity, urban spaces and the claim to a livable environment.

The society of care

Italy represents a case in point for investigating how the COVID pandemic has accelerated the implosion of welfare, and why a basic income can be a preventative tool against gender violence and against the blackmailing of exploitation, work, precarity and harassment[2]. The economic crisis triggered by the pandemic has put to the test the resistance of men and, mostly of women, who have to increasingly shoulder most of their own biological and social reproduction needs. It is not surprising that these themes and claims have been at the core of Non Una di Meno. This past 8th of March, for the fourth consecutive year, in Italy, as in many other countries, was declared women's global strike day, with the demand for self-determination income at its centre. In fact, Italy has been ranked lowest among countries in Europe regarding women's employment[3]. As the feminists Lidia Katia Manzo and Alessandra Minello recently argued:

> the COVID-19 pandemic is teaching us an important lesson about the gendered division of labour, as mothers and fathers are facing the consequences of a new organisation of care and work time imposed by lockdown measures. It is well-known that the gendered division of care was unbalanced before the COVID-19 experience. Care work was not equally distributed between genders across all groups in society, even among highly educated couples, with women devoting significantly more time to household work than men.[4]

In Italy, care-related work (unwaged labour) is divided along traditional lines. Together with Romanian women, Italian women hold the record among Europeans for daily family work at an average of 4.5 hours per day, compared with 1.5 hours for Italian men. Moreover, while Italian women are the most active in care-related work, men are less active than in other countries. Given the low participation of women in waged work, one might think that the difference in household work is due to the fact that women spend more time at home than men. Yet, according to the latest data from the Italian Institute of Statistics[5], even when women contribute to income and work as much as men, they also contribute the bulk of family work.

In the Italian family model, women's ethical and social duties to take care of others prevail over their being recognised as people who might themselves be in need of care, as part of a society which resignifies relations between human beings by building a different society. The gendered definition of care[6] has helped to conflate care with maternal care[7], as women are deemed to perform care work for the family and for the state, particularly in critical times such as during Covid-19.[8] This is connected with the theme of 'double presence', that is, with the fact that Italian welfare is centred on the family so that the care work of mothers and daughters integrates what is not provided by public services. In so doing, they become a constitutive component of the subsidiary processes of privatised welfare.

The notion of self-determination is able to reactivate the political imagination. In the Italian context – as in many others – it highlights subjective choice in relation to reproductive processes. Social reproduction appears to many Italian men as the natural goal of women's bodies. However, women in Non Una di Meno are dissident, driven by the desire to transgress nature and biology, and by the willingness to politicise care work. The analysis of socio-economic contexts today builds on the awareness that the new productive paradigms have intensified the translation of subjectivities and differences, lives and desires, into labour. The precarity of women's labour has replaced waged labour, transforming bodies into the actual matter of the reproductive paradigm.[9]

Global feminist movements have been one of the main driving forces in defence of the environment and sociality, focusing their struggles and claims on the terrain of life, time and income. The ability of feminist movements to diagnose and act is connected to the role acquired by social reproduction in the processes of valorisation at large and exploitation of unpaid labour specifically. Moreover, they are familiar with searching for practices and political outcomes which strive for a collective liberation from dynamics of dependency which are enhanced by processes of precaritisation – namely through unpaid labour (care work) as part of an economy centred on the promise.

All these aspects are tightly connected to each other, because life is translated into labour and labour has become a control on life. The contemporary feminist movements play a leading role in claiming the right to self-determination and (unconditional) basic income also because of the depths of historical memory. Today, such a memory represents a strong (composite) vision in figuring out how the conflicts between people, men and women, and social power, should be translated into freedom to desire. At the same time, it is key to shed light on the interweaving of paid and unpaid labour, namely on the value of living productive activity.

Self-determination income can free the potentialities of a self-regulated and self-managed social context; by doing so, it can foster subjects' autonomy, beyond the dependency and the management imposed by the blackmail (including sexual) that stems from the imposition and institutionalisation of precarity. Building on such an understanding of basic income, it becomes possible to envisage new ways of re-imagining concepts like *labour* in terms of quality and choice.

Capitalism is not 'a way of feeling'

The possible sources of exploitation that capitalism produces today are multiple. If we look at these forms of exploitation from the point of view of the generalisation of free waged labour, we can argue that today *all* labour is apparently consumed in a non-productive manner. At the same time, *all* activities are productive and therefore generators of accumulation. We are witnessing the paradox of a generalisation of surplus value in the age of decline of waged employment, and the consequent tension of contemporary capital towards the mortification of living labour. This is, in fact, *life put to work*, in its multiple articulations.

In order to clarify this paradox, I use the lens of labour and citizenship as they have been articulated by patriarchal society. The above is also useful to shed light on how the dimension of fragility and social risk is growing today, precisely in connection to the crisis of the waged labour framework and the citizenship tied to it – both phenomena caused by the radical shift of the productive paradigm and by the dynamics connected to globalisation. All this occurs through the paradigm of precarity. This means that the labour of precarious women and men, marked by the same fragmentation that has always defined feminine labour, ends up being considered once again as *outside of citizenship*, although this now concerns the majority of the population, and not only women.

It is not a coincidence that Guy Standing talks about the need for precarious workers to become *citizens*.[10] But instead of crying on the ruins of deindustrialisation that shrinks jobs, we should think about the open possibilities of having 'less work, more time'. From this point of view, unconditional basic income is central. With it we aim to evoke a world where desire isn't suppressed, and a worldview that considers capitalism only as an economic force.

'What is a good life, if not a self-determined life, free to express and develop itself'?[11] By asking this, we shed light on a number of problems that risk dramatically setting back societies, both from the point of view of distribution of resources and increase in inequalities,

and due to the violent contradictions produced by these dynamics – such as the rise in violence against women and all Other/Different subjectivities (gay, lesbian, trans, immigrant).[12] A reflection is taking shape around the precarious ontology of the contemporary subject faced with the erosion of waged labour and the existential dimensions (time for life and relations with the surrounding world), precisely through dynamics enabled by new technological processes and capital's *appropriative* capacities. The problem of keeping welfare and law up to date with respect to socio-economic inequalities triggered by productive transformations is therefore one of the most urgent questions for feminist movements.[13] If we look closely, we can trace a historical line of asymmetries and value systems in which the concept of citizenship and the right to citizenship itself constitute a controversial and unsolved element. Citizenship is, in fact, intended as the condition of the physical person – called a *citizen* – as one who is recognised by the state has having full civil and political rights. For a long time, the expression 'income of citizenship' has been used in Italy, precisely in connection to the aspect of inclusion in the community constituted around the right to income.

It can be argued that the main innovation brought by the introduction of social rights granted by the welfare state was simply the state's legal validation of social benefits born in the nineteenth century with an informal and solidarity-focused approach.[14] This was, in fact, a crucial shift that indicated the transformation of social benefits in 'the universal right to a real income not measured through the market value of the subject.'[15] The idea of a social contract progressively born with industrialisation – not surprisingly also called the *Fordist social compromise* – takes as its reference point only the 'productive classes', meaning by that waged labourers. Women (whose 'labour' is neither seen nor calculated) have access to welfare rights only through the mediation of the male worker. Carole Pateman has extensively written on this topic, precisely indicating how welfare was built on the production/reproduction dichotomy. In fact, welfare was intended to integrate the wage of the worker as the beneficiary of these measures. The worker's wife could enjoy these rights only as a consequence, despite the fact that her domestic and care work, alongside her sexual, psychological and affective services, are not retributed and despite the fact that she is, in fact, the backbone on which 'waged serfdom' was built, and also the secret of the worker's real productivity.[16] As the Marxist autonomist feminism of the seventies has already pointed out, the worker's wage could not fully cover similar care work on the market. The presence of a woman who carries out these tasks gratuitously is crucial for the balance of the entire system.[17] This series of acts that form emotional labour have been called 'deep acting' by Arlie Hochschild,[18] then Wendy Chapkis[19] and Elizabeth Bernstein,[20] which resonates once again with what I call *the economy of interiority*.[21]

Today, starting from these frameworks, it is increasingly clear that in relational bio-cognitive capitalism, it is the concept of productive waged labour itself that has become inadequate. By this I mean that the concept of labour that we are familiar with, or that we believe we know through the shared meanings of a language mirroring hierarchies of domination, derives from the waged relationship, which is in decline – unlike profits. This familiar concept of labour also resonates with interiorised models that oppose forms of autonomy and liberation of the people.

The economic violence of the present

Although today we should be able to grasp the horizon of a *post-work* society, in the past years the Left has unfortunately lacked both imagination and strategy, as it has continued to promote a world of full-time employees, structured around traditional sexist organisations. This world overlooks forms of labour that could potentially be non-alienated (including reproductive labour and other activities that are autonomously chosen). This has also pushed aside the concept of *freedom from work*, previously central to the analyses and claims of the socialist, communist and labour parties.[22]

Italy is the only European country, alongside Greece, where a measure of income support is missing, although the European Union had already suggested the introduction of a minimum income in 1992 (94/441 CEE). The centre-Left, which had been in power until May 2018, has only introduced the inclusion income (*Reddito di inclusione* or REI), basically a measure of poverty management. In fact, the government hasn't taken that extra step towards alternative forms of welfare and social inclusion, rendered imperative by the country's labour transform-

ations. By drawing attention to the current context, in which different forms of poverty are undoubtedly increasing even at the heart of Europe,[23] we can restore a sense of interdependence between subjects, which has been dissolved precisely by the domination of uncertainty imposed by neoliberalism through the generalisation of precarity stretched way beyond the boundaries of traditional waged labour.

Contemporary capitalism occupies spaces of life by multiplying differentiations and progressively disintegrating, for an increasing part of the population, the possibility of caring for one's health, of studying, of having a hom, and a 'good life', as Judith Butler aptly puts it.[24] It is not a coincidence that global environmental and feminist movements are making claims about life, social reproduction and the conditions of existence. These movements can be considered as an 'emerging continent', where feminist struggles play a paramount role in articulating claims that oppose the historical and 'naturalised' destiny of discrimination and exploitation of women in heterosexual patriarchal society.[25]

What we are talking about are struggles against the violence of an economic, social and development model that is currently attempting to take ownership of people as a whole (regardless of their gender and/or sexual orientation). Today, the machine-body from which profit is extracted is the social human being, namely the singularity which is immersed in an interconnected environment through new technologies.

This bio-economic model incorporates in increasingly pervasive ways not only the labour power of individuals, but also their vital, intellectual, sexual, emotional, affective and imaginative energies. Emotional production (hopes, plans, individual choices) is translated into an emotional surplus intended as an economic element directly produced by the individual. Since subjects are faced with a constantly dramatic nature of everyday life increasingly marked by anxiety, fear, insecurity and impending wars, they tend to act in a polarised, thus predictable, manner. The more predictable the behaviour, the more it can be exploited economically by those who financially speculate on the prediction of social behaviour, something platform capitalism is highly capable of doing.

To use Shoshana Zuboff's eloquent description, the *surveillance entrepreneurs* (Google and Facebook among

others) have taken ownership of us for our lives, not just for our labour.[26] In other words, it is life that has become directly profitable, precisely as waged labour is going through a crisis that appears to be irreversible. New technologies allow for the most immediate and direct socialisation of labour that has ever been seen and for profit that doesn't require any mediation, especially in terms of formal wages. The twentieth-century framework based on the connection between the worker's performance and the employer's obligation to retribute it has disappeared. Thus, the system of collective bargaining, the recognition of the social stakeholders involved, the public space connected to it and its representation, have disappeared as well.

The crucial point lies in the shift produced by the different devices that we use in our everyday life, and in the transformation of linguistic-relational products into *commodities*, alongside the modification of relationships themselves into commodities. Therein lies the historic change of the productive paradigm that has so far unfolded in the sense that reproduction has become production, and the labour theory of value has touched upon new fields.[27] This has been accompanied by a curious overturning of perspectives, thanks to the role of the above-mentioned social networks, processes of financialisation and privatisation of the welfare state.

The value fixed in this linguistic/semiotic/relational commodity that has been subtracted by contemporary biocapitalism is time or, in other words, *life*. Life is surplus value, as formulated in Melinda Cooper's analysis.[28] In other words, the social reproduction chain – formed by relationships, exchanges, care, people's dependency on each other, relations with the environment – acquires a leading role within the new productive system. The content and form of social, cultural and biological reproduction represent more than ever before the raw material that is processed by bio-capitalism, inextricably correlated to, added to, overlaid onto life and its becoming, made of affects and needs. In this manner, life becomes the very synonym of raw material.

Translated by Oana Pârvan

Cristina Morini is a journalist, essayist and independent researcher, and a founding member of the Bin-Italia association (Basic Income Network Italia). Her books include La serva serve *(2001),* Per amore o per forza: Femminilizzazione del lavoro e biopolitiche del corpo *(2010), and the collection* Lo sciopero delle donne: Lavoro, trasformazioni del capitale, lotte *(2019).*

Notes

1. https://www.bin-italia.org/nonunadimeno-un-piano-reddito-autodeterminazione/

2. Non Una di Meno, *Abbiamo un piano. Piano femminista contro la violenza maschile sulle donne e la violenza di genere* (2017), 29, accessed 11 January 2021, nonunadimeno.wordpress.com

3. Only 42.1 % of women are employed and 56.2 is the percentage of women's labour-related activities. Fondazione Censis, *Respect. Stop Violence Against Women*, Summary Report, Rome (November 2019), 6, accessed 14 January 2021, https://www.censis.it/sites/default/files/downloads/Sintesi_def_0.pdf

4. Lidia Katia C. Manzo and Alessandra Minello, 'Mothers, Childcare Duties, and Remote Working Under Covid-19 Lockdown in Italy: Cultivating Communities of Care', *Dialogues in Human Geography* 10:2 (June 2020), 120.

5. Istat, *I tempi della vita quotidiana. Lavoro, conciliazione, parità di genere, benessere soggettivo* (Roma: Istituto nazionale di statistica, 2019), https://www.istat.it/it/archivio/230102

6. Nel Noddings, *Caring: A Feminine Approach to Ethics and Moral Education* (Berkeley, CA: University of California Press, 1984).

7. Silvia Federici, *Wages Against Housework* (Bristol: Power of Women Collective and Falling Wall Press, 1975), accessed January 2021, https://caringlabor.files.wordpress.com/2010/11/federici-wages-against-housework.pdf

8. Cristina Morini, 'Take Care: Society of Care and Self-determination Income', Cogut Institute for Humanities, Brown University, accessed January 2021, https://blogs.brown.edu/humanities/archives/344

9. See Sandro Mezzadra, 'How Many Histories of Labour? Towards a Theory of Postcolonial Capitalism', *tranversal texts* (January 2012), https://transversal.at/transversal/0112/mezzadra/en

10. Guy Standing, *A Precariat Charter: From Denizens to Citizens* (London: Bloomsbury, 2014).

11. Judith Butler, *A chi spetta una buona vita? (Who gets a good life?)* (Milan: Nottetempo, 2013).

12. Monique Wittig, *Il pensiero eterosessuale* (Verona: Ombre Corte, 2019), 49–50; *The Straight Mind and Other Essays* (Boston: Beacon Press, 1991).

13. Nancy Fraser, *Fortunes of Feminism. From State-Managed Capitalism to Neoliberal Crisis* (London: Verso, 2013).

14. Karl Polanyi, *The Great Transformation* (New York: Rinehart & Company, 1944).

15. T.H. Marshall, *Citizenship and Social Class and Other Essays* (Cambridge: Cambridge University Press, 1950).

16. Carole Pateman, *The Sexual Contract* (Stanford: Stanford University Press, 1988); Carole Pateman, *The Disorder of Women: Democracy, Feminism, and Political Theory* (Stanford, Stanford University Press, 1989).

17. Maria Rosa Dalla Costa and Selma James, *The Power of Women & the Subversion of the Community* (Bristol: Falling Wall Press, 1972); cf. Silvia Federici, *Revolution at Point Zero: Housework, Reproduction, and Feminist Struggle* (Oakland, CA: PM Press, 2012); see also Antonella Picchio and Giuliana Pincelli, *Una Lotta Femminista Globale: l'esperienza dei gruppi per il Salario al Lavoro Domestico di Ferrara e Modena* [A Feminist Global Struggle: the experience of the groups for Wages for Housework in Ferrara and Modena] (Milan: FrancoAngeli Press, 2019).

18. Arlie Russell Hochschild, *The Managed Heart: Commercialization of Human Feeling* (Berkeley, CA: University of California Press, 1983).

19. Wendy Chapkis, *Live Sex Acts: Women Performing Erotic Labour* (New York: Routledge, 1997).

20. Elizabeth Bernstein, 'Sex Work for the Middle Classes', *Sexualities* 10:4 (October 2007), 473–88.

21. Andrea Fumagalli and Christina Morini, 'Anthropomorphic Capital and Commonwealth Value', *Frontiers in Sociology* (April 2020).

22. Standing, *A Precariat Charter*.

23. Publicly available datasets were analysed in this study. This data can be found here: H2020-ICT-2015, ICT10—Collective Awareness Platforms for Sustainability and Social Innovation (CAPSSI), Grant Agreement No. 687922: Title: PieNews-Commonfare.

24. Judith Butler, *Notes Toward a Performative Theory of Assembly* (Cambridge: Harvard University Press, 2015).

25. Cristina Morini, *Le pillole azzurre del capitale* [The Blue Pills of Capitalism] (May 2016), Effimera.org, http://effimera.org/le-pillole-azzurre-del-capitale-cristina-morini/

26. Shoshana Zuboff, *The Age of Surveillance Capitalism: The Fight for a Human Future at the New Frontier of Power* (New York: Public Affairs, 2019).

27. Cristina Morini and Andrea Fumagalli, 'Life Put to Work: Towards a Life Theory of Value', trans. Emanuele Leonardi, *Ephemera: Theory & Politics in Organisation* 10:3-4 (2010), 234–52.

28. Melinda Cooper, *Life as Surplus: Biotechnology and Capitalism in the Neoliberal Era* (Seattle: University of Washington Press, 2008).

Rethinking basic income

Federico Chicchi and Emanuele Leonardi

For what is possibly the first time in history, we have been living for the last few years in a social system that could easily provide for its own needs by working considerably less than in the past, if it was equipped with fair modes of distribution and was reasonably planned. Why is it then that, despite the fact that labour today no longer ensures social integration and the diminishing of inequalities, we are increasingly pushed to transform the time of life into a productive time? It is in relation to this question that our own proposal for basic income becomes meaningful and acquires its practicability.[1]

Basic income is an unconditional money transfer financed through taxes. It is distributed to all the residents of a given political community and the recipients can spend it according to their own preferences. Ultimately, it aims to guarantee them a sufficient sum of money in order to live an autonomous and dignified life. Yet this is still not exhaustive enough as a definition. Basic income takes on different meanings according to the context in which it is situated: it is not desirable in itself, but it becomes so only if it is lodged within a process of de-commodification of capitalist society. In this sense, first, basic income is not to be superimposed upon or confused with the different public policies to fight poverty. Rather, it must become an instrument of struggle against new forms of exploitation of socialised 'industriousness',[2] where this term is to be understood as the whole set of cooperative and/or productive practices that are performed without necessarily being formally regulated and remunerated by a work contract. If adequately designed, basic income could become an effective weapon to be deployed in trade union struggles in defence of workers' dignity. Equally, as already claimed by feminist movements such as Ni Una Menos [Not One Woman Less], it can promote subjective self-determination and freedom of choice. Moreover, it retains an extraordinary and inherent vocation for convergence in an era characterised by a heightened fragmentation of work and subjects, as it provides a common ground on which it would be possible to link together numerous anti-capitalist struggles which break out every day and everywhere, locally and globally.

In other words, what is at stake in basic income does not solely affect the quantitative relation between poverty and wealth in a specific community but concerns the opportunity to modify, qualitatively, the relations of force [rapport di forza] between exploited and exploiters in contemporary society. Its main purpose is thus to foster the autonomy of producers, their ability to have an impact (from below) on the *qualitative composition of production*, which is to say their ability to exert an influence on how, what, where and for whom one produces. In the following we will attempt to present, genealogically, the terrain on which such a project should be shaped.

The wage-institution in Fordism

Capitalism is a mode of production whose end-goal is the creation of a *surplus* of value, that is to say, the presence at the end of the economic cycle of a quantity of money which is higher than what had been advanced in order to set in motion capital's production process. The spasmodic hunt for surplus value, in fact, requires that the organisation of production privileges the accumulation of capital at the expense of the use value of commodities (i.e. of the needs they satisfy). What is more, the quantitative logic of value – according to which 'everything has a price' and thus could be bought – is altogether indifferent to the qualitative one of real wealth – grounded in the multifarious experiences of well-being which different communities, autonomously and in every specific case, decide to pursue. Put differently, when the capitalist decides what to invest money in, the fundamental criterion that directs the decision is not the product's utility but rather its profitability. 'Do weapons bring good business? It matters little that people die.'

For a long time, however, the search for the logic of value partially overlapped with the multiplication of the logic of wealth. This is not to say that it was a linear process; on the contrary. More than ever, it is evident today that capitalist development necessarily entails the depletion of the two sources of every wealth, nature and human labour power,[3] not to mention leading to the colonisation of, and genocides in, the so-called New World. On the other hand, it is nonetheless undeniable that, with respect to previous modes of production, capitalism has significantly improved the life conditions of a broad population strata across vast areas of the planet.

This double-sidedness of capitalist development emerges clearly in the Fordist period – in Western Europe, from the Marshall plan to the oil shocks of the 1970s – and the social compromise by which it was distinguished, between productive capital and wage labour (obedience in exchange for security, salary increase offset by the surrender of decisional autonomy, and, hence, relative prosperity exchanged for discipline). This process can be defined as the *wage-institution*, since integration, in the form of social rights and access to mass consumption, was ensured to the working class by means of acquiring the status of 'wage-labourer'.[4] But it should also be noted that (predominantly female) domestic work, slave work and a concern for the environment were excluded from the Fordist pact.[5] Actually, the pressure on the planet dramatically increased with the paradigm of growth, which transformed the political conflicts around income distribution into technico-managerial issues concerning ways in which to increase the GDP.[6] Instead of struggling over an increase in wages to the detriment of an increase in profits, the workers' movement found itself endorsing in this way the cause of a quantitative growth that would make everyone happy – aside from the biosphere, that is.[7] Such a social pact based on the centrality of wage labour could be termed a *productivist syndrome*, which hinges on the link between social redistribution and value-oriented economic development.[8]

And yet reality never perfectly corresponded with this model. Particularly in Italy, the Fordist period was a time of terrific attacks upon the endurance of the wage-institution. The legendary struggle of the workers in the electromechanical sector in Milan in the 1960s, for instance, sparked a cycle of conflicts – the so-called Red Decade – which came to a close with the extraordinary creativity of Bologna's 1977.[9] The feminist movement was fundamental to this, with its refusal of the social 'reproductive' role invented for women by capital. More specifically, a catalyst was provided by the Wages for Housework international campaign which, behind the ostensible request to participate in the Fordist compromise, revealed the invisible foundation of the latter in its violent subordination of the sphere of reproduction. 'Rewarded' by care labour, the angel in the house was denied any autonomy.[10] A further catalyst could be found in the ecological crises whose discussion had become inescapable after the 1972 publication of the Club of Rome's report, *The Limits to Growth*, and which was forcefully brought to public attention by environmentalist groups that often belonged to the workers' movement. Consider, for instance, the important season of struggles against the harmful effects of heavy industry on health and the environment.[11] Finally, it is important to stress the centrality of the working class politically exercising its power, as negotiations around salaries were coupled with claims for freedom, against the capitalist organisation of labour and for a less dehumanising pace of work and tasks. Even more radically, other struggles would not settle for the sole objective of emancipating labour, but rather argued for its refusal in the name of an unwillingness to produce value for capital and the experimentation with new forms of autonomous activity and cooperative production of wealth.[12]

Though very different from one another, these struggles shared an anti-capitalist aspiration and the backdrop of the wage-institution. Did they succeed in modifying relations of force? Certainly they did not. Capital is still alive and kicking and the waged labour force, while very shrunk in size and shattered in the West, has not globally decreased in number. Nevertheless, this was a peculiar, ambiguous defeat. On the one hand, it brought about the progressive dismantling of the welfare state while, on the other, it involved a radical reconfiguration of social practices for the extraction of value, namely, of those very processes that found their defining model in the factory.[13] This does not mean that the factory became extinct. Rather, the crisis of the link between employment and citizenship determined the dissemination of the factory beyond its gates and into urban spaces, and, later, its transfiguration within the digital universe of the Internet.

The separation between value and wealth

In the 1980s, the socialisation of the factory – the expansion of its productive logic in new social spaces and temporalities – allowed capitalism to widen and, at the same time, reconfigure its base for the extraction of value chiefly in a *post-* and *neo*-waged sense. Put differently, what was radically transformed were the social mediations that presided over the encounter between labour and capital. In this regard, the most significant issue is the thinning out of the boundaries between production and reproduction. In the neoliberal society these two social spheres – work and life, one could say – immediately take part in the new dynamics of valorisation. This is exactly what the phenomena of precarisation and feminisation of labour point to: the *becoming productive of social reproduction*. It is here that capitalist exploitation pours out beyond the limits maintained, for better or worse, by the wage relationship and invades even the most intimate aspects of subjectivity.[14] In this regard, basic income could easily be termed *reproductive income*.[15]

Industrial society produced commodities and made them social; post-Fordist capitalism produces society at once in the form of a commodity. One should refer to the ways in which so-called big data have been transformed in an immense commercial enterprise transforming people into providers of unpaid and continuous information (24/7).[16] But let us consider, more generally, how absurd and symptomatic is the existence of an expression such as *human capital*. How can we comply with the fact that affects, relationships, skills and talents are recognised and supported *if and only if* the performance society can extract value from them?[17] In the straitjacket of success-at-all-costs, which is validated by economic triumph, women and men in the flesh become crippled subjects, lose their sense of solidarity and of a passion devoid of second aims. They lose the sense of being gentle, as Brecht would put it. We are facing an actual paradigm shift: driven by the logic of value, economic growth is no longer accompanied by an increase in social well-being. Private profits and collective wealth take inexorably different paths.

This situation is evident, for instance, in the sectors of scientific and cultural cooperation. Knowledge could freely circulate at insignificant costs, and partially it does thanks to peer-to-peer networking and information piracy. In addition, since it is a non-rival good – which is to say that its sharing does not diminish its quality but rather increases it – knowledge would by itself encourage cooperative practices more than competitive ones. It could easily create new forms of sharing rather than destroying social bonds.[18] Only the coercive imposition of copyright and other property devices enacted by big editorial groups ensures the profitability of these products. Capital resolutely creates scarcity when there is none. Still, this is at the expense of the good, as nowadays the promise of more efficiency and quality inherent in the transformation of objects in commodities is often not maintained. Therefore, the logic of value does not overlap with that of wealth, not even partially. The confirmation of their divorce is definite.[19]

This is not to imply that, as Gorz optimistically believed, capitalism is on the edge of the abyss or that we are already starting to get out of it. Unfortunately, at present, nothing prevents the logic of value from flourishing. However, it seems clear that the driving force of such logic is withering away, and that the political space for a new social compromise within it is growing smaller. Why? It is because wage labour lost the centripetal force establishing it as the model towards which all the other forms of socialised industriousness had to lean, in order to be recognised at the institutional level. The global economic crisis accelerated this deflation. Indeed, the growth registered in some countries, which was achieved thanks to austerity measures implemented on the shoulders of more fragile economies as in Greece or Italy, not only has not markedly raised the rate of employment but, rather, it fed itself with a further multiplication of inequalities.

For these reasons, it is somewhat bizarre to discuss basic income solely by asking whether it would be technically feasible. Of course, it is of necessity to make precise calculations, put in place intelligent experimentations, accurately calculate the risks of failure and, if need be, arrange plans for dealing with it. Yet these discussions become ridiculous if we detach them, for instance, from the scandal of the public bail-out of different American banks which, between 2008 and 2016, had a cost to the tax-payer of an 'investment' of thousands of billions, whether one counted them in dollars or in euros.

Labour and income: a rapidly transforming relation

Basic income is thus a political mechanism that is adequate to the ways in which value is currently produced and, therefore, appropriate to the transformations of labour. The latter is increasingly more fragmented and under attack – to the point of normalising the figure of the *working poor* – but also increasingly more interconnected, both as regards the digital world and within global value chains. Nonetheless, the adequacy of an instrument by itself does not confirm the extent to which such an instrument is desirable. For instance, the idea of full employment was very appealing in the golden age of the wage-institution, yet it yielded positive results only where the effects of its partial realisation were foisted from below through struggles – just to refer to an example from Italy, one should think about the Statute of Workers in 1970.[20] Conversely, in those instances when it was lowered from above, full employment generated conformism and social passivity. Those who oppose basic income on the grounds that it would weaken the exercise of political class conflict are confusing causes and effects. As with any other measure, basic income works well when snatched through struggles, and badly if it is capital granting it.[21] We would argue that, in this context, there are three possible scenarios for a potential implementation of basic income.

First, there is a *digital-capitalist* scenario, recently advanced by the tycoons of the Silicon Valley and whose argument could be approximately expressed as follows: if manufacturing work is fading away under the blows of automation, collective online activity produces data from which the monopolists of the web and digital platforms are extracting astronomical amount of profits, thus it would be only fair to let a few crumbs end up feeding the actual producers. This is a proposal which seems to be founded on a specific claim or could even be regarded as progressive, but which instead confirms the parasitic model of digital capitalism. This would be a case of accepting a meagre gratuity from terribly rich entrepreneurs in return for the renunciation of decisional power on society's modes of life and labour.

A second option could be termed *social-democratic 2.0*. Finally recovered from the neoliberal hangover, the State would come back and do its job, which is to reduce the ratio of exploitation in order to stabilise the regime of accumulation (driven by finance, in this case). Once again: obedience in exchange for social peace, validation of the new forms of diffuse productivity, integration by means of consumption patterns always more apparently personalised yet always more identical to themselves, no autonomy and insufficient power over the qualitative composition of production. This would lead to a new social compromise based on a *post*-waged mediation presumably managed by a yet-to-be-imagined *post*-representative democracy. We are dealing with an attempt of high reformism to which we wish the best of luck but which we believe will be difficult, if not impossible, to realise. The divorce between the logic of value and logic of wealth substantially reduce the room for manoeuvre. How much economic growth can the planet still endure and, most importantly, how much commodification can still be inflicted upon the social body?

It seems to us that democracy and autonomy of the producers are to be found elsewhere, and could be built based on a third kind of basic income, a *conflictual* one. In any case, such basic income cannot be considered as an alternative to the traditional welfare state. Whereas the latter redistributes a part of the value produced by the waged labour force, the former directly distributes a part of the value produced by diffused socialised industriousness. This is the value originating from undisputedly productive social labouring activities which are however not framed in a wage labour contract, and which these days remain an exclusive prerogative of network capitalism and platform monopolies. Consequently, those who reject basic income because, as they argue, it would end up demolishing the tools for social protection that are currently still available, albeit gradually diminishing, are making a grave mistake. The funding of the *conflictual* basic income, for instance, does not involve a transfer of the resources that today still guarantee social rights. On the contrary, it would be a matter of levying taxes

on the lords of the boundless digital revenues (Google, Facebook, Amazon, and so on), so as to limit new exploitative practices and in order to find in social equality an indispensable goal.[22]

After forty years of the socialisation of costs and privatisation of earnings, it is time to reverse this tendency. This is a difficult yet necessary challenge. Only a strategy that is capable of articulating welfare and basic income can hope not to be defeated. Their relationship must be set in terms of complementarity, never in terms of substitution. In this sense, basic income must be understood from the start as a device which makes visible concealed social productivity in order to then remunerate it in the form of primary income.

For all these reasons, it is clear that the classic objection to basic income – 'nobody would be doing anything anymore, freeloaders will get by on the efforts and struggles of those who still work' – goes dangerously around in circles. This is so not only for the pathetic moralism of the wealthy person devoted to luxury, who also brands as lazy or a slacker the poor who refuse to have their own life eaten away by work. But, chiefly, it is because such an objection is incapable of recognising that contemporary accumulation relies always more consistently on non-waged and non-remunerated activities. *Already now* there is nothing passive in the socialised industriousness that would be at last recognised by basic income.[23] And this is not even the whole story. By weakening the blackmail of *poor labour* – that is, the obligation to accept humiliating salaries rather than no salary at all – basic income would open a crucial space for social mobilisation. This space would be radically other to the punitive and blameful version put forward by neoliberal workfare, which markedly affects the economic support given to the actual and active search for employment.[24] *This* way of living and taking action in collective participation claims for itself the right to autonomously decide ways of being together, in addition to what is to be involved in producing in order that everyone may enjoy freedom from need.

In a nutshell, the conflictual basic income does two things. It frees the right to a dignified life from participation as a wage-labourer (or 'entrepreneur of herself'), as well as defuses the sense of guilt affecting many among us when the labour market hands us over to precarity. It reminds us that we are collective producers, not inadequate individuals as we are usually depicted, and improves the conditions of our lives. The overall effect is that of some fresh liberty.

Yet, it is not for these reasons that basic income can lay claim to a strategic centrality. For example, it would be just as useful to introduce a minimum wage which is transversal to different economic sectors so as to avoid the devaluation of labour and, thus, in order to effectively and efficiently reduce the workers' chances to be blackmailed by companies. In sum, basic income plus welfare equals the production of a society beyond the maximisation of profits. What is more, these two measures could also reinforce each other.

This is not just a marginal issue, and it appears to us that it is the same point Guy Standing is emphasising when he insists on the necessity of an 'integrated approach' between contrasting precarious conditions of work and supporting income.[25] When the blackmail of poor labour drops in intensity, the deserters of the industrial reserve army multiply and trade union consultations can become more effective in their negotiations and gain organisational creativity when facing the new scenarios of the post-industrial urban economy. ('Let's stop production!' means very different things depending on whether it is shouted in factories that are increasingly emptied of labour, in logistic warehouses progressively filled up with commodities, or in hospitals, universities and shopping malls). Furthermore, basic income can function as a solidarity fund in cases of prolonged and harsh strikes, that is to say, it can serve as an immediate and concrete resource that reinforces the resistance capacities of workers and the communities they belong to.[26] Besides, a more just labour market multiplies the possibilities of using this income. It also fashions into practicable diverse forms of co-existence between waged and socialised industriousness labour, forms which would be freely experimented with by different individuals within their collective groups. From this standpoint, basic income is an important yet not self-sufficient element in a rudimentary programme to fight exploitation. Such a plan, besides a minimum wage, must introduce a cap on unreasonably high salaries[27] and a drastic reduction in working hours. This is the way forward to enforce the autonomy of producers and thus the democratic exercise of the right to decide how, what, when, where and for whom one produces.

There is, however, a further aspect of basic income that contributes to making it both an important social claim to be used in conjunction with others and a political catalyst for an anti-capitalist plural strategy. We are referring here to basic income's ability to seize time from the logic of value and thus represent a cure for the aforementioned *productivist syndrome*, which is leading us to an ecological and social collapse. That which the feminist movement Ni Una Menos calls 'self-determination income' is the picklock whereby the plural voices of the social conflict can *interrupt* their forced participation in the perverted mechanism of capitalist accumulation. It becomes easier from there to talk to each other, recognise each other, fight together and design non-predatory forms of production and reproduction of wealth. Here the analysis must stop, and the conflictual practice be turned back on.

Conclusion

Today, social integration and the satisfaction of basic needs is no longer required to pass exclusively through the wage-institution, that is, through the access to income provided by *labour*. This terrain is still important, but it must be flanked by a new social and political space where the experimentation with alternative forms of work allows for the multiplication of the ways in which each individual and their collectivities experience well-being.

This is a possibility. In order to actualise it, however, a broad social conflict must necessarily be re-activated, a social conflict which works towards inverting the tendencies that inequalities have to spread. The word 'conflict', coupled with the idea of an unconditional basic income, serves the purpose of reiterating that this is not a 'reasonable' option for everyone, as the advocates of the digital-capitalist scenario would want us to believe. These, indeed, while with one hand conceding a minimal access to the shining world of consumption, with the other steal labour and social security from the many. In reality, basic income as presented and understood in our contribution here, is 'reasonable' only for a part of society – those whose socialised industriousness is being exploited – as it must be snatched collectively, not meekly requested. An impressive process of redistribution from the financial elites to the proletarianised masses is the necessary condition so that basic income may sustain the production of social wealth against the capitalist imperative of profit at all costs.

Translated by Yari Lanci

Federico Chicchi is Associate Professor at the Department of Sociology and Business Law of the University of Bologna. His books include Karl Marx *(2019) and (with Anna Simone)* La società della prestazione *(2017).*

Emanuele Leonardi is an affiliated researcher at the Centre for Social Studies of the University of Coimbra and a research fellow in Sociology at the University of Parma. He is the author of Lavoro Natura Valore. André Gorz tra marxismo e decrescita *(2017).*

Notes

1. This text is a revised and updated version of Chicchi Federico and Leonardi Emanuele, *Manifesto per il reddito di base* (Roma-Bari: Laterza, 2018), with a postface by Marta Fana and Simone Fana. Many thanks to the publisher for permission to translate it here.

2. Federico Chicchi, Emanuele Leonardi and Stefano Lucarelli, *Más allá del salario. Lógicas de la explotación* (Montevideo: Azafran Editorial, 2019).

3. Karl Marx, *Capital, Volume I* (London: Penguin Classics, 1990; reprint of Pelican Books edition, 1976).

4. Robert Castel, *From Manual Workers to Wage Labourers* (London: Transactions, 2003).

5. Emanuele Leonardi, 'Bringing Class Analysis Back In: Assessing the Transformation of the Value-Nature Nexus to Strengthen the Connection between Degrowth and Environmental Justice', *Ecological Economics* 156 (2019), 83–90.

6. Mathias Schmelzer, *The Hegemony of Growth* (Cambridge: Cambridge University Press, 2016).

7. Andrè Gorz, *Ecology as Politics* (Boston: South End Press, 1980).

8. Claus Offe, 'A Non-Productivist Design for Social Policies', in *Arguing for Basic Income, Ethical Foundations for a Radical Reform*, ed P. Van Parijs (London: Verso, 1992), 61–78.

9. Franco 'Bifo' Berardi, *Futurability: The Age of Impotence and the Horizon of Possibility* (London: Verso, 2017).

10. Silvia Federici, 'Social reproduction theory', *Radical Philosophy* 2.04 (Spring 2019), 55–57.

11. Lorenzo Feltrin, Book review of *Quando il potere è operaio: autonomia e soggettività politica a Porto Marghera (1960-1980)*, *Toxic News* (2019), https://toxicnews.org/2019/05/28/book-review-quando-il-potere-e-operaio-autonomia-e-soggettivita-politica-a-porto-marghera-1960-1980-edited-by-devi-sacchetto-and-gianni-sbrogio-2009-roma-manifestolibri/

12. Kathi Weeks,*The Problem with Work: Feminism, Marxism, Antiwork Politics, and Postwork Imaginaries* (Durham, NC: Duke University Press, 2011).

13. Andrea Fumagalli and Cristina Morini, 'Life put to work: towards a life theory of value', *Ephemera* 10:3-4 (2011), 234–252.

14. Melinda Cooper and Catherine Waldby, *Clinical Labour: Tissue Donors and Research Subjects in the Global Bioeconomy* (Durham, NC: Duke University Press, 2014).

15. Giacomo D'Alisa, 'Towards a Reproductive Income', presentation at the conference *Ambientalismo operaio e giustizia climatica*, Centro Studi Movimenti, Parma, June 14th 2019.

16. Burkhardt Wolf, 'Big data, small freedom? Informational surveillance and the political', *Radical Philosophy* 191 (May/June 2015), 13–20.

17. Pierre Dardot and Christian Laval, *The New Way of the World: On Neoliberal Society* (London: Verso, 2016).

18. Andrea Fumagalli, Alfonso Giuliani, Stefano Lucarelli and Carlo Vercellone, *Cognitive Capitalism, Welfare and Labour: The Commonfare Hypothesis* (London: Routledge, 2019).

19. André Gorz, *Ecologica* (Chicago: University of Chicago Press, 2010).

20. In 1970, Italian laws partially incorporated radical demands advanced by the Labour Movement during the 'Hot Autumn' of 1969, especially pay rises. Shortly after, most pay scales were indexed to inflation for wage and salary earners. Jobs were virtually guaranteed in the official economy, and trade unions became influential on a host of planning bodies. The firing of workers became difficult in many sectors.

21. For this reason, too, basic income must necessarily be *unconditional*, as Guy Standing maintains in his interview in this issue.

22. Antonio Casilli, *En attendant les robot : Enquête sur le travail du clic* (Paris: Seuil, 2019).

23. Basic Income Network, *Big Data, WebFare e reddito per tutti. Siamo in rete, produciamo valore, vogliamo reddito*, Quaderni per il reddito 9 (2019), https://www.bin-italia.org/quaderni-reddito-n9-big-data-webfare-reddito-tutti/.

24. Ursula Huws, *Labour in Contemporary Capitalism: What next?* (London: Palgrave McMillan, 2019).

25. On this, see the first part of the interview with Guy Standing elsewhere in this issue.

26. Erik Olin Wright, 'Basic Income as a Socialist Project', https://www.ssc.wisc.edu/~wright/Basic%20Income%20as%20a%20Socialist%20Project.pdf

27. Hubert Buch-Hansen and Max Koch, 'Degrowth through Income and Wealth Caps?', *Ecological Economics* 160 (2019), 264–271.

Reviews

Gimmickification

Sianne Ngai, *Theory of the Gimmick: Aesthetic Judgement and Capitalist Form* (Cambridge, MA: The Belknap Press of Harvard University Press, 2020), 416pp., £28.95 hb., 978 0 67498 454 7

'[I]f only we could forget for a while about the beautiful and get down instead to the dainty and the dumpy'. In this oft-cited remark, made in the context of his 1956 paper 'A Plea for Excuses', J. L. Austin glancingly alludes to a subclass of 'minor' aesthetic categories, suggestively hinting at, yet in the end failing to elaborate on, their critical significance for the philosophy of aesthetics. The theoretical investigation of 'minor' aesthetic categories, as Sianne Ngai notes in *Our Aesthetic Categories: Zany, Cute, Interesting* (2012), 'remains surprisingly marginal to philosophical aesthetics', which has, since the discipline's emergence in the eighteenth century, continued to be organised around two primary aesthetic categories, the beautiful and the sublime, and their respective moral and theological resonances. Indeed, as Ngai observes, philosophical aesthetics typically appeals to these rare and powerful aesthetic experiences as models for theorising aesthetic judgement in general, paying little attention to how more 'trivial' or 'affectively equivocal' aesthetic categories 'might put interesting new pressure on the theory of aesthetic judgement', as well as 'the role aesthetic judgements might play in criticism with explicitly extra-aesthetic goals'.

In *Our Aesthetic Categories* Ngai singles out three everyday aesthetic categories – the 'cute', the 'interesting' and the 'zany' – whose aesthetic judgements are underwritten by 'mixed or equivocal feelings'. In doing so, she challenges 'the longstanding assumption that aesthetic judgements must always be based on a single and unequivocal feeling', such as the disinterested or strongly visceral feelings of pleasure or displeasure that give rise to judgements of the beautiful or the disgusting. The aesthetic evaluations of cute, interesting and zany, by contrast, can take either a positive or negative form, and are accordingly capable of functioning as both praise or criti-

cism, something that is not the case for other 'minor' aesthetic categories (like 'dumpy'). As in her earlier study, *Ugly Feelings* (2005) – in which Ngai explores how a range of negative emotions and dysphoric affects can be interpreted as indexing the 'suspended agency' and 'social powerlessness' of individuals living in 'late modernity' – the affective uncertainty at the heart of 'our' everyday aesthetic categories, as Ngai suggests, critically points to how aesthetic experience has been radically 'transformed by the hypercommodified, information-saturated, performance-driven conditions of late capitalism'.

In *Theory of the Gimmick: Aesthetic Judgement and Capitalist Form* (2020) Ngai continues her critical inquiry into how everyday aesthetic categories encode larger social and historical processes by turning to the 'gimmick'. The gimmick, as Ngai claims, is 'capitalism's most successful aesthetic category'. Its 'flagrantly unworthy form can be found virtually anywhere': from manufacturing and finance, to mass culture and contemporary art. We encounter gimmicks in the form labour-saving contraptions, financial strategies and artistic techniques. As Ngai explains,

> Gimmicks are fundamentally one thing across these instances: overrated devices that strike us as working too little (labour saving tricks) but also working too hard (strained efforts to get our attention). In each case we refer to the aesthetically suspicious object as a "contrivance", an ambiguous term equally applicable to ideas, techniques and things.

As an '*ambivalent* judgement tied to a *comprised* form', the gimmick names 'a relationship between a relatively codified way of seeing and a way of speaking that the former compels'. As such, it renders explicit how aesthetic categories always have two sides: 'the form we perceive, a way of seeing' and 'the judgement we utter, a way of speaking'. This latter discursive 'side' of aesthetic experience – originally identified by Kant in the *Third Critique* in terms of the compulsory sharing of pleasure that attends judgements of taste – has typically been neglected by both aesthetics and art theory, where scholars have focused predominantly on 'forms of appearance'. Going against the grain of such literature, *Theory of the Gimmick* continues to develop an argument that is central to *Our Aesthetic Categories*: namely, 'that ways of speaking tethered to specific ways of perceiving are as meaningful as the latter'. Here Ngai follows Stanley Cavell in his emphasis on the 'dialogical' and 'performative' dimension of aesthetic judgement as what makes an aesthetic encounter socially significant: namely, 'the way in which we face or address others to appearances we can only perceive for ourselves'. The gimmick, as Ngai underscores, uniquely reflects this intersubjective dimension of aesthetic judgement in a 'redoubled way', registering how our 'encounter with a form making wrong claims to value that our judgement refutes' implicitly evokes 'the image of other judges who evaluate differently'; judges who *buy into* whatever it is that the gimmick is promising or selling. The gimmick is thus always also a 'metajudgement' – 'a judgement on and about judgement' – that highlights 'how other judges, abstract figures standing in for our relations to others in general, are already "inside" our most spontaneous, affectively immediate experiences of form'.

If aesthetic judgements are evaluations based on feelings related to how things appear, and not on concepts of what they are, nonaesthetic or cognitive judgements (whether historical, political or moral in kind) are, as Ngai outlines in *Our Aesthetic Categories*, nonetheless a constitutive part of an aesthetic judgement's 'discursive and narrative aftermath'. This 'toggle' between aesthetic and nonaesthetic judgement is, as Ngai shows, 'internal' to a category like the 'interesting', 'an ambiguous feeling tied to an encounter with difference without a concept, which then immediately activates a search for that missing concept'. In the case of the gimmick, specifically, our aesthetic appraisal of an object's form as unsatisfyingly compromised 'quickly morphs into ethical, historical, and economic evaluations of it as fraudulent, untimely, and cheap'. While all aesthetic categories presuppose some relationship to social norms, what distinguishes the gimmick, then, is the way in which its judgement of

'aesthetic worth aligns with a judgement of economic worth'. Although distinctively capitalist aesthetic categories like the 'cute' and the 'zany' speak, respectively, to 'our equivocal relation to the commodity as consumers' and the 'ambiguous borders separating work from nonwork', the gimmick, as Ngai writes, is 'our culture's only aesthetic category … in which our feelings of misgiving stem from a sense of overvaluation bound to appraisals of deficient or excessive labour encoded in form'.

Such appraisals are based on the perceived 'deviation from a tacit standard of productivity'. If a gimmick 'seems to be working too hard or too little', as Ngai notes, 'it is because the social timing of its appearance is off'. A gimmick can accordingly strike us 'as technologically backward or just as problematically advanced: futuristic to the point of hubris, as in the case of Google Glass'. When a technology is judged to have 'arrived too early', what is typically meant here, as Ngai explains, is 'that its cost is proving too high'. Such 'metrics' are specific to a capitalist mode of production 'that binds value to labour and time', and which is structured by an historical dynamic of 'unceasing innovation' and 'increasing productivity'. In capitalist societies, these 'ratios get filtered' – via the mediating abstractions of the rate of profit and price – 'into the conscious and unconscious decisions of all producers and consumers'. In expressing 'how a kind of quantitative measurement can persist, abstracted, inside qualitative judgements', the aesthetic judgement of the gimmick, as Ngai contends, reveals how 'the basic laws of capitalist production and its abstractions' come to structure the 'way we perceive the world, seeping into how people share their pleasures and displeasures'. Indeed, as a 'moving measurement of labour … that binds this abstraction of labour to value', our everyday judgement of the gimmick, as Ngai suggestively puts it, 'has, or *is*, a "value theory of labour"', in that it 'encodes' something 'strikingly akin' to what Marx terms 'socially necessary labour time'.

As in her previous publications, Ngai deepens her analysis of the gimmick as an aesthetic judgement and capitalist form by attending to an eclectic range of modern and contemporary artistic, literary and cultural artefacts that not only represent the capitalist gimmick as an object or idea but 'riskily instrumentalise' its compromised form, 'deploying it to think through other aesthetic, conceptual, or historical problems'. The gimmick, as

Ngai observes, is endemic to art under capitalism, its compromised form reflecting art's 'equivocal' relation to the commodity form. Gimmicky as we might find them now, it is only with the maturation of capitalist relations of production that a pre-capitalist artistic device like the *deus ex machina* comes to be viewed with 'suspicion or contempt', becoming 'the name for a "cheap" or aesthetically unconvincing contrivance for achieving narrative closure'. Artistic devices that appear as 'neutral' can 'flip into problematic gimmicks (and vice versa) with remarkable ease in artworks made, circulated, and consumed in capitalism', as is exemplified by the culture industry's tendency to 'degrade' formal techniques to the status of gimmicks through 'perpetual reuse'. However, the accusation of gimmickry 'haunts' artworks that make claims to being 'advanced' in an especially 'intense' way, hovering over modernism and modernist techniques in particular. For Ngai, this is connected not simply to modernism's affirmation of the new, but to what Cavell (echoing Adorno) characterises as modern art's 'rising technicism', whereby the continuing production of art becomes increasingly dependent on its internalisation of 'a thicken-

ing critical apparatus' – a phenomenon that Ngai further elaborates on in a chapter considering the exceedingly gimmick-prone 'novel of ideas'. This structural intimacy between artistic technique and theoretical criticism results in the growing suspicion of the artwork (particularly the conceptual artwork) 'as always possibly fraudulent', an 'uncertainty about trickery that becomes extended to the idea of art in general, retroactively affecting our relation to works of the past'.

There is a continual slippage in the book, left largely uninterrogated by Ngai, between aesthetic judgement and what Peter Osborne terms 'art-critical judgement'. For as the history of modern and contemporary art makes clear, to judge an artwork as *aesthetically* unconvincing is rarely the same thing as judging it *artistically* or *critically* so. While Ngai is careful not conflate art with aesthetics, or to reduce art to its aesthetic dimension – a commonplace error in the fields of philosophical aesthetics and art theory alike – her discussion of particular artworks routinely shuttles between these two forms of judgement in a way that sometimes leaves their borders and relationship unclear. Do, for instance, aesthetic judgements ground art-critical judgements, as Ngai sometimes suggests, or should they be comprehended as merely a condition or aspect of the latter (relating to art's necessary aesthetic appearance and the registration of feeling in our experience art)? If, like Adorno and Cavell, Ngai is aware of the dangers of thinking the unity of art as a generalised aesthetic, always insisting on the conceptual, historical and social character of art, these cognitive and nonaesthetic aspects of the work tend to be subsumed by the aesthetic, or restricted to its interpretative aftermath. This stands in contrast to Osborne, who contends that the artistic significance of the aesthetic in modern and contemporary (or post-conceptual) art be understood as both ontologically partial and historically relational.

While Marx's value-theory of labour underpins Ngai's general theory of the gimmick, this comes most to the fore in the chapters that focus on capitalist abstractions. For Ngai, the 'relation between mystified and objective valuation' in our aesthetic encounter with the gimmick 'pedagogically underscores' something crucial about Marx's critical theory of capitalist social forms, wherein 'economic essences must appear as something other than themselves': value as money or price, surplus value as profit, and relations of exploitation as ones of equal exchange. For Marx, financial capital emerges as an intensified version of the fetishism underlying value's various 'forms of appearance', in that surplus value generated within the sphere of production appears to the financial capitalist to be generated within the sphere of circulation through the mere exchange of promises, creating the illusion of 'self-valorising value' or 'money breeding money' (M-M'). As a form of appearance making aggrandised claims to value, finance, as Ngai observes, thus 'confronts us with an interestingly amplified instance of the gimmick's structure and ambiguities'. These ambiguities are compellingly explored in a chapter focusing on Robert Louis Stevenson's story 'The Bottle Imp' (1891) and David Mitchell's psychological horror film *It Follows* (2014): both debt-driven tales, written in the wake of financial crises, that route their representations of finance through structurally similar narratives about 'the circulation of deferred reckonings'. In striking contrast to popular depictions of financial products as impossibly complex and abstract, both 'The Bottle Imp' and *It Follows*, as Ngai's close reading of these two texts foregrounds, 'take the sublimity out of finance' by mobilising 'exaggeratedly crude' story-telling devices to portray the 'ambiguous interval' that defines the aftermath of financial crises (and their attempted deferral), when credit is confronted with its material limits.

In two subsequent and equally compelling chapters, Ngai reflects on how particular artistic instantiations of the gimmick in Rob Halpern's book-length poem *Music for Porn* (2012) and Stan Douglass's video installation *Suspiria* (2003) have their own unique ways of illuminating the 'peculiar ontology' of capitalist abstractions like 'abstract labour' and 'value'. Focusing on Halpern's extravagant employment of the poetic device of 'catachresis' to portray the male body as an eroticised capitalist abstraction, reading *Music for Porn*, as Ngai suggests, helps clarify what is at stake in Marx's notoriously contradictory presentation of 'abstract labour' in *Capital*, *Volume 1* as both a '"suprasensible or social" *and* sensuously material' *substance*. Both Halpern and Marx, as Ngai contends, intentionally mobilise a 'catachrestic image' of abstract labour as a 'congealing substance' in order to emphasise 'the synthetic or *plasticising* action' of an abstraction like value, which, despite being a social relation of validation established in exchange, comes to 'palpably' shape 'the empirical world of collective activity to which it belongs and in which it acts'. In *Suspiria*, Douglas likewise employs a gimmicky special effect to 'allegorise' what Marx terms the 'ghostly' or 'phantom-like objectivity' [*gespenstige Gegenstandlichkeit*] of value, by manipulating outmoded analogue technology to create a blurry spectral image wherein colours escape their bodily containers. This 'comically bungled' looking effect is notably set in tension with a complex, variation-intensive script, whereby a digital algorithm creates a viewing experience of 'computer-driven endlessness' that evokes a feeling of the 'sublime'. In pitting this 'temporally unstable' and 'transient "special effect" against the infinity of the digital/automated machine', Douglas, as Ngai observes, deflates the seeming 'invulnerability of capitalist "value machines"', pointing, once again, to the gimmick 'as the aesthetic flipside of capitalist sublimity'.

There are moments in Ngai's impressively intricate and yet occasionally extravagant readings of artworks and literary texts when the analytical category of the gimmick disappears from view or is stretched beyond recognition, appearing as either an under- and over-performing heuristic device. In the book's concluding chapter, for instance, Ngai interprets Henry James's late fictions – whose elaborate narratives of coincidence regularly feature instances of 'occulted' domestic and service labour – as indirect indexes of the author's shift from 'writing longhand, silently and alone, to dictating to a hired typist' (the typist and type-writer both representing instances of labour-saving techniques), as well as 'the rise of an incipient service economy that would come to supersede manufacturing and industry in Great Britain and other wealth nations'. This contrived, if always engaging, reading of James's late narratives stands in contrast to an earlier chapter focusing on the Norwegian post-conceptual artist and photographer Torbjøn Rødland, whose kitschy yet enigmatically seductive photographs of people and objects serve to illustrate the gimmick's comprised form in a relatively straightforward manner. Despite the capacious and eclectic character of Ngai's study, there remains, moreover, a latent provincialism in the book's archive, which comprises artists and writers deriving exclusively from North-America and Europe, as well as Ngai's retention of 'postmodernism' as key periodising and critical category in the face of its critical displacement by the globalisation of the resurgent concept of modernity. For if the aesthetic judgement and form of the gimmick tells us something central about 'the basic laws of capitalist production and its abstractions as they come to saturate everyday life', it makes sense to ask in what ways 'capitalism's most successful aesthetic category' comes to be unevenly registered beyond the metropolitan centres of the capitalist world-system? Or does the judgement of the gimmick, like the phenomena of postmodernism before it, name a narrowly conceived Euro-American capitalist modernity exhausting itself?

Alex Fletcher

Normativity at the edge of reason

Cecile Malaspina, *An Epistemology of Noise* (London: Bloomsbury, 2018). 256pp., £90.00 hb., £28.99 pb., 978 1 35001 178 6 hb., 978 1 35014 176 6 pb.

In recent years noise seems to have become an interdisciplinary concept *par excellence*, apt to capture important dynamics at work whether in technological, scientific, social or aesthetic domains. But when economists, biologists, psychologists, and musicians speak of noise, are they all referring to the same thing? Cecile Malaspina takes this dispersion of the notion of noise as a starting point, accepting that, when removed from its mathematical formulation in information theory and spread into diverse disciplines, noise takes on a metaphorical ambiguity. Yet rather than eliminate this ambiguity, Malaspina sets out to account for it. The key problem in *An Epistemology of Noise* is not to identify the legitimate usage of the concept of noise, but rather to examine what happens when noise moves between disciplines, and what the 'noisiness' of this movement tells us about the conditions for interdisciplinary knowledge. Noise here is both an object (or many objects) of inquiry and a condition for that inquiry, and presents us with the problem of how knowledge can find its ground in these 'shifting sands'.

While not aiming to dispel the ambiguity that noise takes on when adapted for new fields, Malaspina does differentiate her overall theoretical perspective from the notion that has allowed much of this adaptation to take place: that is, is the 'negentropy' associated with cybernetics and Norbert Wiener, where noise is opposed to information. Negentropy, or the negation of entropy (the tendency towards disorder), describes the means by which machines or systems, as bearers of information, self-regulate. The interdisciplinary concept of noise is often posited in relation to such a notion of negentropy, with noise being what forms of organisation, 'from the organism to the ecosphere, from socio-political to economic relations, from networks to the idea of globalisation', fend off in their processes of self-regulation. Malaspina proposes that in the information theory of Claude Shannon we find something quite distinct from this uptake of Wiener's thought. In Shannon's work we find a profoundly counterintuitive proximity between information and noise, and *An Epistemology of Noise* follows the consequences of this counterintuitive formulation.

Part 1 of *An Epistemology of Noise* commits to the careful work of definition and distinction around the notions of information entropy, negentropy, and noise. A first disciplinary translation takes place when, aiming to define information, Shannon adopts Ludwig Boltzmann's mathematical formulation of physical entropy. It is not a direct adoption: Shannon subtracts from Boltzmann's formula the physical constant, in so doing increasing its ambiguity. The ontological arbitrariness that Shannon introduces thus makes this definition less constrained and more apt to adoption in other fields, and this constraint reduces further still when entropy is translated from a mathematical notion into a discursive one. This is already an instance of what Malaspina consistently highlights in the notion of noise: that an increase in noise, in ambiguity and uncertainty, serves as a condition for novelty. Noise comes to be associated with 'freedom of choice'.

By then defining information not in opposition to noise or entropy, but as itself 'information entropy', Shannon can be seen to face head-on a certain paradox of information. Information is associated with order – as for instance when the philosopher of information Luciano Floridi argues that information must be 'well-formed' – but in a purely ordered system nothing novel could take place, and so no 'new' information could be transmitted. In rejecting the intuitive association of information with order and certainty, and noise with disorder and uncertainty, Shannon avoids this paradox, but leaves his readers with the problem of dealing with a lack of clear distinction between what counts as information and what counts as noise.

This, for Malaspina, is to Shannon's great merit. Such ideas have further provenance in French philosophy – take, for example, Bergson's rethinking of the distinction between order and disorder – and Malaspina bolsters her examination of noise by turning to that tradition, with particular reference to the thought of Gilbert Simondon (whose *On the Modes of Existence of Technical Objects* she translated in 2017) and Georges Canguilhem. Simondon's notion of metastability is introduced, almost in passing, to show how noise within a system allows for the system to respond to a changing environment. Metastability, a term also used in Wiener's *Cybernetics*, names a state 'between entropic dispersion and structural iner-

tia', at the fuzzy border between noise and information, and so, despite receiving little further explication, the notion of metastability underlies much of the inquiry that follows its introduction. Simondon is also significant later, with his concept of transduction helping account for the translations that noise undergoes between fields. Transduction is a concept that Simondon uses to think across domains without reducing them to each other, and for Malaspina it is crucial that 'thinking in terms of noise differs from domain to domain' and that no 'universal key of conversion' will be easily found. Transduction thus provides for Malaspina the principle of transdisciplinary movement.

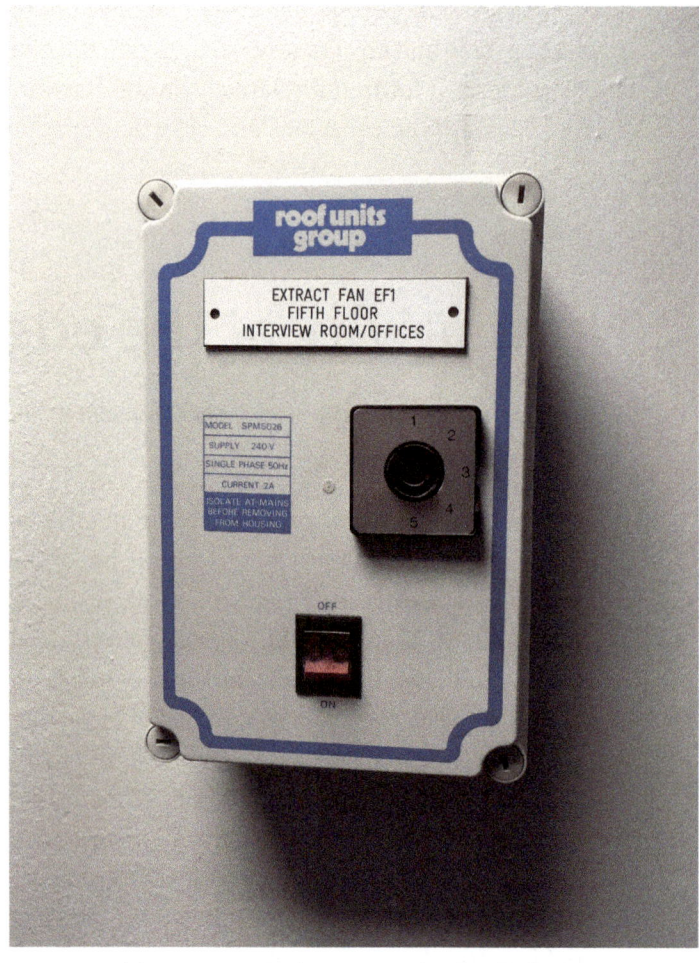

Arguably even more important is the short discussion of Canguilhem that closes the first part of the book. Foucault's now well-known summation of Canguilhem's philosophy, where error is said to be 'at the root of what makes human thought and its history', is taken by Malaspina to be key to understanding the varied conceptualisations of noise. It is here that the epistemological stakes of her project become clear. For Shannon information, formally speaking, is not about meaning, and on his terms the meaningfulness of a message is not the concern of information theory. What in a message is considered to be information and what noise is thus a decision that precedes, and is outside of, the process of transmission itself. As such, with regards to meaning, the distinction between information and noise is rarely ready-made. What Canguilhem brings into focus is how the relation between information and noise, or, in terms closer to Canguilhem, between reason and contingency, is, moreover, always a *normative* relation. Thought is said to involve 'the act of generating new norms', of refiguring the line between information and noise. In this act, reason opens the question of its own grounding: for Malaspina a key distinction here is between a philosophy that aims to provide foundations for certainty and a philosophy that shows the limits of established norms and produces systematic uncertainty, and in the thought of Shannon and Canguilhem she finds a basis for the latter approach.

As information is a normative category, noise is often presented as its abnormal, even immoral, outside. Part 2, 'Empirical Noise', examines in different fields and disciplines the drawing and redrawing of the distinction between information and noise. After the detailed conceptual explication of Part 1, Part 2 captures the expansive reach of the notion of noise, dealing with discourses of noise in finance, statistics, biology, physics, and more. Throughout the question of normativity remains prominent, as in the 'moral caveat' that is widely and diversely inserted into common definitions of information. In statistics, for example, 'the objective of maintaining stability of power through knowledge becomes a culturally determining factor for the definition of information and noise', while strategies of 'noise abatement' have drawn an intrinsically political line between acceptable social sounds and unacceptable social noise.

Yet in contrast to these distinctions by which noise is taken as something to suppress or eliminate, what emerges in the process of Malaspina's inquiry is a reinforcement of the notion that, following Shannon's formulations, noise is not an object to be identified and studied, but a relational figure. Addressing the links between the psychology of acoustic perception and the use of noise as a deterrent or even a weapon, Malaspina identifies instances when acoustic noise is clearly decoupled from information theory's conception of noise in the channel of communication: the meaning of the noise made by acoustic weapons is clear, as it is intended to threaten or to injure. But where noise continues to be found here is how it is received, not as an object perceived or cognised, but as the incapacitation of perception and cognition itself. The closing pages of Part 2 introduce, via the sound theorist Steve Goodman, practices of inaudible sound being used to subvert conscious perception and rational cogency. Whether deployed by artists, the defence industry, or mass media, inaudible or barely audible sound has been shown to be able distort the critical faculties of those subjected to it. Here noise becomes not only a normative problem in various fields, but a problem for thought itself.

This theme transitions into the third and final part of *An Epistemology of Noise*: 'The Mental State of Noise'. Yet while one might suppose that the concern here is going to be with the troubled condition of thought in an age of information overload, Malaspina adopts a quite different perspective. The starting point is a little-discussed 1986 article by the psychologist Steven Sands and the psychiatrist John Ratey, entitled 'The Concept of Noise'. In this article Sands and Ratey define the 'mental state of noise', as a condition of distress caused by a sense of crowding and confusion in response to stimuli that the subject fails to tolerate and organise. As Malaspina points out, Sands and Ratey's definition is implicitly in terms of a cybernetic sense of homeostasis, where the failure on the part of the self is a failure to self-regulate in relation to its environment. Noise here is, again, not an object of perception, but a disruption to perception, and thus at stake are 'not the noises we perceive, but the noise of cognition constituting itself, against the always looming crisis of its dissolution'. In describing this state Sands and Ratey will speak of the 'vicious whir of sensations' supposed of infant experience, and thus the mental state of noise is understood as a kind of regression.

Yet Malaspina finds in Sands and Ratey's account an ambivalence between the mental state of noise as an excessive openness and a healthy openness associated with both infant learning and the poet John Keats's notion of 'negative capability'. For Malaspina, negative capability supposes a more radical perspective than Sands and Ratey assume. Rather than only affirming a 'tame liberal motto of refraining from preconceptions', for Keats negative capability involves existential risk, a putting in jeopardy of one's stable identity in the name of artistic creation. Here the implicit cybernetic frame of Sands and Ratey's account is key: what is at hand with negative capability is not a question of a negentropy by which a system sustains itself in relation to its outside, which itself risks the 'catastrophic reaction' of shutting the self off from the outside, but a negation of negentropy, a step into 'the abyss of reason'.

This clearly distinguishes the project of *An Epistemology of Noise* from much of the recent work that has applied the cybernetic notion of negentropy beyond its original domain. In cybernetics information is said to counteract entropy 'in the service of an already constituted and correctly functioning entity', and at its limit, where the cybernetic account of man-made machines becomes a paradigm for social systems, this is linked to a logic of control as 'the idea of totalitarian domination without noise'. Just as calculating the level of contingency, or noise, in a mechanical system renders the system predictable, so this is supposed of social systems: we might picture here individuals as mere nodes in the circuits of an increasingly precisely controlled social system. Yet Malaspina highlights that such a high degree of control is only feasible when mathematical standards apply, and the application of a cybernetic model will be incomplete if it does not have an account of the *limits* of control, which, as Malaspina's transdisciplinary explorations show, are significant when working in discursive rather than mathematical terms. The adoption of notions of negentropy and control into the analysis of social systems may suppose that noise can be tamed far more than is the case.

Here Malaspina's emphasis on noise as 'freedom of choice' is key. The presence of noise ensures that a system cannot proceed mechanically, and that the opportunity of choosing between possibilities exists. The problem is not one of maintaining a system in the face of outside noise, but of facing up to the proximity and shifting line between information and noise that Shannon's definition of information as information entropy presents us with. In this light Malaspina can return again to Canguilhem for a crucial definition of normativity: normativity is to be understood as 'the individual's reassertion of his or her power to act, judge and decide, in other words, the power to generate new norms in answer to

life's contingent events'. What *An Epistemology of Noise* thus provides is a compelling instance of what Ian James has called 'the technique of thought', a concern with how reason constitutes its own grounds that James identifies as a key theme in recent French philosophy. While not denying that thought faces many mechanisms of control, at the core of Malaspina's project is a faith in reason to constitute new norms for living.

This places *An Epistemology of Noise* in an interesting position in relation to some other theoretical discourses on noise. Malaspina acknowledges that her entry point into the problem of noise was noise music and noise art, but sets aside direct engagement with scholarship in that area. What is distinctive in this scholarship is that noise is often not viewed as a problem, as it tends to be in other fields. For example, the editors of the 2012 collection *Reverberations: The Philosophy, Aesthetics and Politics of Noise* speak of 'the pleasures of transgression and subversion', and more generally the transgressive capacities of noise are celebrated by theorists including Greg Hainge, Paul Hegarty, and Jacques Attali. Malaspina's project, to an extent, goes along with this, aiming as it does to retrieve noise from 'the theoretical exile of negation into which it was thrown'.

Yet the logic of transgression behind this work has been subject to significant critique in scholarship on sound, with theorists including Eric Drott, Robin James, and Marie Thompson highlighting how, among other instances, Jacques Attali's fantastical yet widely influential account of music anticipating social change relies on attributing to music the logic of capitalism's self-transgression and self-transformation. *An Epistemology of Noise* is doubtlessly more subtle and measured in its dealing with the critical potential of noise than is this work, and moreover it suggests crucial questions for these champions of noise – where does the normative element lie if not in pure transgression? And where do we want it to lie? – but its own confrontation with 'the abyss of reason' requires a careful consideration of the limits of a logic of transgression. *An Epistemology of Noise* does not present any easy answers to these questions, but, in its series of asymptotic approaches to the shifting problem of noise, it makes clear their significance to any attempt to engender new forms of thought.

Iain Campbell

Cyborgs without organs

Legacy Russell, *Glitch Feminism* (London and New York: Verso, 2020), 192pp., £9.99 pb., 978 1 78663 266 1

In her endorsement of *Glitch Feminism: A Manifesto*, culture and media theorist McKenzie Wark locates its author Legacy Russell among those who are 'playing in the ruins' of 'the old empire of imperatives about both flesh and tech'. The book, she seems to warn, will walk you through the walls of an established theoretical tradition, all the while casting shade on its crumbling masonry.

And yet, while Russell's prose is as determined as any good manifesto's in containing the force of rupture its existence must imply, and while an entire chapter is committed to the glitch 'throwing shade', any takingdown of predecessors is minimal and gracious. Russell saves her word count for better things: for celebrations of radical art and injunctions to political creativity. But to adequately affirm her success in this project – which offers an alternative to decades of tortured Theory – I feel I must recall some of the empire of problems amidst which the book was born.

Like most who have located their intellectual innovations within a history of cyberfeminism (the site of many an imperative on flesh and tech both), Russell acknowledges early in her book an important, if ambivalent, relationship to the thought of Donna Haraway. *Glitch Feminism* mines internet-based artistic practice in arguing for the online space as a liberatory site of experimentation in 'glitching', or subverting, the binarily gendered body. Haraway, of course, remains best known for her 'Cyborg Manifesto', an essay that in 1985 responded to what the author had been tasked with identifying as the Reaganera's central challenges to socialist feminist politics. Her manifesto was a call to leftist feminists to reimagine themselves as political subjects by imaginatively reconceiving the boundaries of their bodies. As Russell phrases it in a reframing of de Beauvoir's old adage: '*One is not born, but rather becomes a body*'.

Haraway, observing how immiseration was being wrought differentially among feminised agents by the globalisation and de-industrialisation of capital, proposed that resistance to these new forms of damage demanded a new kind of political identity. Neither 'woman' nor 'proletarian', in her view, was adequate to capturing the complex and complexifying affinities of queer women or women of colour, not least those assembling computer chips in East Asia. Conjuring the image of the cyborg as imaginative aid, Haraway asked her readers to recognise all living organisms as necessarily hybrid, enveloping and smudging falsely circumscribed identities, just as the cyborg – both human and machine – necessarily dissolves the definitive boundaries of the 'natural' and the 'synthetic'. Hers was a vision of multiplicity and infinite permutation across the spectrum of the feminised and within each feminised subject, giving political agents an appreciation of difference around which, paradoxically, they might be better placed to collectivise.

The advent of the internet, however, invigorated among feminist artists, coders, gamers and writers inspired by Haraway a more literal idea of the political subject as both organism and machine. Cyberfeminism, a school of both theory and praxis, unified itself in 1997 when 38 of its proponents convene at Documenta X. While the shared manifesto they produced betrayed varying notions of cyberfeminism's definition, all sought to emphasise the necessary role of internet technology in feminist revolution. It was clear that information and communication technologies were not only developing in the mould of the human nervous system, but were also themselves effecting the kinds of alteration in the human field of perception that gave the figure of the cyborg vivid new meaning.

In redefining the cyborg simply as she who operates online, most cyberfeminisms of the '90s and early 2000s had effectively dispensed with Haraway's concern to sustain an account of difference, allowing the vision of emancipatory ends pinned on techno-optimism to license its divisive means. As cyberfeminist artist Faith Wilding pointed out, the net was '*not* a utopia of nongender', but rather an entity 'already socially inscribed with regard to bodies, sex, age, economics, social class and race'. And as Russell adds, summarising cyberfeminism's historical limitations, '*white women = producing white theory*

= *producing white cyberspace'*. Even as artists such as Wilding began to range further than the net, confronting other technological frontiers of feminist practice (notably that of biotechnology), the problem of reconciling difference with a unified feminist project endured. In 2021 it feels almost platitudinous to state that the absorption of 'technology' in untrammelled techno-capitalism has enhanced the latter's potential to redouble divisions between women along the lines of employment status and labour conditions. As technologies of exploitation flourish at a quickening pace, the degradation of some women's labour collides more horribly than that of others with the exploitation of their race, sexuality and class.

The practice of 'embracing technology' has never uniformly enthused the left. In 2015, Laboria Cuboniks' *Xenofeminist Manifesto* (XFM), which positioned its techno-accelerationist vision as 'the only true suspension of inequality', was lauded by many – not least among them Mark Fisher – for aspiring to break through the kind of unambitious melancholia that had stalled the turn of the millennium's cyberfeminist zeal. '[T]he machines are so alive', wrote Haraway, 'whereas the humans are so inert!', and in that sense XFM seemed to kick against the posture of leftist listlessness that redefines the 'Luddite' in the present. Its rhetoric scorned those who allowed essentialised, oppressed identities to limit the horizon of leftist struggle to 'survival' (rather than transformation). And yet, as Annie Goh has argued, XFM's explicitly 'rationalist' project of universalised feminism makes no new intervention to mitigate the costs of its hyperactive approach to those whom techno-capital most exploits. Indeed, what of those on the left to whom there remains no choice but to prioritise survival?

Russell opens her set of artist-led meditations by referencing E. Jane, who she affirms is not being hyberbolic in asserting, as 'a Black artist with multiple selves', that 'we are dying at a rapid pace'. 'Pushed to the margins', Russell agrees, 'we find ourselves as queer people, as people of colour, as femme-identifying people most vulnerable in weathering world conditions, ranging from climate change to plantation capitalism'. But while she is for this reason unable to gloss over the ways in which cybertechnologies serve to accelerate violent 'world conditions', her response is far from technophobic. As Russell sees it, for the specific 'we' that crests an intersection of gender and racial oppression, facing down architec-

tures of power requires, as an urgent prerequisite, finding 'techniques that provide space for ourselves' to do so. If reality happens (and power lies) online as well as 'away from the keyboard' (AFK), some of these spaces of cover and resistance will inevitably rest in cyberspace. The question of engaging with the online world while sustaining a critique of power thus becomes the motivating force behind Russell's signal concept.

Enter 'Glitch Feminism', an idea Russell conceived in 2012 that in the intervening years has blossomed with artists' use of it as creative material. Where Lucca Fraser of Laboria Cuboniks brashly insists that 'Yes', the master's tools can dismantle the master's house, Russell offers the more sophisticated suggestion that what institutions of power require may be not so much dismantling as 'strategic occupation'. Beginning with an understanding of gender as a disciplinary technology – a core cog within capitalist society's wheel, and the body as a weapon of that technology – giving form to 'an idea that has no form', Russell proposes the glitch as a means of taking that form and, through rupture, rendering it abstract once more. The technological glitch – a form of 'machinic anxiety' – serves in this sense as a portal of imagination, suggesting applications of error and strategic nonperformance in cyberspace to the violently normative world in which lives are lived AFK.

Recognising, as Foucault did, that power can be both restrictive (*potestas*) and productive (*potentia*), Russell targets the internet as a central site of both types, looking to the productive force of artistic representation online as the basis of art's more general *potentia* to offer modes of refusal. Summoning to her argument a panoply of philosophical men (Édouard Glissant, Gilbert Ryle, Timothy Morton, Henri Lefebvre, Jean-Luc Nancy...), Russell's theory of parts and wholes brings to their incomplete theories an alternative framework for imagining autonomous political participation in 'reality'. This framework is formed both by and for queer and female-identifying women of colour, and plots the sphere of agency as occurring dynamically both on and away from the keyboard.

Mobilising her own experiences of self-formation through artmaking, nightlife and internet living, Russell's emancipatory vision is animated by the work of an eclectic chorus of contemporary artists. As Deleuze, inspired by the Surrealists, saw in art the potential

Thomson & Craighead, *#screaming* (2020)

for advancing a relationship with technology radically detached from functionalism and organised efficiency, a process of becoming 'bodies without organs', these artists engage in the digital remix of what Russell calls 'corpo-realities', reforming these in opposition to techno-capital's rabid opportunism. Stretching the body's resonance to cosmic registers, these artists draw on the peculiar potential in the aesthetic to create new ways of imagining what the body can do beyond our calcified norms.

In the glittering land of the glitch, artist and drag queen Victoria Sin exposes the seams of gender-prep through hyperbolic re-performance both online and off, showcasing cracks in 'the gloss and gleam of capitalist consumption of gender as product'; Sondra Perry uses 3D graphics to highlight encrypted signifiers of lost Black traumas, manipulating technology's rhythms of repression and surveillance; Shawné Michaelain Holloway's 'cam girl' adventures tug at the lines between vulnerable selves and impenetrable digital skins; American Artist poses a challenge to search engine coloniality; and POWRPLANT attempts to trailblaze dissolution and re-distribution in digital education. Through each artistic exposition, Russell demonstrates that digital activity can neither be unlinked from the world of AFK, nor dismissed as somehow 'immaterial'. Her frames of reference for illustrating this range from Zach Blas's 'collective masks', which effectively undermine the requirements of biometric data gathering, to Simone C. Niquille's digital avatar modelling, which intervenes in the forensic ambitions constructed by the defence in the trial of George Zimmerman.

Such feats of critical artmaking are of course far from devoid of their own internal scepticisms. Holloway's 'fantasy-fetish' underscores, as Russell puts it, 'the implausibility of ever being able to fully dictate or refuse how one's body can and cannot be digested through a digital platform'. Among theorists of contemporary biopower, progressively accustomed to the problem of resistance from within the neoliberal frame, there emerges a growing consensus that the absorption of the psychic self in a power apparatus that encourages auto-oppression obviates any possibility of resistance on the level of corporeal gesture. The subject, immersed in the institutional apparatus that seeks to subject them, now becomes indistinguishable from the institution itself. Russell is not blind to the truth in this negative corpo-reality.

What *Glitch Feminism* offers, however, is a commitment to exploring where channels of resistance might still be forced open. While it is central to Russell's argument that, the machine being 'the material through which we process our bodily experience', bodies are 'as much computational as they are flesh', she refuses to accept this as cause for surrender to certain malign strains of computational power. 'We are standing inside the machine', she writes, and every day we make a choice whether or not to rob ourselves'. Similarly, while acknowledging that it becomes difficult to see the artificiality of gender when submerged within its omnipresent and overwhelming logic, Russell sustains an account of gender as not only as a tired fantasy, but one whose relinquishment will amount to an escape from manifold modes of regulation, management, division of labour, exchange of value and control.

Glitch Feminism, while an invocation of the 'cosmic', is all about 'finding one's range'. As such, it is vitally aware of its own boundaries and limitations. Neither a blueprint for overthrowing global capitalism, nor a set of infrastructure-level demands (in the vein of the Cyborg Manifesto's call for the unionisation of office workers), it rather renews the serious call for new forms of subjectivity that white cyberfeminisms dropped. This is not an alternative to proposing new forms of (secure, de-centralised) digital infrastructure, but rather a prerequisite for such projects. Proceeding from the self-

constructive power of her earliest chatroom handle, Russell's interest is in nascent performances of selves – gestures of digital self-determination – as necessary forms of world-building. Through her text she enters, like the early-twentieth-century artist of Saidiya Hartman's *Wayward Lives, Beautiful Experiments* (2019), 'the intensity of creating and inhabiting a world with others, a domain of collective bodies, kinaesthetic experience and gestural language'.

In the process of becoming political subjects who enact the requisite 'failure to function within the confines of a society that fails us', the glitched bring into being the kinds of subjectivity that are necessary conditions of the largest anti-capitalist visions – moves towards transforming partially shared agendas such that political unity on the left might one day be more than fantasy or lie. While a latter-day Haraway, to the disappointment of her followers, ultimately draws from intersectionality only a deepening sense of cyclical, inescapable domination, Russell holds liberation on her horizon. Her achievement amounts to what Toni Cade Bambara once affirmed as the very 'task of the artist': if the task is determined by the status and process and agenda of the community that [the artist] already serves', the task for the artist whose community's survival depends upon political change is 'to make the revolution irresistible'.

Amber Husain

All that Hegel allows

Robert Pippin, *Filmed Thought: Cinema as Reflective Form* (Chicago: University of Chicago Press, 2019). 312pp., £79.00 hb., £28.00 pb., 978 022667 1 956 hb., 978 022667 2 007 pb.

The course of the relationship between philosophy and film studies never did run smooth. The encounter of these two disciplines, while producing both influential and exciting work, has often been beset by mistrust and misapprehension, ruptures, rejections and partings of ways. For all the promising developments made by the likes of Gilles Deleuze, Alexander Kluge, Miriam Hansen, and others, mutual mistrust remains. In recent years, much of the work attempting to rekindle this interdisciplinary flame has been markedly political, with thinkers

like Jacques Rancière, Alain Badiou and, perhaps most visibly, Slavoj Žižek, exploring cinema as a path to ideological critique: reflecting on the social relations of the present and the modes of being which arise from them.

Beyond his extensive work on Hegel, Nietzsche and the problem of modernity, cinema has remained one of the focal points of Robert Pippin's critical attention across the last decade, during which time he has created a body of work that engages with the possibility of staging a productive encounter between the two disciplines as a route to reflecting on, and changing, human self-understanding. This has led him to publish books on the American Western, *Fatalism in American Film Noir*, and Hitchcock's *Vertigo*. The most recent addition to this body of work, *Filmed Thought: Cinema as Reflective Form*, continues this line of inquiry at a more general philosophical level than his previous books, taking the question of what kind of philosophical reflection cinema makes possible as the primary object of attention. Specifically: the book asks to what extent cinema can be considered a mode of expression capable of the 'non-empirical exploration of meaning and value'.

Pippin's corpus is drawn largely from canonical and mainstream works of US film: two more Hitchcock films, two films by Nicholas Ray, Terence Malick's *The Thin Red Line* and Roman Polanski's *Chinatown*. There is, in addition, an essay on Pedro Almodóvar's *Talk to Her* and one examining the depiction of action in the work of the Dardenne brothers. The essays themselves comprise a set of discrete and intricate close readings, and as such resist summary. There are however a number of common threads which guide these readings.

Pippin, as one might expect, describes his approach to cinema as broadly Hegelian, specifically: 'Hegel on the link between self-knowledge, agency and knowledge of others'. The epistemological preoccupation evidences Pippin's position as an analytic Hegelian of a neo-Kantian/non-metaphysical persuasion. Pippin's overarching characterisation of film's potential is its ability to present a challenge to what he considers a fundamental principle of Hegelian thought, that: 'there is nothing in principle unknowable, and that the logic of the knowable can be determined'.

Throughout *Filmed Thought*, Pippin's most common touchstone in the film-philosophy canon is Stanley Cavell. Pippin credits Cavell with providing a useful terminology for expressing the Hegelian notion of subjectivity, and, more specifically, the idea that: 'that what it is to know oneself as a subject is wrongly conceived at the outset if understood as some sort of particularly intimate relation between a thinker or agent and itself'. Instead, Cavell argues, any understanding of the subjectivity of the other requires a kind of *acknowledgement*: its dimension is not merely cognitive but ethical. The claims human beings make on one another, and the responses to those claims engendered in experience, *are* the substantive matter of our knowledge of others.

At the core of Pippin's mode of reading is what, in *The Philosophical Hitchcock*, he terms the 'struggle for mutual interpretability'. This struggle is the one into which human beings are thrust in their relations with one another in trying to know and be known. Part of a film's philosophical work, if it can be said to have any, is its capacity for giving expression to the complexity of this interpretive struggle, plagued by social convention and pretence, anxieties about betrayal and concealment: the tendency toward unknowingness inherent in human intersubjective relationships. The immanent mechanisms of filmic depiction by which film explores the struggle for interpretability, and the manner by which it reveals the criteria underlying it, is the problematic which moves through all the essays of *Filmed Thought*. It is through this struggle that the reflective capacity of cinema is articulated.

Pippin shares with Cavell a resistance toward over-theorisation when analysing works of cinema. As a result, much of the philosophical work is left 'behind-the-scenes' in allusions and footnotes, making *Filmed Thought* both analytically assured and compulsively readable. The essay on Ray's *In a Lonely Place* is perhaps the most explicitly theoretical in the book and is where Pippin most clearly details his affinity with Cavell. Essential to this is the latter's concept of scepticism. Pippin outlines Cavell's delineation of 'passive' and 'active' scepticism: active being the question of the other, of how one can know the true nature of another's inner life, the former, conversely, being the anxiety of 'whether *I am ever truly known* ("as I really am") by an other.' Re-deploying Cavell's arguments under the aegis of the struggle for interpretability, Pippin draws out the deep narrative complexities of Ray's film and the love between Humphrey Bogart's Dix Steele and Gloria Grahame's Laurel Gray. Pippin's reading is both effective and affecting. Most impressive is the manner in which the meta-filmic aspects of the films are drawn into the operative movement of the works themselves. For Pippin, these elements of 'self-awareness' are never devices of fixity, never *merely* ironising the film's narrative content or de-realising its emotive depth, but an integral part of the way those films complicate and develop the question of human relations. In the case of *In a Lonely Place* this includes Ray's deliberate utilisation of Bogart's 'type' in setting up and confounding audience expectations, and the staging of the murder re-enactment (by a Hollywood screenwriter no less) as a demonstration of audience vulnerability to the conventions of Hollywood and hasty interpretation; conventions which Dix and Laurel are forever contesting, overturning and lapsing back into.

In the early essay on *Rear Window*, Pippin's reflective unfolding entails a convincing re-casting of the stereotypical reading of *Rear Window* as a portrayal of the sinful condition of the cinema viewer as, rather, a distinction between two kinds of viewing: one merely spectatorial, voyeuristic, the other involved, engaged. Here the question of scepticism resurfaces: the first, disengaged, mode of reading, which views the world merely as a set of impressions to be tested, can only lead to futility and cynicism. It leaves the viewer desperate for a definitive truth in a world where any possible proof can always be discounted. The contestation takes a more socio-political turn in Pippin's examination of Douglas Sirk's *All That Heaven Allows*, which focuses on how the film constructs 'a politics of American emotional life' around the two lovers and the multilayered irony of melodrama. The two also become stand-ins of two divergent visions of the American dream: Connecticut white picket bourgeois suburbia and unreconstructed Thoreauvian primitivism. Pippin impressively draws out from this a demonstration of how, in Sirk's hands, the very self-narration of America, its deepest understanding of itself, becomes a form of melodrama.

Pippin is keen to avoid any immanentist/contextualist dualism in his mode of reading, asserting that an immanent analysis of film's reflective capacities can illuminate the mechanisms by which the films thematise socio-historical issues, but it is in these moments that the weaker elements of *Filmed Thought* emerge. The analysis of class in *All That Heaven Allows* is limited, staying merely within a question of authenticity and a liberal sociological conception of class as opposed to a structural relational concept of social being. More interesting though are the examples where the immanent depiction of the socio-historical forces within the film might present a challenge to the reflective Hegelian method itself. This is most evident in the case of *Chinatown*.

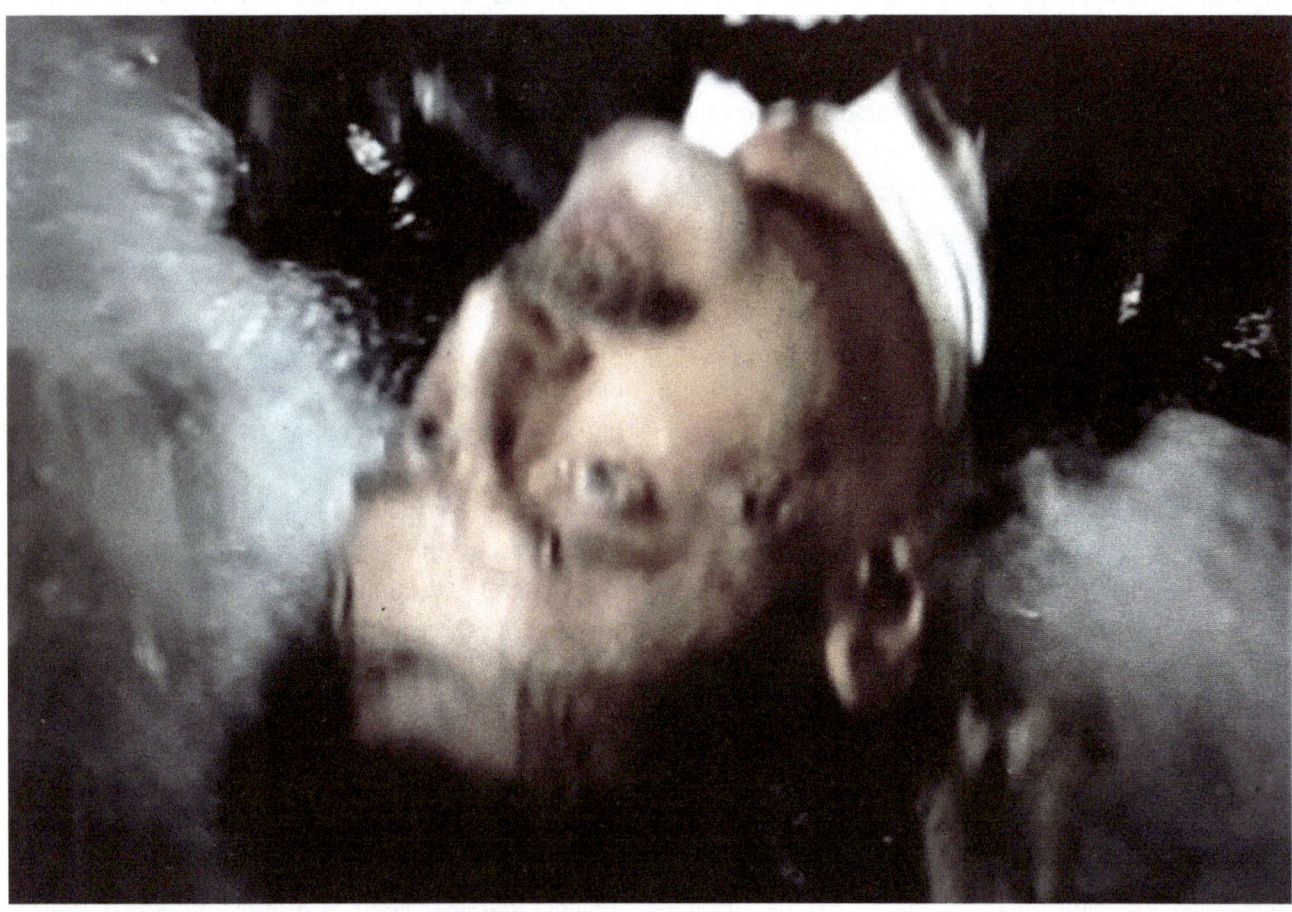

In his analysis of the unsettling mood pervading *Chinatown*, Pippin unpicks the ways the idea of 'Chinatown' casts its shadow across the film, not merely as a specific place within LA, a confusing web of lawlessness where one has to do 'as little as possible', but as a condition of existence, a word for the ominous and threatening atmosphere of a life gone wrong. Here Pippin draws on Adorno's preface to *Minima Moralia* and the capitalist instantiation of a life that, in some sense, cannot be lived. However, one might argue that Pippin fails to fully accord this incoherence the 'dignity of its notion'. *Chinatown* depicts the ruin of its own world, certainly, but this incoherence, effected by the dissolutive power of the subsumptive accumulatory logic of capital, potentially erodes the possibility for reflection itself. To return to the terminology of viewing in *Rear Window*, the question *Chinatown* poses through this contaminating incoherence is the way in which the historical social relation of capital deforms the reflective, active relation to the world back towards the spectatorial, towards futility.

The ominous collapsing mood of *Chinatown* is acted out at the level of narrative structure, depiction and at the level of genre. It is a film which dissolves the noir genre from within. From Jack Nicholson's Jake Gittes and his bewilderment at the case presented to him and the deliberate narrative incoherence, to the ludicrous cut nose and the preponderance of bright, burning daylight. Gittes, for his part, attempts to instantiate a noir, trying to engage with Evelyn and have a relationship, but is forced back into clumsy detection and proofs, even typecasting Evelyn as a typical *femme fatale*. *Chinatown* immanently, through the very mechanisms of noir, forges a world where noir is no longer possible. Inimical in this regard is the infamous tide pool which is the site of the murder of Hollis Mulwray. Pippin includes this as part of his reading of the film's depiction of life becoming false, a place where 'the source of life now...is the place of death'. However, such inversions of symbolic coding would leave us still in the domain of noir. Instead, what is most important about the tide pool is its *material composition*: that it is tidal and therefore cannot be leveraged into agricultural profit. The point then is not a question of life, death, or life become death, but rather the capacity of the historical materials to elicit an erasure of the possible meaning of the distinction.

The figure who could and, in the ordinary course of things, should shed some light on all this confusion and doom is Noah Cross, the 'villain' of the film (though such a term seems decidedly irrelevant here). However, the motives for his criminal acts are equally incoherent. The reason he gives for his actions, like accumulation given voice, is simply 'the future'. This future is the force that leaves several people dead, erodes familial bonds and cheats people from their land. Pippin is right in identifying the simplistic nihilism of Cross's 'most people never have to face the fact that at the right time in the right place, they're capable of anything' speech, but he goes on to say that such an emptiness becomes the 'point of view' of the film when the reality is more dispiriting. The film depicts a place where something like the reverse is true: where people constantly have to face the fact that, at the right time in the right place, they are incapable of doing anything. The 'Chinatown' which haunts the characters' minds is a kind of spectre of a universal idea of exteriority, of a place of lawlessness and confusion, a fragment of a past when such a geographical and moral distinction could still be made. Evelyn's denial of the term 'rape' in reference to her relationship with her father, would thereby not necessarily imply an element of complicity, or even the internalised guilt of a traumatic condition, but, rather, that for Cross the term rape has no meaning. Just as there is no longer any identifiable Chinatown, there is no longer any rape or even the incest taboo, there is only 'the future'. The possibility of relating to the world has been swept up by the subsumptive thirst of accumulation. All we can do is watch.

Filmed Thought is an important contribution to film-philosophy that attests to the difficult relationship between the two disciplines. Indeed it puts the difficulty of relationships at the centre of its analysis. Cinema here is not a tool for escapism or empty voyeurism, but reflects and *works* at forcing a confrontation with the complex problem of inter-subjective reality. Perhaps this reflective mode of reading could be 'stood on its head' by examining how the dynamics of socio-historical relations work in tension with the struggle for interpretability, how social forms pervert our impulse to be understood, turning us back towards escapism and spectacle.

Daniel Fraser

Whose law is it anyway?

Nadine El-Enany, *(B)ordering Britain: Law, Race and Empire* (Manchester: Manchester University Press, 2019). 312pp., £20.00 hb., 978 1 52614 542 0

On the 11th August 2020, in the midst of a tabloid maelstrom around people travelling from Calais to Dover in small boats, the UK Home Office released a statement that departed from their usual bureaucratic evasiveness: 'We want to see migrants who have illegally and dangerously crossed the Channel returned to mainland Europe. While we are unable to comment on ongoing legal proceedings, it is the case that the current legal framework is often abused by activist lawyers to frustrate the government's attempts in this regard.' The phrase 'activist lawyers' caused a ripple in certain legal circles, where the tacit rules of the game preclude such open criticism between the government, civil service and legal profession. The Tories, so keen to position themselves as the party of 'law and order', were framing certain laws, and lawyers, as somehow of the 'the left'. A few days later it emerged that Home Secretary Priti Patel had told a meeting of Conservative MPs that she was planning to fix the 'broken' asylum system with laws that would 'send the left into meltdown', complaining again about 'judicial activism' where laws were 'exploited by leftie Labour-supporting lawyers.'

The response from NGOs and legal firms to this framing of 'illegal crossings' was to use the law to push back, pointing out that such a phrasing is a legal misnomer, as the current asylum and immigration system has definitive protections for those who make such journeys to Britain. Many argued that it was in fact the Home Office's attempt to remove people at speed, during a pandemic that many felt the 'crisis' in the Channel was being constructed to obscure, that was breaking laws and regulations. While the Home Secretary made clear her ambitions to change the existing legal structure, the 'lefties' she wanted to send into 'meltdown' turned back to those very laws. The picture is the same at a far more everyday level, as campaigners, NGOs and legal firms working with people in the system utilise an ever-narrowing set of asylum and immigration criteria to try and justify individual claims for humanitarian protection, refugee status and wider citizenship. While many mount open criticisms of the provisions within such legislation, this most often manifests in reactive moves against particular government measures, rather than attempts to unpack the wider asylum and immigration system itself. Through all these contestations, and attempts to accuse or reclaim a sense of the lawyer as 'activist', the left position around immigration law often remains unclear. Just as worryingly, such debates seem to obscure the experiences of those actually crossing into Britain, and the histories that underpin this.

As such, Nadine El-Enany's *(B)ordering Britain* could hardly be more timely. That rare thing, an academic monograph that has quickly become a word-of-mouth sensation, passed around reading groups and campaigning organisations well outside the academy, the book is a brilliant exposition of British immigration law's role in a violent system of racial and colonial exclusion. At its core, *(B)ordering Britain* argues for a profound shift in how we consider what and who constitutes Britain, offering what El-Enany calls a 'counter-pedagogy' to that of law, framed in terms of racial justice and a reckoning with Britain's colonial past and present. The book begins with an invitation to the 'racialised others' who have been denied access to Britain's concentration of colonial wealth:

> Law's lesson is that some people are entitled to space, presence, resources and opportunities and others are not. Immigration law in particular teaches white British people that Britain and everything within it is rightfully theirs. 'Others' are here as their guests. Yet Britain would not be the wealthy, plentiful place that it is without its colonial history. We should not wait for the law to rule on our entitlement to colonial spoils. Even when we are granted access, we are not seen as belonging in Britain. And yet a Britain understood as the spoils of empire already belongs to us.

El-Enany sets up her audience for the book in such a way because *(B)ordering Britain* fundamentally speaks to those who, in the famous phrasing often attributed to Ambalavaner Sivanandan, might say, 'we are here because you were there'. While readers from across the social sciences, history and law will gain much from reading *(B)ordering Britain,* it is with those who have been partially and violently interpolated by the colonial project of Empire that El-Enany anchors the book.

(B)ordering Britain's cover – a picture of the British Isles without Ireland, floating in white space – speaks to one of the book's central questions: 'can we imagine Britain without its colonies?' Clearly, argues El-Enany, we cannot and should not. While these islands have become the locus for a centrifugal regime of colonial extraction that pooled 'resources, healthcare, welfare, security and opportunities, all of which can be understood as modern-day manifestations of stolen colonial possessions', it is only a pervasive colonial amnesia that allows people to imagine Britain as somehow separate from such processes.

(B)ordering Britain thus positions the country as a repository of colonial wealth, 'a young nation state, but an old imperial power', that has established its shifting national boundaries and access to these resources through historical and deeply racialised categorisations of 'subject', 'citizen' and 'refugee'. El-Enany invites the reader to reconsider the borders of Britain in a temporal and spatial sense, but also through analogy to those normatively white settler-colonies that are less quickly scrubbed from British history. Drawing on how a range of scholars of indigeneity in the contexts of Canada, Australia and the US have attempted to reckon with the legacies of violent settler colonialism, El-Enany argues that Britain itself should be contested in similar ways, for instance in a rejection of white supremacist regimes of legal status recognition. As she explains, 'while there are important and complex historical differences between settler and non-settler colonial contexts, British immigration law is part of a colonial legal system' that creates similarly 'colonised subjects' who are forced to engage in limited processes of legal recognition that tacitly reinforce the colonial state. Such comparisons, along with the notion of a 'neocolonial' present, could become flattening in a less deft analysis, reducing different contexts and historical moments to a blurry similarity – but situated within El-Enany's counter pedagogical project they productively evoke the shared if distinct threads which have upheld the British state *as* a colonial project throughout its history.

With this theoretical structure in place, the main bulk of *(B)ordering Britain* works as a sweeping counter-history of immigration law. El-Enany goes as far back as the 1705 Aliens Act and 1707 Act of Union to consider Britain as a formatively colonial enterprise, before examining how considerations around preserving the movement of 'free white men' and Britain's dwindling Empire influenced the establishment of the foundational Aliens Act of 1905 and British Nationality Act of 1948. While the latter is often presented as a generous act of inclusion, or economically motivated post-war push to fill gaps in the labour market, El-Enany argues that it was predominately an attempt 'hold together what remained of the British Empire and the Commonwealth' and to maintain 'white British supremacy', in the face of countries like Canada putting in place their own citizenry frameworks, which were seen as a threat to the primacy of the 'British Subject'. The subsequent arrival of racialised members of the new category of 'Citizen of the United Kingdom and Colonies', including those on the HMS Windrush, was treated as an unexpected and unwelcome effect by the majority of those in government. As racist agitation around these arrivals mounted, legislators moved from the officially 'race neutral' notion of equity in the eyes of the Empire's 'motherland', to more explicit protections of whiteness. The 1971 Immigration Act, argues El-Enany, 'made whiteness intrinsic to British identity' through a patrilineal clause – which meant that 'only patrials, those born in Britain or with a parent born in Britain, had a right of abode, and therefore a right of entry and stay in Britain.' At this time, El-Enany points out, despite decades of colonial rhetoric of 'inclusion', those eligible for the patrilineal clause were 98% white, ensuring the exclusion of racialised colonial subjects. It is then only with the 1981 British Nationality Act that Britain's 'post-colonial' separation from its colonies is formally enacted in law, with the first distinct legal conception of British citizenry, no longer automatically granted to those born on British soil. El-Enany goes on to critique how legal frameworks of asylum and refugee provision then moved to position Britain as a magically wealthy and benevolent host to 'spontaneous' arrivals from countries that had formed a part of the British colonial polity for decades.

Underpinning El-Enany's analysis are a range of insights from critical race theory and colonial studies, with a focus on 'racial capitalism', whereby migrants are 'shunted into precarious labour market conditions or excluded from the market entirely' through a system of racialising differentiation and exclusion. El-Enany is clear that this manifests in acute material forms, arguing that immigration law is 'racialising violence' in itself, drawing on Ruth Wilson Gilmore's definition of racism to argue that, 'inside Britain's borders, the racialised poor are differentially yet systematically vulnerable to being marginalised, controlled, policed, deported and killed.' Such a seemingly materialist approach, with its focus on resources, exploitation, and extraction, could lend itself to an exploration of reparations. Yet, while El-Enany does speak at various points through the book about 'redistributive and reparative justice', her focus is more on the conceptive shifts of her 'counter-pedagogic' project. Partly this must be down to scope – *(B)ordering Britain* is an expansive and ambitious piece of work and it would be wrong to begrudge El-Enany for not going wading into the lengthy debates around reparations – but the book is also clear about the importance of a 'radically altered subjectivity in the Fanonian sense of what people desire, consider themselves as entitled to and understand themselves to be.' This implies a question of

emphasis: can subjectivity be altered in advance of material redistribution? How might anti-racist movement address both the discourse of entitlement, and material inequalities on the ground? El-Enany's reading of this problem leads her to a cautious celebration of 'irregularised migration' as 'radical, anti-colonial' resistance and reparation in itself – rejecting the assimilationist frameworks of legal recognition in favour of a reclamation of stolen wealth. While critics may argue such an approach risks exposing migrants to the very violence El-Enany vividly depicts, her argument speaks to a long history of critical self-organisation amongst people in the asylum and immigration system, many of whom balance a range of tactics including strategic narratives of colonial entanglement, practical 'irregularised' support networks and ways of moving, and attempts at legal recognition where necessary. El-Enany is not arguing against the strategic utility of the legal recognition, rather that it can be 'counterproductive', diminishing movements for migrant justice when it becomes the sole focus. While 'activist' lawyers may do great individual casework, a left reliance on Immigration Law, so clearly built through the scaffolding of colonialism and violent exclusion, is a dangerous cul-de-sac.

El-Enany partly focuses on the reinforcing ways law and 'common sense' visions of collective entitlement overlap because this has been such a key feature of right-wing nationalism in the decades since 1971. Politicians ranging from Jack Straw to Priti Patel know the power of ensuring a racialised sense of entitlement to Britain's resources amongst key parts of the populace, regardless of how narrowly such resources may actually be distributed. This is often interwoven with a tacit and partial understanding of legal frameworks, for instance with the EU's Dublin Regulations, which allows countries like Britain to send people back to peripheral EU countries if they were fingerprinted for asylum there en route. Such laws, while materially harmful for those moving through 'fortress Europe' when drawn on by the state, also buttress an opaque racist sense of 'illegal' migration on the ground. Despite the regulations' complexity (involving shifting time-frames and varying legal procedures), and relative newness (the current iteration only came into place in 2013) countless tabloid comments sections and vox-pops are now full of complaints around how 'genuine' asylum seekers would claim in the 'first safe country' they passed through – as the legal and everyday blur into one another. El-Enany demonstrates how 'street and state racial terror are thus mutually reinforcing', prefiguring how the Covid-19 pandemic has seen far right groups increasingly positioning themselves in Britain as an auxiliary police and border control force, protecting colonial statues, patrolling the English Channel, and attacking those they deem 'illegal'. It remains to be seen how this may mutate in the aftermath of Britain's departure from the EU, but specific policies like the Dublin Regulations will presumably be re-drawn, creating heightened contexts for racist violence on the ground, but also room for anti-racist counter-arguments that must avoid a romanticisation of EU law.

In a wider sense, Theresa May's Hostile Environment policies were an extension of the way that British governments have repeatedly used vague and shifting immigration controls as a tool to encourage a sense of 'good' citizenry as predicated on the everyday policing of borders, in ways that go far beyond the actual terms of legislation. As the recent narratives around 'activist lawyers' prove, the government is well aware that law is a contingent and shifting thing, though it operates through a pretence of fixity, with the effects of new legislation (of which there will be plenty by the start of 2021) percolating through people's everyday lives, as much as through the grand halls of law. Contesting such moves through the domain of immigration legislation alone will only allow the state to continue to position itself as both arbiter and moral critic of an ahistorical 'law', that, when it comes to force, gunboats and border guards, it will always control. While recent 'left' push-backs to the unending so-called 'migrant crisis', have been to call for more safe legal migration routes, a return to 'free movement' (for some) within the EU, or for variants of an exclusionary 'civic nationalism' – the need for a far more ambitious, anti-racist, internationalist and critical approach is clear. *(B)ordering Britain* is a vital building block for a such a project, demonstrating how any vision of a truly 'post' colonial future must reckon with the violence, exclusion and extraction that has sustained the British state since its inception.

Joel White

The sociality of theory

Fadi A. Bardawil, *Revolution and Disenchantment: Arab Marxism and the Binds of Emancipation* (Durham: Duke University Press, 2020). 280pp., £83.00 hb., £21.99 pb., 978 1 47800 616 9 hb., 978 1 47800 675 6 pb.

A Flood in Baath Country, the 2003 documentary by Syrian filmmaker Omar Amiralay, opens with a stark confession on the director's behalf. His career had begun in the early 1970s with a panegyric to the Baathist project of modernisation glorifying the construction of the Tabqa Dam on the Euphrates, near the northern Syrian city of Raqqa. Revisiting his directorial debut, Amiralay assumes personal responsibility for echoing the state's once alluring rhetoric of progress: 'I blame myself for what I did', he reflects forty years later. This acts as the premise for his return to the towns and villages neighbouring the dam, half of which – in a poignant allegory for the history of Syria under the Assad dynasty – now languish underwater due to the deliberate flooding caused by its construction. Far from idiosyncratic, Amiralay's self-critique chimes with the dominant sentiments of those Arab intellectuals, militants and artists whose political coming of age intersected with the high tide of postcolonial state-socialism of the 1950s and 60s.

Whilst the director might have sought atonement for his self-avowed complicity in state violence, the organisational legacy of democratic centralism, paired with a lingering theoretical economism, were the object of no less remorse from members of more outwardly oppositional groups in Syria, Egypt and Lebanon, who began processing their failure to deliver on the promise of postcolonial emancipation at the start of the 1990s. The recently translated memoirs of the Egyptian Marxist feminist Arwa Salih are but the most recent example of this retrospective clairvoyance and anguish, rendered all the more painful if read against the backdrop of the brutal reaction that swept Syria and Egypt in the second half of the last decade. Inaugurated by successive military defeats at the hands of both Israel and ascendant Syrian proxies, rather than through direct pressure by the repressive state apparatuses of neighbouring states, the demise of the Lebanese left, which began in the early 1980s, generated a similar affect of introspection among the ranks of its former conscripts.

Given the ubiquity of these tropes of defeat and self-criticism, it would be tempting to read Fadi Bardawil's recent work, *Revolution and Disenchantment: Arab Marxism and the Binds of Emancipation*, as another episode of this transnational story of radicalisation, militancy, defeat and despondence. But the life and work of the young cadres that formed the group *Lubnan Ishtiraki* (Socialist Lebanon) in the mid-1960s is atypical of the trajectory of left-militants in this period, and whilst the political present in which their work is revisited – in Lebanon, at least – teeters between revolutionary openings and the intractability of recent decades, the unprecedented popular uprising of the past year cannot but lend a renewed urgency to the collective's theoretical output.

At the core of the book lies a series of interviews with members of what Bardawil terms the Lebanese New Left, figures such as Waddah Charara, Fawwaz Traboulsi and Ahmad Baydoun, better known today as accomplished scholars and public intellectuals. Their upbringing was marked by parallel experiences growing up in and around Beirut during the 1950s, the aftermath of the *nakba* of 1948 having a particular effect on those, such as Charara and Baydoun, whose families hailed from southern villages with ties to Galilee and the northern Palestinian ports of Haifa and Acre. As students in Britain and France, Traboulsi and Charara worked with clandestine networks of Arab nationalist party officials, émigrés and exiles (the well-known *Réseau Janson* in France, for instance) co-ordinating support from the metropole to popular fronts in Algeria and Yemen. Almost all of the members of Socialist Lebanon were initially affiliated with the Ba'ath Party, but encounters with Marx, another defining feature of their experiences abroad, armed them for their return to Lebanon in the early 1960s, whereupon they identified and critiqued the party's opacity over the issue of private property.

The politics of nationalism were increasingly tainted by a slanted emphasis on independence from foreign domination at the expense of meaningful social change locally, but defection to the Lebanese Communist Party (LCP) was not so straightforward for the rebellious young militants. Beholden as it was to Stalinist evolutionism, the LCP's insistence on the historic role of the bourgeoisie in laying the foundations for communist revolution represented the very denial of the autonomy of the working class which, as Bardawil explains, had exposed nationalism as an 'instrument of rule', rather than a 'tool for revolution'. It was this critical insight that brought Socialist Lebanon together.

Its best expression was found in their collectively penned *Introduction to Reading the Communist Manifesto* (1969); a '*retour aux sources*' in which the sphere of the political is endowed with the ability to develop the forces of production, authorising a politics of immediacy in which workers would no longer be condemned to wait for 'correct conditions' to seize power. The text also articulated the group's commitment to a dual process of translation; that of an increasingly eclectic corpus of theory into Arabic – Gramsci, Mao, Bourdieu; essays from the *New Left Review* and *Le Monde Diplomatique* – but also the conceptual formulations necessary to reanimate the corpse of Marx from the stifling political alignments of the Arab communist parties.

By the mid-1960s, Socialist Lebanon had crystallised around a broader group of disaffected radicals who published regular bulletins and pamphlets critiquing the theoretical fallacies of the LCP and the excesses of the increasingly powerful Arab regimes in equal measure. Writing in 1966, the group observed that 'the rule of the Ba'ath in Syria is the rule of the rural segment of the petite bourgeoisie that appropriates surplus production through the army and the state apparatus', shifting analytical priority to the Arab regimes' military-bureaucratic ruling classes. This did not only allow Socialist Lebanon to expose the ways the socialist revolutions of Egypt and Syria reproduced relations of exploitation they claimed to be subverting; it also broke with the dominant left discourse of national independence, which, articulated in isolation from broader economic and social demands, only legitimated the regimes' revolutionary posturing.

Indeed, this ability to ground anti-imperialism in a consistent analysis of local configurations of power is what Bardawil points to as the most instructive aspect of Socialist Lebanon's collective *oeuvre*. The group's penchant for immanent critique is posited as part of a 'minoritarian tradition' in need of recovery in the wake of the revolutions of 2011, referred to by Bardawil as a similar (if far more generalised) moment of clarity, in which the primary object of political critique was no longer an abstracted imperial metropole but the local, authoritarian vassal.

With Lebanon playing an increasingly prominent role as a front in the Palestinian Revolution at the turn of the 1970s, Waddah Charara began a gradual withdrawal from quotidian political struggle, in stark contrast to many of his comrades, who played leading roles in integrating disparate leftist factions into a united front against Christian antagonism to the anti-colonial struggle maturing on Lebanon's southern border. In this period, Charara began to elaborate answers to questions that continue to define political struggle in Lebanon today: the relationship between sectarianism – enshrined into an arrangement of political power-sharing in the Lebanese National Pact of 1943 – and capitalism, and the proper form of organisation that might best lead to the overcoming of both. The Lebanese left of the 1960s and 70s considered sectarian solidarity a vestige of pre-modernity which

hindered the development of class consciousness, and Bardawil notes the emergence of a mainstream strategy of constitutional reform to prevent its 'veil' from obstructing the interests of the exploited masses. Secular citizenship would rid sectarianism of its institutional scaffolding, thereby limiting its reproduction in society, the position dictated. Invariably, this was to be achieved with the help of an external agent; if the secularising tendencies of capitalist expansion could not render sectarian affiliation obsolete on its own, it was hoped that rallying around the Palestinian Revolution could, in Charara's words, 'eradicate the fragmentation of the popular masses by regional and kinship relations'.

Charara drew explicit connections between his dissatisfaction with the vanguardism of groups such as the Organisation of Communist Action in Lebanon (OCAL, which he and his comrades helped found in the early 1970s) and the poverty of their analyses. His assessment of the role of communal bonds in the peasant upheavals of Mount Lebanon during 1860s, published in *Origins of Sectarian Lebanon: The Right-Wing's Mass Line* (1975), to him demonstrated sectarianism's origins as an insurrectionary force; the same type of solidarity Charara would witness in his own time, when observing how 'familial [ties] are overturned against the factory owner... and workers use it as a strong pressuring measure on the factory owner'. This ambivalence could not possibly have been grasped, argued Charara, by a left which increasingly held its base at arm's length from its project of reform.

To be sure, Charara's contributions to a critical theory of sectarianism effectively marked the end of his engagement with politics. Bardawil is quick to observe that rather than devising ways of broadening its allegedly oppositional scope, Charara's insistence on the immediate validity of the masses' lived experience led him to explain Lebanon's fragmentation during the Civil War as an inevitability, transforming the once engaged militant-intellectual into a passive observer of foretold events. But as recent mobilisations in Lebanon have once again attempted to undermine sectarian relations Charara's theory of sectarianism as a resource – varyingly used by both power and people – helps clarify the specificity of this recurring object of resistance, whose very 'polyvalence' might well account for its tenacity beyond any formal abolition.

As tempting as it might be to draw parallels between the revolutionary moment of the early 1970s and the present day, these are certainly imposed by circumstances that have developed since the completion of this work, and are admittedly not its primary focus. Bardawil is motivated by an altogether different question: to what do we owe the relative absence of Charara and his comrades from the annals of Marxist theory? More broadly, what obstacles prevent us from reading political thought from the Arab world, and the Global South more generally, as critical theory in its own right? Echoing his teacher and collaborator David Scott, Bardawil identifies what he calls the 'metropolitan unconscious' of academic theory, which measures the sophistication of intellectuals in the periphery in terms of the latest theoretical innovations forged in the academy. Susan-Buck Morss' call to include Shariati and Qutb in the canon of twentieth-century theorists in her *Thinking Past Terror: Islamism and Critical Theory on the Left* (2003), for instance, hinges on a characterisation of a Eurocentric Arab Marxist tradition which is epistemically irreflexive, and thus unable to provide the tools necessary to make sense of anti-imperialism after 9/11.

Paradoxically, this impulse of theory to invalidate radical secular thought from the postcolony is traced back to the afterlives of the work of Edward Said, whose most politically charged work was informed by the very same events that triggered Socialist Lebanon's militancy: the Arab regimes' defeat in 1967 and the ensuing Palestinian Revolution. Although written in political solidarity, the effect of Said's epistemological critique – ubiquitous in the West as it is in the Arab world – was often theoretically at odds with local radicals. Read uncritically, for instance, Charara's account of the persistence of communal affiliation might come under attack for its culturalist essentialism, an oft-repeated charge of Saidian critique.

Yet for Bardawil this disregards both the historicity Charara attributes to sectarianism, and, more importantly, his commitment to an analysis of the lived reality of the society in which he was embedded, whose demands were more urgent than those of academic fashion. The author thus claims to abstain from any retrospective appraisal of Socialist Lebanon's normative claims, exchanging an analysis of their work's 'political performative powers' for a thick description of how theory 'seduces intellectuals, contributes to the cultivation of their ethos and sensibilities, and authorises political practices for militants'.

For Bardawil, what limits conventional histories of intellectuals (and often precipitates their hasty dismissal) are narrow evaluations of the descriptive force of their theoretical tools, rather than a broader inquiry into how those tools either multiply or circumscribe their ability to *act* in the world. It is this tendency of theory to extend itself beyond its own analytical contours that Bardawil considers the major corollary to his historical narrative, and he wields this insight both in his critique of the interpretative failures of postcolonial theory, and in his repeated rejection of the impulse to canonise an 'Arab theory', which would likely reflect concerns markedly different to those originally articulated by its exponents.

But does a recognition of theory's largely autonomous 'social life' necessarily preclude a critical intellectual history which would seek to uncover, adapt and submit past thought to present concerns? There seems to be a tension that runs throughout *Revolution and Disenchantment,* in its attempt to encourage 'an intergenerational conversation' between the 1970s and the present day, and its investigation into theory's varied mechanisms of (in)validation amongst militants, intellectuals and academics. Implicitly, however, this is resolved through Bardawil's own use of retrospective judgement when pointing to Socialist Lebanon's heterodoxy – their ability to *distinguish* themselves from majority of the left of their day – as what qualifies their oeuvre for present consideration. More than just amounting to a defence of Socialist Lebanon against the condescension of posterity, his understanding of theory's sociality ultimately supplements his efforts to shed light on a localised tradition of thought that might well inform struggles currently unfolding, as well as those yet to come.

Francesco Anselmetti

Migrant multiplicities

Martina Tazzioli, *The Making of Migration: The Biopolitics of Mobility at Europe's Borders* (London: Sage, 2019). 184pp., £79.00 hb., £25.99 pb., 978 1 52646 403 3 hb., 978 1 52646 404 0 pb.

It has been five years since the peak of what European states labelled a 'refugee crisis'. The idea that this was an exceptional time, a spectacle of suffering, or a moment of reckoning in the EU's border regime gained centre stage in public imagination in 2015 and has not really disappeared since. Punctuated by smaller 'crises' off the Libyan coast, in Greek island camps, or more recently in the English channel, such grammars of political and humanitarian 'crisis' and 'emergency' lend themselves to both an unhelpful presentism and essentialisation of 'migrants' in hegemonic discourse. The 'migrants' in question are known in advance, the time is always now. The questions asked are often narrow, even within so-called critical scholarship. Spatial analyses remain central and the imperative to 'undo' methodological nationalism remains a key concern, as explored in the recent work of Bridget Anderson.

But who is a migrant today in Europe? And how are they 'made'? With these deceptively simple questions, Martina Tazzioli troubles the canonical scholarship on migration and mobility, collapsing the many binaries which animate the literature: crisis vs. routine, the migrant victim vs. the migrant activist, freedom vs., control, mobility vs. immobility. Moving away from thinking of 'migrants' as individuals with a fixed identity or as already constituted groups, Tazzioli instead probes the many ways migrants are brought into being by technologies of governance, and racialised as such. Using a broad, biopolitical lens, the author points to the duplicity of this process of 'making' – the myriad political, legal and material practices through which migrants are governed, but also, following Ian Hacking, the way that migrants both 'live in', appropriate and exceed these categories.

Tazzioli's motivation in making this move is clear: 'migration' is not a phenomenon that should be seen through the lens of how to 'govern' it, even how to 'govern' it more fairly, or humanely. Instead, we should resist the imperative to 'see like a state' and try to disentangle the phenomenon of migration from the state gaze. Thinking in terms of processes of subjectification and subjec-

tion on one hand, and objectification-subjectification on the other, Tazzioli takes a step back and pays attention instead to the types of knowledge produced around migration. Following Janet Roitman in her book *Anti-crisis*, and Joan Scott's 'History Writing as Critique', Tazzioli aims to reopen spaces of political action and knowledge production away from the restraining punctual moment of 'crisis'. She is tremendously careful not to inadvertently reproduce the object or discursive framing upon which her critique intervenes.

What is exceptional about *The Making of Migration* is the way it brings together different strands of scholarship on mobility, collectives and critique, literatures which are usually kept separate. Instead, Tazzioli ricochets between these approaches at high speed, weaving in ethnographies of border enforcement and migrants' struggles and movements with oral histories of citizen-allies of migrants in Alpine villages and European capitals. With such a radical relational approach, Tazzioli effortlessly dismantles and rethinks the taken-for-granted categories of political theory used to talk about migration, mobility and borders. In short, the book not only takes migration simply as its object of study, but also mobilises lived experiences of migration as an analytical lens to shatter so many of the frames we think through and with, building new categories of subjectivity from radical heterogeneity and the traces. The author's aim, to 'de-fetishise migration', to view migration with a more lateral gaze, and in relation to intertwined struggles and transversal alliances, is perfectly executed. Instead of reified, neatly demarcated groups and people, we get fluid, highly entangled sets of actors and relations which are constantly in flux.

The refusal to superimpose an analytical grid and pre-fabricated political and epistemological boundaries sees Tazzioli instead ask how we can think about the 'politicalness of collective subjects that are temporary and on the move.' Through the language of (migrant) multiplicities and singularities, the author pokes at the ambivalences which subjectify and objectify migrants,

both as individuals and as part of 'temporary collective formations'. Not simply a spatial analysis, this framing also depends on capturing the importance of temporality in these processes – the transient and fleeting spaces, the enduring memories of solidarity practices, but also the 'stolen time' – to use Shahram Khosravi's term – frittered away from migrants' lives leaving them unable to think about possible futures. The concepts of 'multiplicities' and 'singularities' also encapsulate paradoxes around political visibility and invisibility – the tactics used by migrants to become or be (in)visible without perhaps identifying with this status or actively striving for it.

How to begin thinking in terms of migrant multiplicities? What Bernd Kasparek and Marc Speer referred to as the 'long summer of migration' in 2015 brought into being so many new ways of conceiving migrants as a collective group. No longer described as much as intangible flows and channels to be managed and manipulated, migrants began to be increasingly referred to as a 'swarm' or infestation of undesirable bodies to be

chased away, or a crowd or mass congregating on the border. Tazziloli reminds the reader of Katie Hopkins' hateful UK tabloid column at the time, likening migrants in Calais to 'cockroaches', a register which quickly became normalised when the UK Prime Minister referred to the same migrants as 'swarms of people' .

In using 'multiplicities' as a conceptual framing, the author not only deconstructs these deeply problematic framings, but also departs from standard collective terms such as community or assembly to capture the non-homogenous and highly precarious nature of collective formations. This endeavour is not without peril: in discarding so many standard political categories, the author opens herself up to being accused of losing some of the critical purchase that these labels provided in the first place. However, Tazzioli's onto-methodological move, placing primacy on migrants' grounded experiences of political subjectivity, means that this critique can never really take hold. The empirical for Tazzioli is never purified or flattened to fit an existing concept of political collectivity or way of 'doing' politics. The rich, ethnographic grounding of unmaking and making migrant multiplicities is always paramount. The author skilfully retraces the ambivalences of the term 'mob' to further this very point, an idea that captures the ephemeral and heterogenous nature of migrant collective subjects which are brought into being through governmental techniques though exceed these mechanisms of control nonetheless.

In this vein, so much attention around the subject of migration has been paid to death and dead bodies, to those who have drowned or are conceived solely in terms of bare life in what Nicholas De Genova has called the 'border spectacle'. The other side of this coin sees migrant agency and resistance celebrated, the migrant 'activist' who claims citizen rights in a disruptive, punctual 'moment'. What to make then of all the other modes of governance and modes of struggle that do not fit into these frameworks? It is through a rethinking of biopolitics beyond the making live/letting die couplet, Tazzioli proposes, where so much of the manifoldness of biopolitical technologies can be empirically captured: the 'cramping, choking, hindering, chasing away, constricting, confining, dismantling' of migrants' mobility and presence and the incessant exposure to violence and vulnerability leaving migrants 'de-socialised' and prevented from forming solid networks.

To 'singularities' then, where Tazzioli captures the ways migrants are individualised, subjectified and objectified. Like her mobilisation of multiplicity to get away from standard categories through which to think of migrant collectivities, singularity seeks to escape the methodological individualism which permeates so much of migration scholarship and political theory. Focusing on the ways migrants are targeted by specific technical and political actions, as well as the ways they are coerced to speak (whilst nonetheless treated as deceitful subjects, unable to tell the truth), thinking in terms of singularities also brings to light that individual migrants are digitally scattered across databases into discombobulated pieces of 'data'.

For this reason, there are no accounts of migrants' narratives or trajectories in Tazzioli's conception of singularities. Instead, the author speaks of 'hit without interpellation'; drawing attention to the many ways that data is extracted and circulates without the migrant being asked to respond, which shapes their subjectivity

nonetheless, albeit from a distance. In this respect, one of the most powerful parts of the book presents two fictional geographies, that of S. and M., migrants who land in Italy and Greece respectively. Drawing on what has been captured, physically and digitally by national authorities, NGOs or European agencies, Tazzioli retraces the steps of what happens to migrants who land by sea and then try to move on. The use of fiction in this way, albeit a fiction written from the archives, forms an intriguing rupture here in its pushing of social sciences towards the humanities and creation of a disparate truth regime within the book. The medium manages to capture the human experience of migration, its contingencies and possibilities, whilst avoiding reifying the individual migrant or fetishising migrants' stories. It is through the geographies of S. and M. where Tazzioli's overall thesis is perhaps also encapsulated in its fullest form: migrant singularities are not some sort of antithesis to multiplicities and the two can only ever be seen as mutually constitutive and interactive.

Tazzioli's style presents a powerful way of writing social science, avoiding the imperative to write in a linear way, to have one 'main' argument and to clearly state two or three interventions into a specific literature. Indeed, the author's skipping and rebounding between different dynamics of migratory governance and resistance, taking into account their historicity and complexity is as non-compliant as the 'migrant spatial disobedience' she describes in her final chapter. The book operates through multiple vectors, across many different layers.

This refusal to enclose must be applauded in the way it rejects so many arbitrary conventions or being bound by discipline or methodology. We are not really told much about the author's 'fieldwork', how many weeks or months were spent in various camps or zones of transit. We do not know the exact number of interviews that took place. Style and form are as much part of Tazzioli's political intervention in de-reifying migration as the content itself. The many different frontiers of Europe in which the author spent time – the French-Italian and Swiss-Italian borders, Calais, Paris, Sicily and on several Greek islands – are not reduced to 'case studies', nor are they subsumed under a single overarching analysis of Europe's border regime. Instead, these different sites are analysed in terms of their resonances: 'showing patterns of similarity among them in light of the political technologies deployed for containing unruly mobility and highlighting what each of them reveals about *the making of migration'* (author's emphasis).

To be sure, though these migrant multiplicities and singularities are characterised by fragmentation, heterogeneity and disjuncture, Tazzioli succeeds in piecing them together to form a strong, political intervention. Readers are pushed to understand the European social, political and historical present in different ways, a provocation which though somewhat exhausting in its constant impulse to put things on the move, is also highly original and galvanising. *The Making of Migration* mobilises radical relationality and transversal connections to study emerging political formations and the subjects that inhabit them.

Emma Mc Cluskey

Homo desiderans

Miguel de Beistegui, *The Government of Desire: A Genealogy of the Liberal Subject* (Chicago & London: University of Chicago Press, 2018). ix+295pp., £34.00 hb., 978 0 22654 737 4

Miguel de Beistegui's new book is one of the most important contributions to the study of desire since the publication of René Girard's *Things Hidden Since the Foundation of the World* (1987). The central argument of the work is that the creation – through specific rationalities of knowledge and technologies of power – of a type of subjectivity (*homo desiderans*) is the mechanism that allowed modern capitalism to transform into neoliberalism and power to translate into its biopolitical double. For, if neoliberalism is essentially characterised by a form of governance that privileges the management of productive subjects over their repressive control (the carrot instead of the stick), then it is crucial to understand the mechanisms that push individuals to move relentlessly according to the models and the new economic geography created by neoliberal capitalism. Desire is precisely one of these mechanisms in that it is constituted as a *structural negativity* (i.e., as an infinity of always different carrots, or, to speak more directly, as an 'ontological lack' construed by the various *epistemai* of power) – which generates *hyper-positivity* at the subjective level through the incessant individual search for pleasures and products that the 'free market' constantly manufactures.

Drawing on the late Foucault's work on sexuality, de Beistegui traces a convincing genealogy of this transcendental-historical *dispositif* by examining three fundamental assemblages or regimes of desire: the economic, the sexual and the symbolic. As he demonstrates, these three regimes are interdependent and self-reinforcing because they are born out of the same paradigm, i.e. the disciplinary rationality that characterises modern bio-power. Thus, for example, starting from the eighteenth century, the emergence of liberal political economy (i.e. Physiocracy) established a new discourse on negative freedom that, on the one hand, seemed to free individuals from the control of the state, but, on the other, subjected them to the new rules set by the market. Self-interest and utility thus become the watchwords of a libidinal economic system based on the 'free maximisation' of desires, which can now be purchased for money. In this way, desire 'is naturalised, and seen as a form of positive energy, that is, as a spontaneous mechanism generating its own norms'.

This new paradigm of governance allows, in turn, the birth of a science of sexuality, which is no longer repressive but normative. Indeed, the problem of 'natural' interest creates the need for further rationalisations and normalisations: if individuals are maximisers of pleasure and utility, how to explain the motives behind 'aberrant' crimes and, so the narrative goes, sexual acts 'against nature'? It is precisely at this historical juncture that, according to de Beistegui, new concepts such as 'sexual perversion' and 'abnormality' appear in the psychiatric literature in order to create further barriers of exclusion between 'good' (i.e. natural and economic) and 'bad' (i.e. perverted and criminal) desires. In short, the discursive occupation of 'desire' generates a new totalising system of norms, which branches out into different fields of knowledge following the trajectory indicated by economic rationality.

Mirroring this development is the birth of a type of subjectivity characterised by the constant affirmation of the 'self' as the ultimate source of authority. For, within the network of desires, *homo symbolicum* is a creature that must constantly individualise herself by knowing what she wants. The struggles for recognition that occur on both the individual level (through practices of self-esteem, self-management, self-respect, mindfulness, etc.) and the collective level (through the recognition of one's minority rights, one's culture, one's identity, e.g. LGBT+ rights) can be read, first and foremost, as self-individualising processes. According to de Beistegui, this politics of self-identification involves serious limitations in that it pushes socio-political minorities to play by the rules, assumptions and models of the same assemblage of power that had initially excluded them. This critique of identity politics has the undoubted merit of exploring, in a new light, some of the fundamental issues that animated the debate between Habermas and Taylor on the political role of minorities. (Although it should be said that, in rule of law systems, there can be no *pure individuals* but only *legal persons*, i.e., access to rights is only possible by identifying oneself as belonging to specific socio-political categories: BAME groups, disabled people, single mothers, etc.)

The Government of Desire is an exceptionally rich *tour-de-force* of a complex history – that of the naturalisation of desire, which the book subjects to critical scrutiny. This intellectual operation is more notable if one considers that even Marx had ignored the fundamental difference between wants, needs and desires. As he writes in the opening of Capital, volume 1: 'A commodity is … an object outside us, a thing that by its properties satisfies human needs of whatever kind. The nature of these needs … *whether they arise from the stomach, or the imagination, makes no difference*'. De Beistegui shows quite convincingly that it is precisely in the chasm between 'natural needs' and 'artificial desires' that the forces, discourses and models of liberalism have managed to transform the repressive forms of power into neoliberal governmentality *by* and *for* desire.

Nonetheless, if the book's genealogy stands out for its theoretical richness and analytical acumen, de Beistegui's *pars construens* seems to take a step back from its initial assumptions. For, it remains somewhat unclear how and, above all, on what grounds, we may activate strategies of desubjectivation. In the final pages of the book, the uncomfortable legacy of Kojève's metaphysics of Desire, which has so much influenced and limited French thought in the last fifty years, still seems to resonate. Consider, as an example, the following passage:

> Become in order not to recognise (even yourself)! Lose yourself, undo yourself! For only then – when experimentation replaces normalisation, and when the processes of subjectivation are traversed and overwhelmed by life lines, untamable intensities – *can desire reveal its immanent voluptuousness* (emphasis added).

This possibility of desubjectivation by means of individual forms of resistance raises two fundamental questions: 1. If, as the book argues, desire is always a historical assemblage of specific rationalities of power and knowledge, how can a 'sovereign', a sort of zero degree, or anarchic form of Desire exist or be accessed? 2. In a slightly abstract way, de Beistegui places within the subject the endogenous possibility of liberation from precisely those mechanisms that had constituted its 'self'. The fact is that desire, being an assemblage of historical power relations, can never be Desire (as de Beistegui, following Deleuze, seems to indicate). In fact, the potency of desire lies in its being a *relational dispositif*. Girard is perhaps the scholar who has considered this issue in the closest detail in recent years. Reflecting on the epistemic and sociogenetic role of desire, he writes in *I See Satan Fall Like Lightning*:

> Humankind is that creature who lost a part of its animal instinct in order to gain access to 'desire', as it is called. Once their natural needs are satisfied, humans desire intensely, but they don't know exactly what they desire, for no instinct guides them. We do not each have our desire, one really our own. The essence of desire is to have no essential goal. Truly to desire we must have recourse to people about us; we have to borrow their desires. [...] If our desires were not mimetic, they would be forever fixed on predetermined objects; they would be a particular form of instinct. Human beings could no more change their desire than cows their appetite for grass. Without mimetic desire there would be neither freedom nor humanity.

According to Girard, desire is part of human nature and, as such, is a transhistorical dimension. At the same time, however, being an 'empty' dimension, so to speak, desire constantly varies its morphology under the pressure exerted by historical configurations of power. In other words, desire is both historical and phylogenetic; it is, in Foucault's parlance, a transcendental-historical *dispositif*. Yet, precisely for this reason, the subjective overcoming of the regimes of power and desire is not possible through a simple distancing (i.e. play or Bar-tleby's 'I would prefer not to'), an escape (i.e. idleness or inactivity) or a leap into an undefined Becoming (which would be nothing but a leap into the void of Desire). The liberation from the regimes of desirability created by neo-liberalism cannot take place (to use a metaphor dear to Nietzsche) *à la* Munchausen, which is to say by means of a metaphysical lifting of the subject who, pulling herself up into existence by the hair, out of the swamp of desires, is able to access the Impersonal, the Singular, the Outside – as de Beistegui suggests, in the wake of Foucault and Deleuze. The point is that a form of power that controls – and develops inside – *omnes et singulatim* requires a resistance that acts on both these levels (the individual and the masses).

It is at this level, then, that de Beistegui's argument meets its limitations: what *concrete* models can we imagine and, above all, embody in order to create alternative forms of life to the hedonism-consumerism-productivism that characterises the society of the integrated spectacle? The answer to this question remains open. Yet, if it is true that 'the real voyage of discovery consists, not in seeking new landscapes, but in having new eyes', this book is an excellent guide to start imagining a novel geography of resistance. The ways to inhabit it, inevitably, will have to be decided through historical and social conflict.

Antonio Cerella

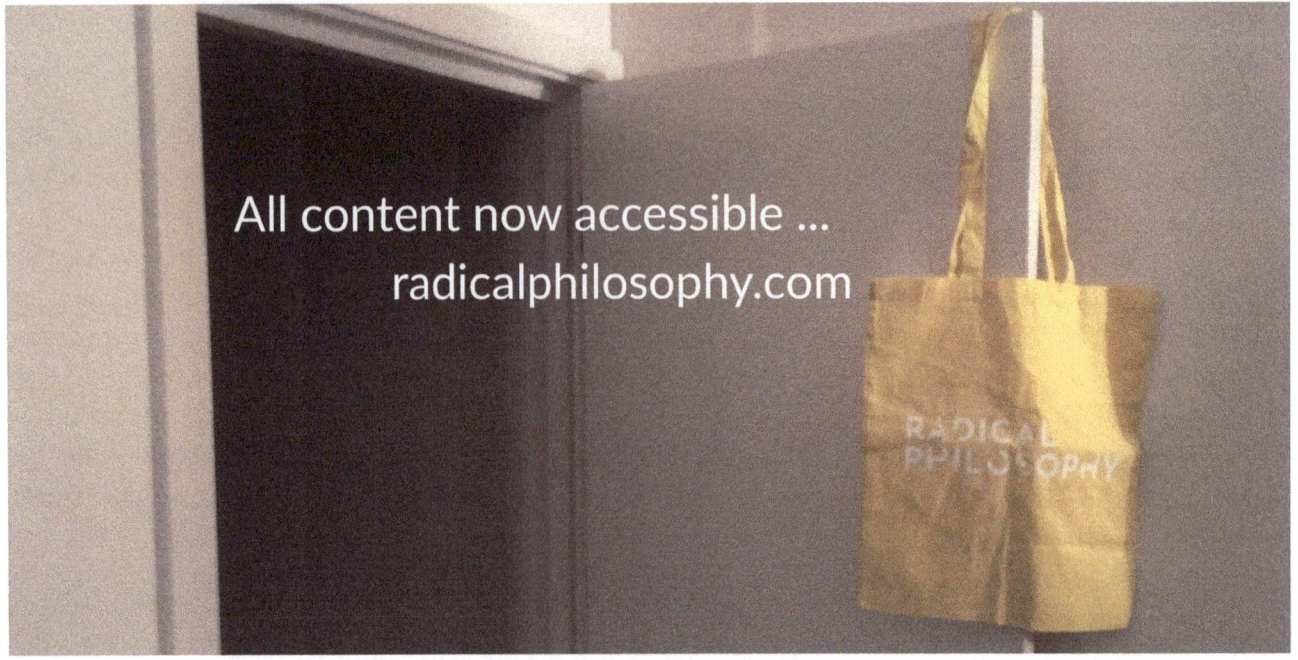

All content now accessible ...
radicalphilosophy.com

María Lugones, 1944-2020

Françoise Vergès

The task of remembering one's many selves is a difficult liberatory task.[1]

María Lugones, a feminist philosopher, sociologist, activist and Professor of Comparative Literature and Women's Studies at Binghamton University in New York State, died on July 14 2020. Sadly, she did not live to see the victory of feminists in her country of birth, Argentina, who have won a decades-long battle to legalise abortion, and the replacement of the once popular hashtag *#SeráLey* [#ItWillBeLaw] with *#EsLey* [#ItIsLaw]. But she has left an important legacy in philosophy and decolonial feminism with her theory of 'multiple selves' and concept of the 'coloniality of gender'.

Born in 1944 in Moròn, near Buenos Aires, to parents who had migrated from Catalonia – part of the large migrations from Europe to Argentina between 1880 and 1940 which contributed to the fiction of a 'white' society and erased the presence of indigenous peoples and Afro-Argentinians – María Lugones grew up in a country governed by the military since 1930. Inspired by the ideology of Mussolini, they imposed a nationalist, corporatist, conservative, racist and sexist regime with the help of the Catholic Church. Thus, when Lugones at 17 said to her parents that she wished to have sexual relations, her father put her in a psychiatric hospital where she was given electroshock therapy and forced into a straitjacket. 'They will not tame me', she repeated to herself throughout the ordeal.[2] Once released, Lugones decided to escape Argentina and left for California, writing her PhD on moralism and interpersonal and institutional relations at the University of Wisconsin in the 1970s.

Her interest in race and gender, which developed during her studies and was anchored in her rejection of heteropatriarchy (for which she had paid a heavy price), led her to join the growing group of feminists of colour who were critical of a white feminism that made women into a unified, homogenous and fixed category. Race was a modality in which patriarchy was lived, they argued, and the racialisation of patriarchy meant that all men did not belong to the dominant group and all women did not experience patriarchal oppression in the same way. Along with Gloria Anzaldùa, Audre Lorde and the authors of the Combahee River Collective, Lugones looked at the ways in which slavery, colonialism and racism had impacted genders, affecting the ways in which heterosexuality, masculinity and femininity were conceived, and in which lesbian, trans, gay and queer sexualities were criminalised.

'The creation of "women" as a category was one of the very first accomplishments of the colonial state', Lugones wrote in 2007. It was an important argument that added to the critique that Black, racialised and colonised women had historically made by insisting on the role and place of slavery and colonialism in the making of genders, sexualities, social classes, races, the division between culture and nature, of the cartography of the world, in the erasure or appropriation of non-European epistemologies, knowledges and techniques. To develop her argument on the coloniality of gender, she drew from the work of sociologist Oyèrónkẹ Oyěwùmí, who had argued that the binary organisation of society (man/woman) was imposed on Yoruba society during colonisation and that the dichotomy of gender went along with racial domination and sexual subordination of the colonised, and from Paula Gunn Allen's work on indigenous peoples of North America.

'Colonialism did not impose precolonial, European gender arrangements on the colonised. It imposed a new gender system that created very different arrangements for colonised males and females than for white bourgeois colonisers. Thus, it introduced many genders and gender itself as a colonial concept and mode of organisation of relations of production, property relations, of cosmologies and ways of knowing', she wrote.[3] Indeed, the differences that gender binarism created – complementarity of men and women, different 'natural' inborn qualities, biological maternal attachment – have never been universal. Under colonial slavery, Black people, and under colonisation, indigenous peoples, were gendered differently from whites. When white women were seen as fragile, sweet and delicate, enslaved women were seen as devoid of maternal sentiment, were worked as hard as enslaved men, punished as harshly as men, were raped, abused, killed, as men were tortured, trafficked, killed. Both were worked to death, were forbidden to create a family or kinship, were denied rights. Men were deprived of paternity rights, and if a non-white man could be a domestic tyrant, once in the street, he was a Black, brown, Asian, Arab man, in other words not quite a 'Man'. Colonised women were not women but 'females' and colonised men were not men but 'boys' or 'males'.

With her essay on the coloniality of gender, Lugones considerably enriched decolonial theory. To her, Anibal Quijano, the leading theorist of decoloniality, had made a mistake in his account of the coloniality of power by assuming that gender and even sex share the same organisation in all human societies. With this assumption, he had accepted without hesitation the patriarchal, heterosexist and Eurocentric understanding of gender. Lugones disagreed with his radical replacement of class by race as the central notion to understand modernity and cited the work of Black feminists who had demonstrated the entanglement of different forms of oppression, what came to be known with Kimberlé Crenshaw as intersectionality. Lugones' analysis of 'the modern/colonial gender system' showed that 'colonisation was a twofold process of racial inferiorisation *and* gender subordination' that had ultimately benefited colonised men whose machismo in social and revolutionary movements had been denounced by women. White feminism, blind to its own racial history, has also benefited from the Eurocentred conception of gender, family, sexualities and patriarchy. Yet, to Afro-Brazilian or Afro-Dominican feminists, Lugones had minimised the heterosexual and patriarchal elements in Afro communities which had to be fought against alongside the fight against western global modernity. Decolonial indigenous feminists have also challenged the idealisation of 'pre-Hispanic' communit-

ies and the invention of patriarchal oppression as tradition.[4] No decolonisation without de-patriarcalisation.

In recent years, the theory of decolonial feminism, to which María Lugones brought so much, has informed political practices that are deeply transformative. Her focus on collective thinking, on the fact that the self is always multiple and cannot be framed into narrow categories, her attention to the coloniality of gender and to the intersections of race, class, genders, sexualities and spiritualities, produced enlightened work and contributed to the conversation on a feminism that seeks the liberation of all. The convergent and massive struggles worldwide against femicides, extractivism, anti-migrant policies, the construction of walls, the expansion of surveillance and control by the neoliberal state, racism, Islamophobia, capitalism and imperialism, show what decolonial feminism brings to thought and practice: a committed intersectionality, a rejection of dominant hierarchy, and a practice that does not ban joy, desire, pleasure and love. Lugones wrote beautifully about the practice of 'playfulness, "world" travelling and loving perception' that advocated cross-cultural and cross-racial loving, the need to embrace the plurality among women: 'We are not self-important, we are not fixed in particular constructions of ourselves, which is part of saying that we are *open to self-construction*. We may have no rules, and when we do have rules, *there no rules that are to us sacred*.'[5]

Françoise Vergès is a decolonial feminist activist, political theorist and co-founder of the collective Decolonize the Arts (Paris). Publications include Une théorie féministe de la violence: Pour politique antiraciste de la protection *(2020).*

Notes

1. María Lugones, *Pilgrimages/Peregrinajes: Theorising Coalition Against Multiple Oppressions* (London: Rowman & Littlefield, 2003).
2. Claudia Acuña, 'Maestra: María Lugones, teórica feminista', *Lavaca*, 19 August 2019, https://www.lavaca.org/mu138/maestra-maria-lugones-teorica-feminista/
3. María Lugones, 'Heterosexualism and the Colonial/Modern Gender System', *Hypatia* 22 (2007), 186–209.
4. Aura Cumes, '"Sufrimos vergüenza": mujeres k iche frente a la justicia comunitaria en Guatemala', *Desacatos* 31 (Sept-Dec 2009), 99–114; 'La "india" como "sirvienta": servi dumbre doméstica, colonialismo y patriarcado en Guatemala', Doctoral thesis in Anthropology, (Mexico: CIESAS, 2014).
5. María Lugones, 'Playfulness, World Travelling and Loving Perception', *Hypatia* 2:2 (1987), 3–19.